HOSTAGE

HOSTAGE

My Nightmare in Beirut

by
David Jacobsen
with
Gerald Astor

DONALD I. FINE, INC.
NEW YORK

Library of Congress Cataloging-in-Publication Data
Jacobsen, David (David P.)
Hostage : my nightmare in Beirut / by David Jacobsen with Gerald
Astor.
p.   cm.
Includes bibliographical references and index.
ISBN 1-55611-265-3
1. Jacobsen, David (David P.)—Captivity, 1985–1986. 2. Hostages—
Lebanon—Biography. 3. Hostages—United States—Biography.
I. Astor, Gerald, 1926–   . II. Title.
DS87.2.J33A3   1991
956.9204′4′092—dc20   91-2315
CIP

Manufactured in the United States of America

10 9 8 7 6 5 4 3 2 1

Designed by Irving Perkins Associates

The Western world thinks only of its own citizens taken hostage in Lebanon. Forgotten, or worse yet, never recognized are the thousands of young Lebanese Christian and Moslem men who have been kidnapped, tortured, and murdered. History will never record their names or their pain; evidence of their existence on this earth will never be etched on a grave marker. Future generations will have nothing to remember the lives of these young men who desired to be free.

Hundreds of thousands of Lebanese civilians have been casualties of the viciousness of international politics. No decent human being can escape grieving for the innocent children of Lebanon who cannot play out-of-doors without the fear of metal in the air. They, too, are victims of terrorism, held hostage in their own land.

Also victims of hostage-taking are the family members. These people suffer more than the hostages. They are powerless to change the course of history. They are ignored and all too frequently patronized by their governments. Their privacy is destroyed by the curiosity of strangers. The bodies of William Buckley, Colonel William Higgins, and Alec Collett were never returned home for burial; it is a perpetual sorrow for their loved ones.

Hostages develop a bond with one another that transcends political, economic, and religious differences. I owe my survival to my brothers in captivity, Terry Anderson, Tom Sutherland, Ben Weir, and Marty Jenco, who strengthened me with their courage and determination. My best friend Joe Cicippio remained in Lebanon after my abduction so that he could work for my release. He too became a hostage. That marvelous man of the Lord, Terry Waite, sacrificed his freedom in attempting to liberate the Americans held in Lebanon.

It is to all of these victims of terrorism that this book is dedicated.

Acknowledgments

The many people to whom I am indebted for my freedom are named within the text of this book.

While the opinions and the interpretation of events in this book are mine, there are also some individuals who contributed information or assisted me in putting it all together.

My son Eric, who published his own account in England, supplied me with details about his efforts on my behalf and those of his brother Paul and sister Diane.

General Richard Secord was a generous source of information about the negotiations that led to my release. So was Albert Hakim, who also contributed to my knowledge of the personalities of the people running Iran and Hizballah. Oliver North and John Poindexter are two other insiders who furnished me with details about hostage negotiations.

Dr. Calvin Jeff Frederick contributed to my understanding of the effects of terrorism and kidnapping upon the victims.

Peggy Say, that dauntless champion of her brother Terry Anderson, was always willing to talk about what she had learned during her efforts to free Terry.

Ahmad Nasrallah kept me informed of events after I left Beirut, a free man. Cannon Samir Habiby, past Executive Director of the Episcopal Church's Presiding Bishops Fund for World Relief, was another source of information. Robin Wright, who has covered the Middle East and has written several books on events in that part of the world, generously shared her insights.

My agent Frank Weimann served me well as did my co-author Gerald Astor. I am also grateful to David Gibbons, our editor, for his encouragement and the commitment of publisher Don Fine, who enabled me to make public my story.

Contents

Preface

Quiet Diplomacy is Deadly Silence

The Department of State claims that publicity only increases the value of hostages and encourages additional acts of terrorism. Philosophically this might be true, but it could be wrong as it appears to be in Lebanon. The kidnappers are not demanding a ransom in the classical sense, but the return of assets claimed to be legally theirs. Abduction of Americans was intended to increase pressure on the U.S. government to return those assets. The Iranians, who ordered the hostage-taking, long ago established a multi-billion-dollar price. Iran now values the property and cash, tied up a decade ago by President Carter, to be worth many billions. The demand by Islamic Jihad for the release of the Dawa prisoners in Kuwait was nothing more than a smoke-screen for Iran.

Iran is the "Great Satan" of terrorist acts in Lebanon. It was the force behind the murders of our marines and the bombings of our embassy. Iran should be severely punished for those acts of terrorism. It is ironic that delays in the return of Iranian assets may be the reason for the prolonged captivity of Americans in Lebanon.

It is our policy not to negotiate with terrorists for the release of the American hostages in Lebanon, but we are negotiating with them on a case-by-case basis for the return of money and property. The hostages should be a quid pro quo in those discussions. That was the French solution and the French hostages were freed.

Congress should investigate the handling of the Iranian assets and claims. What were the conditions imposed on the Iranians for the release of these assets and to what degree have they complied? There should be a complete public accounting with details of control and daily management of those funds. What is the status of current negotiations? Congress could be the force to free the hostages.

Why are Anderson and Sutherland now in their seventh year as hostages? That's correct; as I write these words, it will soon be seven years! They haven't been forgotten, but it appears that they have been abandoned by their own government. Continued delays in liberating these men only increases the chances that they will suffer the same fate as Higgins, Collett, Kilburn and Buckley. Quiet diplomacy has become deadly silence.

Chronology

History and Hostages in Lebanon

1975

APRIL: The Lebanese civil war begins with clashes between the Christian Phalangists and Arafat's Palestine Liberation Organization. Beirut is partitioned by the Green Line.

1976

OCTOBER 18: Peace conference in Riyadh, Saudi Arabia, ends with an ineffective "no victor and no vanquished" truce.

1979

FEBRUARY 1: Ayatollah Ruhollah Khomeini returns to Iran ending fourteen years of exile.

MARCH 30–31: Formation of an Iranian Islamic Republic is approved in a national referendum.

MARCH 5: Iranian Revolutionary Guard Corps is created.

AUGUST 10: Iran cancels the Shah's $9 billion arms deal with the United States.

AUGUST 18: Khomeini becomes commander-in-chief of all Iranian armed forces.

SEPTEMBER 7–8: Lebanese Shiites hijack an Alitalia airplane to protest the disappearance in Libya of the Lebanese religious leader Musa Sadr. The plane is diverted to Tehran and surrendered to Iranian officials.

OCTOBER 22: Mohammad Reza Shah Pahlavi flies from exile in Mexico to the United States for cancer treatment.

NOVEMBER 1: Khomeini urges student attacks against the United States for not returning the Shah to Iran.

NOVEMBER 4: Iranian students seize the U.S. Embassy in Tehran.
NOVEMBER 14: President Carter orders a freeze on an estimated $10 billion worth of Iranian assets in the United States.

1980

MARCH 24: Shah Pahlavi undergoes surgery in Cairo.
APRIL 7: United States breaks diplomatic relations with Iran, freezes additional assets and imposes sanctions.
APRIL 24–27: U.S. rescue of Iranian hostages fails.
JULY 20: Iranian parliament elects Ali Akbar Hashemi Rafsenjani as its speaker.
JULY 27: The Shah dies in Cairo.
NOVEMBER 2: Iranian parliament approves four conditions for the release of the embassy hostages.
NOVEMBER 20: The United States accepts the Iranian conditions in principle.

1981

JANUARY 6: Khomeini accepts the U.S. proposal for the release of the embassy hostages.
JANUARY 20: Fifty-two American hostages are released by Iran.
DECEMBER 2: Iran denies purchasing arms from Israel.

1982

JANUARY 23: Bahrain charges Iran with instigating Shiites throughout the Middle East to overthrow their governments.
MARCH 7: U.S. media reports that Iran buys millions of dollars of military hardware from Israel, North Korea, Soviet Union, and Europe.
MAY 28: Israeli Defense Minister Sharon claims the United States was aware of the sale of $27 million of arms to Iran.
JUNE 6: Israel invades Lebanon.
JUNE 19: David Dodge, acting president of the American University of Beirut, is kidnapped.
AUGUST 25: U.S. Marines arrive in Lebanon as peacekeeping force.
AUGUST 30: PLO begins three-day withdrawal of military from Lebanon.
SEPTEMBER 10: U.S. Marines leave Lebanon.
SEPTEMBER 18: Lebanese Christian militia massacres 328 Palestinian refugees in camps at Sabra and Shattila, 991 camp inhabitants are listed as missing.

SEPTEMBER 20: President Reagan announces return of multinational peacekeeping forces to Lebanon.

SEPTEMBER 29: U.S. Marines land at the international airport after withdrawal of Israeli forces.

1983

APRIL 18: A suicide car bombing destroys the U.S. Embassy in West Beirut.

JULY 21: French traveler Christian Joubert is kidnapped.

JULY 21: David Dodge is released, after being held captive since July 19, 1982.

OCTOBER 23: A suicide car bombing at the U.S. Marine headquarters at the international airport in West Beirut results in the deaths of 241 Marines.

DECEMBER 12: Dawa terrorists detonate six bombs in Kuwait. Eighteen are apprehended and all but one convicted and sentenced to various terms of imprisonment.

1984

JANUARY 18: Malcolm Kerr, president of the American University of Beirut, is assassinated.

JANUARY 23: United States adds Iran to the list of countries that support terrorism.

FEBRUARY 10: Professor Frank Regier of the AUB is kidnapped.

MARCH 7: Cable News Network correspondent Jeremy Levin is kidnapped.

MARCH 16: CIA Station Chief William Buckley is kidnapped.

APRIL 15: Frank Regier and Christian Joubert are rescued by Amal militiamen.

MAY 8: Rev. Benjamin Weir is kidnapped.

NOVEMBER 30: David Jacobsen arrives at the AUB to assume his duties as director of the medical center.

DECEMBER 3: British citizens Peter Kilburn (AUB librarian), Leigh Douglas and Philip Padfield are kidnapped.

DECEMBER 4: A Kuwaiti airplane is hijacked to Tehran by four Lebanese Shiites. Two American passengers, Charles Hegna and William Stanford, are murdered.

1985

JANUARY 3: Swiss diplomat Eric Wehril is kidnapped, then released less than a week later.

JANUARY 8: American priest Lawrence Martin Jenco is kidnapped.

FEBRUARY 14: Jeremy Levin obtains his freedom.

MARCH 14: Dutch priest Nicholas Kluiters is kidnapped.

MARCH 14: British metallurgist Geoffrey Nash is kidnapped, then released within a few days.

MARCH 15: British businessman Brian Levick is kidnapped, then released within a few days.

MARCH 16: U.S. Associated Press correspondent Terry Anderson is kidnapped.

MARCH 22: French citizens Marcel Fontaine (diplomat) and Marcel Carton (diplomat) are kidnapped.

MARCH 24: Gilles Sidney Peyrolles, a French diplomat, is kidnapped, then freed on April 2.

MARCH 25: British journalist Alec Collett, employed by the UN Relief and Works Agency, is kidnapped.

MAY 22: French journalist Jean-Paul Kauffmann and political studies researcher Michel Seurat are kidnapped. Seurat dies in captivity, apparently of cancer.

MAY 27: British professor Denis Hill of the AUB is kidnapped. Shot through the head, his body is found a few days later.

MAY 28: David Jacobsen is kidnapped. Taken for interrogation to a location near the Sumerland resort, he is moved that night to a location between the Beirut International Airport and the Palestinian refugee camps of Sabra and Shattila.

JUNE 3: William Buckley dies in a room near Jacobsen.

JUNE 9: Professor Thomas Sutherland of the AUB is kidnapped.

JUNE 14: TWA Flight 847 is hijacked and diverted to Beirut International Airport. Passenger Robert Stethem, a U.S. Navy sailor, is murdered by the terrorists.

JUNE 29: Shiite Amal militia attempt to rescue American hostages fails.

JUNE 30: American hostages are moved to new location, one hundred yards closer to the airport.

JULY 1: Thirty-nine American passengers of Flight 847 are released after Israel agrees to free 766 Lebanese Shiite prisoners.

JULY 11: Wadgid Ahmad Duomoni, Syrian born, a resident of Beirut who holds a Kuwaiti diplomatic passport, is kidnapped. He is released August 10.

AUGUST 14: The second of two shipments of TOW missiles is sent to Iran by Israel.

SEPTEMBER 11: Italian businessman Alberto Molinari is kidnapped.

SEPTEMBER 14: The Rev. Benjamin Weir is released as a trade for the TOW missiles.

SEPTEMBER 28: Two British women, Hazel Moss (business executive) and Amanda McGrath (educator) are kidnapped, then released ten days later.

SEPTEMBER 30: Four Soviet diplomats, Oleg Spirin, Valerie Mirikov Arkady Katchkov and Nikolay Svirsky are kidnapped. Katchkov dies in captivity. The other three are released October 30.

OCTOBER 13: Jacobsen, Anderson, Sutherland and Jenco are moved to another location near the old Kuwaiti Embassy in West Beirut.

NOVEMBER 28: Eighteen defective or obsolete Hawk anti-aircraft missiles shipped to Iran by Israel are rejected. Iran demands refund or replacement.

1986

JANUARY 17: President Reagan signs special finding that permit negotiations with Iran for the Lebanese hostages. One thousand TOW missiles are shipped to Tehran in February.

JANUARY 31: South Korean diplomat Do Chae Sung is kidnapped.

FEBRUARY 2: French businessman Marcel Coudari and businesswoman Camille Sontag are kidnapped.

MARCH 9: French citizens Aurel Cornea, Jean-Louis Normandin, George Hansen and Phillipe Rochot (all TV crewmen) are kidnapped.

MARCH 28: British citizens Philip Padfield (teacher at the International Language Center) and John Leigh Douglas (professor at the AUB) are kidnapped.

APRIL 8: French educator Michel Brian is kidnapped, then released four days later.

APRIL 11: Irish professor Brian Keenan of the AUB is kidnapped.

APRIL 15: U.S. warplanes conduct air strikes against Libyan targets as reprisals for state-sponsored terrorism.

APRIL 17: The bodies of Peter Kilburn, Philip Padfield and John Leigh Douglas are found, their murders credited to revenge by Libyan dictator Muhmar Khadafy.

APRIL 17: Briton John McCarthy, acting bureau chief for Worldwide Television, is kidnapped.

MAY 25–28: Former National Security Adviser Robert McFarlane, Lt. Col. Oliver North, and others make secret trip to Tehran to negotiate arms-for-hostages swap.

JUNE 20: French hostages Phillipe Rochot and George Hansen are released.

JULY 26: Father Lawrence Martin Jenco is released. David Jacobsen makes a video that results in his severe beating some weeks later as a result of U.S. media suggestion that he used a code.

AUGUST 4: Hawk missiles are delivered to Iran.

AUGUST 4: Jacobsen, Anderson and Sutherland are moved to a site on the Coastal Road in West Beirut.

AUGUST 23: Gennadi Zakharov, a Soviet physicist attached to the UN, is arrested in New York for espionage.

AUGUST 30: Nicholas Daniloff, Moscow correspondent of U.S. News & World Report, is seized by the KGB and charged with spying.

SEPTEMBER 9: U.S. educator Frank Reed is kidnapped.

SEPTEMBER 12: U.S. comptroller for AUB Joseph Cicippio is kidnapped.

SEPTEMBER 12: Daniloff and Zakharov are turned over to the custody of the U.S. and Soviet embassies, respectively.

SEPTEMBER 29: Daniloff is released and allowed to return to the U.S.

SEPTEMBER 30: Zakharov is released and allowed to return to the U.S.S.R.

OCTOBER 21: U.S. writer Edward Tracy is kidnapped.

OCTOBER 26–29: One thousand TOW missiles are shipped to Iran.

NOVEMBER 2: David Jacobsen is released.

NOVEMBER 3: The Lebanese newspaper *al-Shiraa* reveals the secret swap of arms-for-hostages. Further bargaining for release of those held is halted.

NOVEMBER 7: Jacobsen meets with President Ronald Reagan at the White House.

NOVEMBER 10: French hostages Marcel Courdari and Camille Sontag are released.

DECEMBER 24: French hostage Aurel Cornea is released.

1987

JANUARY 13: French journalist Roger Auque is kidnapped.

JANUARY 17: West German businessman Rudolph Cordes is kidnapped.

JANUARY 20: British hostage negotiator Terry Waite is kidnapped.

JANUARY 20: West German businessman Alfred Schmidt is kidnapped.

JANUARY 24: American professors at the AUB Robert Polhill, Alann Steen and Jesse Turner, along with Indian faculty member Mithileshwar Singh, are kidnapped.

JANURY 26: Saudi businessman Khalid Deed is kidnapped and freed two months later.

JANUARY 30: The U.S. Department of State forbids all Americans to travel to Lebanon and instructs all U.S. citizens to leave.

FEBRUARY 1: The American hostages are moved from West Beirut to south Lebanon.

MAY 17: Iraqi Exocet missile strikes U.S.S. Cruiser *Stark* in the Persian Gulf, killing 37 crewmen. Iraq apologizes for "mistake" and offers reparations.

JUNE 17: U.S. journalist Charles Glass is kidnapped.

AUGUST 17: Charles Glass obtains his freedom.

OCTOBER 26: South Korean diplomat Do Chae Sung is released.

NOVEMBER 27: French journalist Roger Auque is released.

1988

JANUARY 27: West German businessman Ralph Schray is kidnapped. He is freed after five weeks in captivity.

FEBRUARY 5: Swedish UN relief worker Jan Stening and Norwegian UN worker William Jorgensen are kidnapped near Sidon. They are released a month later.

FEBRUARY 17: U.S. Lt. Col. William Higgins, a Marine assigned to the United Nations peacekeeping group in Lebanon, is kidnapped near Tyre.

MAY 4: French diplomats Marcel Fontaine and Marcel Carton, and journalist Jean-Paul Kauffmann, are released.

MAY 21: Belgian doctor Jan Cools, employed by a Norwegian relief agency, is kidnapped near Tyre.

JULY 3: U.S. naval ship *Vincennes*, believing it is under attack, shoots down a civilian Iranian airliner, killing 290 people, the United States apologizes and offers reparations.

SEPTEMBER 7: West German businessmen Rudolph Cordes and Alfred Schmidt are released.

OCTOBER 16: Indian professor from the AUB Mithileshwar Singh is released.

NOVEMBER 17: Swiss Red Cross official Peter Winkler is kidnapped and released after one month.

DECEMBER 21: Terrorist bomb blows up Pan American Flight 103 over Scotland, killing 270 people.

1989

MAY 13: British citizen Jack Mann is kidnapped, and reported dead four months later.

JUNE 15: Belgian doctor Jan Cools is released.

JULY 31: The kidnappers announce the death of Lt. Col. Higgins, claiming they have executed him.

OCTOBER 6: Swiss Red Cross employees Emmanuel Christen and Elio Erriquez are kidnapped near Sidon.

1990

APRIL 22: American Robert Polhill is released.

APRIL 30: American Frank Reed is released.

AUGUST 2: Iraq overruns Kuwait.

AUGUST 8: The United States sends troops to Saudi Arabia.

AUGUST 8: Swiss Red Cross worker Emmanuel Christen is released.

AUGUST 14: Swiss Red Cross worker Elio Erriquez is released.

AUGUST 24: Irish professor Brian Keenan of the AUB is released.

1991

JANUARY 16: U.S. military leads coalition armed forces in Operation Desert Storm to force Iraqi withdrawal from Kuwait.

Chapter 1

The Nightmare Begins

May 28, 1985 was a typical Beirut morning, swiftly brightening as the sun burned off the early mist. Pedestrians and cars sifted through the street between my apartment on the campus of the American University of Beirut and the garage leading to the AUB hospital where I was the CEO. I savored the sweet taste of my pre-and-post-jog tangerines. Dr. Ramez Azoury, chief of the hospital's department of obstetrics and gynecology, sputtered to a halt in his green Datsun 280Z and parked by the curb. He joined me and we snaked our way through the traffic toward the barbed wire intended to deter car bombers from pulling too close to the garage. Because I was a few minutes ahead of my ordinary routine, my usual escort, Hussein Nasrallah, had not yet caught up with me. But with Dr. Azoury at my side, in the warming daylight and bustle of people, I felt secure.

A man abruptly broke into view as he sprinted along the sidewalk between the long tangle of concertina wire and the garage wall. He slipped through one of the narrow openings and suddenly confronted us, pointing a 9 mm pistol at me. He shouted at me in Arabic. I didn't understand his command. But Dr. Azoury knew he was yelling "Get in the van! Get in the van!" Momentarily stupefied, I only stared at him.

"On no, oh no," protested the physician, throwing himself at the man, blocking him with his back. At that moment a

11

My nightmare began Tuesday morning of May 28, 1985 in the street, between the rear of the bus and the second car. Here is where I was grabbed. The low building at left is the AUB garage where a Lebanese soldier stood and watched my struggles. Just down the block, as the arrow indicates, are the offices of Hizballah, the organization behind my kidnapping.

nondescript blue van pulled up from behind me, effectively trapping me against the wire. I couldn't quite grasp that something like this was happening to me. Then a pair of arms encircled me and a small man who weighed at most 130 pounds tried to shove me toward the rear door of the van. A third fellow came to his assistance.

Fight and flight urges flooded me. I resisted furiously, jabbing with my elbows, kicking at their shins with the heels of my shoes, trying to tromp on their toes. I yelled, "Dammit, let go! Let go!" Then it was "Help! Somebody, help me!" During the forty or fifty seconds of this frantic wrestle, I felt

12

no fright. Instead, anger boiled over as I caught glimpses of passersby. Some stared, some headed rapidly off on their own business. Nobody tried to help. Even worse, the Lebanese soldier on duty twenty feet away at the garage entrance, armed with a U.S.-supplied M-16 rifle, ignored my plight. Maybe sixty feet away, a pair of policemen stationed at the gate to the AUB campus clutched their M-16s and did nothing.

The battle ended suddenly as the man with the gun, after failing to push Dr. Azoury out of the way, grabbed him, fired two shots into the ground, then put the muzzle to my friend's head.

"All right! All right!" I abandoned my resistance. I could not allow the doctor to be murdered on my behalf. My captors shoved me into the back seat. One of the pair from

The Lebanese army kept an armored personnel carrier parked near the garage. But it was empty and useless that morning.

behind me scrambled in beside the driver, who'd remained at the wheel. The others, including the gunman, whose name I later learned was Mokmoud, climbed in beside me and the van rattled off, leaving Dr. Azoury futilely crying for help.

A wild flash of agony stunned me. Mokmoud, either irate over my resistance or to insure I remained docile, had suddenly clouted me across the back of my skull with his gun butt. Stunned, I slumped forward, dimly aware of blood dripping down my neck onto my shirt.

Mokmoud now produced a child's tiny red dress. He twirled the fabric, then used it to blindfold me. He thrust a gag into my mouth, pushed me down on my stomach and tied my hands behind my back. With my nose in the van carpet, I smelled oil, dirt and the odor of death.

My abductor went through my pockets. At first I thought it was a weapons search but Mokmoud took everything, including my watch, my shoes, and my necktie. When he finished, he yanked me to a sitting position on one side. Then he rolled back the floor rug and lifted a concealed lid. Underneath lay a small compartment. Mokmoud forced me down into the well, feet first. Only by doubling up my legs and jamming them under the passenger seat could I fit my six-foot frame entirely into the slot.

Another awful moment: Mokmoud slammed the lid down to cover me completely. I was seized by a horrible mix of claustrophobia, nausea from the exhaust fumes spewing beneath the van, and growing dread of the future. Images from those stories of kidnapping, torture and murder, the savage undercurrents to life in Beirut for the last decade, surfaced with all of their terror.

I had been at my post a little more than six months. My chosen profession, after graduating from UCLA, was as a hospital administrator and I had been at it for close to thirty years. Following a bitter and emotionally upsetting divorce that left me with considerable anger against the family court

I was clean-shaven on my passport photo, made in 1984, shortly before I took my post at the American University Hospital in Beirut.

system, I fled the United States for a one-year contract to run a government hospital in Riyadh, Saudi Arabia.

When my stint in Riyadh ended I returned to the States, still restless and bored with a job at a California institution. A friend, Dr. John Mohler, an expert in pulmonary diseases, and as a USC alumnus, a subject for constant needling and practical jokes based on the football rivalry of our alma maters, suggested I investigate an opportunity to run the hospital at the AUB.

After several preliminary interviews in New York with Dr. Raja Khuri, the medical director for the AUB hospital, I was invited to visit the West Beirut site to meet the staff, inspect the facility and discuss the matter further. I figured at worst it would amount to a free vacation in Europe and the Middle East.

Late in September, I arrived at the Beirut International Airport, in the western part of the city. It had been a prime site for the short-lived U.S. Marine presence. The Marines had pulled out in February 1984. The October 1983 truck bomb explosion had killed 241 of the troops in their barracks and a series of firefights with militias had added more casualties.

A delegation from the AUB consisting of Dr. Khuri, Ahmed Nasrallah, an administrator, and Hajj Omar, chief of transportation, greeted me. A Lebanese army captain and a lieutenant whisked me through customs, collected my luggage and most hospitably offered a cup of the local coffee. As we sat in the captain's office exchanging small talk and sipping the brew, a tremendous explosion rattled the windows and caused everyone to leap from his chair. A huge cloud of smoke rose from a vacant lot several yards off. The captain quickly got on the telephone. His anxiety faded to a grin. He announced it was nothing but troops detonating a supply of captured explosives.

The incident provoked a round of comments and hopes for a lasting peace soon. I thanked the military men for welcoming me with fireworks and everyone laughed. Hajj Omar drove us to the AUB. He pointed toward the spot where the marine barracks had been, then zipped through numerous militia checkpoints without slowing down. As I learned later, Hajj Omar knew everyone and they him. He enjoyed such trust that he traveled freely throughout the city. I did not realize, however, that the route he chose for our trip avoided any areas that would have exhibited discomforting signs of the gun fights, shelling and car bombs.

At the hospital I dined with officials and toured the facilities. I reviewed a full portfolio of reports, financial statements, budgets, personnel files and every document relevant to the functioning of the place. I chatted with everyone of any importance. I got the feeling the job was mine if I so desired.

Toward the end of my stay, the government unexpectedly announced a holiday. George Tomey, the assistant dean who served as my host and guide, invited me to accompany his family to Summerland, a beach resort in West Beirut. Sum-

The Sumerland Hotel is part of a beach resort in West Beirut. While I was on a holiday break there, a remark about the future of Lebanese children convinced me to take the job.

erland, with its white sand bordering on the blue Mediterranean, two swimming pools, several restaurants, two discos, shops and a first-rate hotel, had once catered to visitors from Europe and the United States. The fighting had halted tourism but Lebanese still flocked to the place.

Beautiful Lebanese women strolled about in string bikinis and high heels while young bucks, as well as middle-aged men whose overhanging bellies hid their brief trunks, gawked and flirted. Children played all around us. Everyone seemed to concentrate on having fun. War? Who at Sumerland could believe it even existed? It was something from the past. My hosts pointed toward the horizon where Israeli gunboats had appeared a year ago. They laughed sheepishly, recalling the ensuing panic as everyone had frantically looked for shelter. Even as we lolled in the midday heat, a pair of Israeli jet fighters flew over during a routine reconnaissance mission. The Lebanese joked that the sonic booms were an Israeli greeting of "Shalom."

I met folks from all of the major native population groups that day. They unanimously expressed optimism about peace. As we lounged under beach umbrellas to shield us from the hot sun, George Tomey's wife offered a reservation: "I only believe there will be hope for peace and my daughters' futures when the first American comes to stay in Lebanon."

When I boarded my plane for the return trip to California, I had made up my mind to reject the job. It had nothing to do with the danger, since the risks just did not seem very real during my visit. Nor did I have any qualms about the medical center itself. From my inspection, the staff struck me as highly professional and dedicated. What deterred me was in fact a sense that it was not my professional abilities that were desired so much as my presence as an American.

The AUB had been in continuous operation since 1866. As

The AUB upper campus seemed well removed from the turmoil of the Beirut streets.

From the corniche below the AUB campus one looked out to the Mediterranean Sea.

a private, non-sectarian institution, the university and medical center derived some income from tuition and patient payments. But they ran at a considerable deficit, relying on private donations and grants from the United States Agency for International Development to cover the red ink. Obviously an American on-site manager might encourage contributions. But I did not relish the role of being a figurehead for fund-raising.

Just before I boarded the airplane, Ahmed Nasrallah pleaded with me to accept the post. He assured me that security would not be a problem and that the hospital truly needed my services. I lied to him, saying my mind was not made up. Privately, I had no intention of returning to Beirut.

I made myself comfortable on the Lebanese airliner with its excellent service. After a while, as the jet smoothly cleaved the blue sky, I dozed off. When I awakened I looked through the cabin window down upon southern Europe. I

My apartment at the AUB offered a view of the campus and the city beyond.

started to think about the past few days. I recalled the comment of George Tomey's wife. Then I remembered staring at the innocent faces of their two young daughters. At that moment, I reversed my decision. The hopes for the kids' futures overwhelmed me. AUB's avowed mission that they may have life and have it abundantly, firmed my resolve.

Yes, from a financial viewpoint, the job was attractive and there are some tax breaks. But this was not a prescription for easy street and early retirement. I knew it would be hard work under tough circumstances; I was not that naive. And in answer to those who maintain I should have known better and taken the State Department's advice to stay out of Lebanon I can only answer: "My government did not warn me to leave Lebanon until January 30, 1987. That was a full twenty months after I was kidnapped, three months after I was released and after more than thirty Westerners had been taken hostage." The warning, incidentally, was in the form of a press release advising Americans to leave Lebanon.

By the time the kidnappers grabbed me, the word was that at any given moment, perhaps three thousand people, evenly divided among Christians and Moslems, had vanished or were being held against their will. In many cases the victims never surfaced; their mutilated, unidentifiable bodies were

The AUB Hospital was a modern high rise capable of delivering quality medical care.

*I was comfortable in my office at the AUB Hospital, but I could
hear the gunfire when it erupted in the lobby.*

dumped in ditches or the sea. In some instances it was
simply a blood feud between two families; in others collect-
ing ransom was the motive. A major component of the violent traffic in humans was the total shredding of the fragile
fabric of the governing structure of Lebanon. The bloody
wake of the (unwarranted, in my judgment) Israeli invasion
of 1982 had left a ghastly residue of political assassinations
as opposing forces vied for power.

I was aware of carnage in the country but we at the AUB
seemed exempt. Sure, David Dodge, acting president of the
AUB, had been kidnapped in 1982 but he was released. And
when Malcolm Kerr, who became head of the institution,
was assassinated on January 18, 1984, in the hallway outside
of his office, that was chalked up to an aberration by Islamic
Jihad, one of the Iranian-backed groups demanding an end to
any American presence in the country. Some even suggested
Dr. Kerr was murdered either by Christian or Israeli extremists because of his strong and active support of academic

freedom or his willingness to understand the problems of the Palestinians.

While I worked at the AUB hospital, I heard of a few Westerners who had disappeared, like Peter Kilburn, the British-born librarian at the AUB who vanished December 3, 1984. But he had been very ill, having recently suffered a stroke. The talk was that poor Peter had probably experienced a cerebral hemorrhage and collapsed. By the time anyone discovered his body, scavengers most likely had looted the contents of his pockets and the corpse had become one more John Doe. I knew also of a couple of journalists, like Jeremy Levin, snatched March 7, 1984, and Terry Anderson, kidnapped March 16, 1985. Levin gained his freedom even before I was grabbed, while Anderson remained missing. Many felt reporters were at risk because of stories that offended highly sensitive parties who refused to accept the concepts of journalistic objectivity or license.

British-born librarian Peter Kilburn of the AUB disappeared after being kidnapped December 3, 1984. (Courtesy AP/Wide World Photos)

*Protestant pastor Benjamin
Weir had spent thirty years in
Lebanon when he was
abducted, May 8, 1984.
(Courtesy AP/Wide World Photos)*

Two clerics had been taken. On May 8, 1984, Rev. Benjamin Weir, a Protestant pastor who had spent much of his life succoring the downtrodden of the Middle East, was abducted. Then, on January 8, 1985, the Roman Catholic priest, Father Lawrence Martin Jenco, who had recently arrived in Beirut to assist in relief work, disappeared. Again, it was possible for me to distinguish between these cases and myself. The nature of their jobs required Weir and Jenco to travel in the most dangerous areas of the city, putting them at risk the same as good samaritans who labor in high-crime warrens in the United States.

Some of my sense of invulnerability was derived from my job. Never before had I encountered a hospital staff with such great skill and dedication while working under the most adverse circumstances. It was common for the staff to work double, even triple shifts, to voluntarily fill in because the instability of the city produced an absentee rate of thirty percent. Men and women would sack out on the floors or

24

David Jacobsen

Roman Catholic priest
Laurence Martin Jenco had
been in Beirut a matter of
weeks before he was snatched,
June 8, 1985. (Courtesy AP/Wide
World Photos)

Associated Press
correspondent Terry Anderson
was taken on March 16, 1985.
(Courtesy AP/Wide World Photos)

even in bathtubs for a few hours of sleep before returning to the health care wars. And we saw far too many shooting-war wounds. Our 421 beds were always full, with extra patients stacked up in corridors. Most of them were civilians. For all of the shooting done by the militias and armies, the bulk of the wounded were noncombatants with a high proportion carried in from the Beirut suburbs.

Once I observed the tangible results of the medical care extended to a people ravished by bloody strife and saw my own leadership contributions to improved efficiency, I felt I was serving a divinely inspired purpose. It was simply the best job I ever had.

Certainly I figured myself on some sort of "protected list." In fact, when I accepted the medical center's offer I was assured by two of the most powerful elements in the country, the Shiite Moslem Amal Party and the Druse Progressive Socialist Party, that I would be safe. Both of these groups fielded well-armed militias. Like the rest of those performing good works at the hospital I also believed the warring parties would avoid attacks on those engaged in obviously humanitarian activities. Although gunners from East Beirut, the largely Christian sector of the city, frequently lobbed shells into West Beirut, the turf controlled by the Moslem segment, few artillery pieces ever targeted the hospital, located adjacent to Beirut Harbor and near the main shopping and business section of the city.

We treated everyone, regardless of creed or ethnic background. And there was no shortage of victims. Our emergency room saw more people who had been shot or blown up every night than any major U.S. city.

Actually, one day in April 1985, the gunmen brought their wars right into the hospital building. An argument erupted between two groups in the medical center's lobby. From my office, I heard screams, the crackle of breaking glass punctuated by the unmistakable *blam, blam, blam* of small-arms fire. My assistant, Ahmed Nasrallah, rushed into my office.

"Boss, if the shooting gets closer, go out the window, crawl over the high concrete block wall and stay on the ground until I come for you."

However, the fusillade broke off. I asked some staff members to check out the situation and let me know if it were safe for me to inspect the damage. I was advised that the skirmishers had left the building. In the lobby I waded through a carpet of glass shards; every window there and those on the ground floor of the east side of the hospital had been shot out. The ceiling was pocked with bullet holes. Miraculously, no one had been wounded even though the place had been full of people.

As we surveyed the damage, shooting began again outside. Then several gunmen raced into the lobby, pausing only to let loose bursts from automatic weapons at anyone pursuing them. A full-scale panic rattled the staff. It was too dangerous to try the corridor to my office. I ran up a flight of stairs to the second floor clinical lobby where I spent the next hour, hugging the floor, alongside the lab technologists. My friend, Joe Cicippio, controller for the medical center, hid under his desk as one shell caromed off the door jamb to his office.

When the shooters finally left, wondrously with no casualties still, we asked for protection from the government. A brigade of Moslem troops from the Lebanese Army arrived. The commanding officer, known as "Captain Harry," had trained at Fort Knox, Kentucky, and sported a chestfull of ribbons including one from the United States. I was suitably impressed until his adjutant whispered to me that Captain Harry earned his American decoration for his skill at dancing.

Appalled, I whispered back, "You're telling me *I'm* really the company commander?"

"You got it," was the reply.

But in fact, Captain Harry's deputy, a Lieutenant Issa, knew his business. On one occasion, a band of militia brought several wounded comrades to our emergency ward. To the terrified staff, the gunmen announced, "If they die, you die," and trained their weapons on doctors, nurses and technicians.

Lieutenant Issa heard about the situation. He commandeered an armored car, drove to the building entrance, poked the vehicle's nose into the emergency room and pointed its cannon at the interlopers. He ordered them to throw down their weapons and leave. They quickly fled. Unfortunately, I made the mistake of praising Issa's bravery to the authorities. Since the Lebanese Army suffered a severe shortage of courageous and capable officers, he was soon transferred to a more active combat zone.

Another intrusion from the incessant firefights was what I call "The Night of the One Hundred Bodies." Late one evening, while I was in my apartment, someone at the hospital called to tell me one hundred John Doe corpses had suddenly been delivered. All the victims had died of gunshot wounds, many of the bullets delivered at point-blank range. The problem for the hospital was how to handle the bodies; our four-body morgue facilities were already overcrowded.

I came up with a creative solution. We asked for a refrigerated trailer truck from the Red Crescent Society (the Middle East version of the Red Cross). The bodies were then packed into the truck, which was parked on the hospital grounds. The supervising nurse, however, called to tell me that the dead had already begun to stink. She asked if the truck, along with the offensive odors, could be moved a short distance away. I, of course, granted permission.

A few hours later, the entire truck disappeared. It reappeared in the morning hours but now contained only twenty-five bodies. Everyone was puzzled until investigation revealed that every single one of the dead who had been killed at close range was now missing. The circumstances suggested that some sort of mass execution had occurred. The corpses perhaps consisted of Palestinians from one of the refugee camps. We concluded that the murderers had removed the victims, effectively destroying any evidence of their crimes.

For the sixty-some years since France created Greater Lebanon, the country had been a land honeycombed with political and sectarian fault lines. When a civil war erupted in 1958, U.S. troops under orders from President Dwight D. Eisenhower waded ashore in Beirut to protect U.S. interests. It was a bloodless exercise and civilians bestowed garlands upon the bemused Americans.

By 1968, Israel had begun to react to raids upon its territory by members of the Palestinian Liberation Organization operating out of Lebanon. The Israelis bombed the Beirut airport. After King Hussein of Jordan drove the PLO and its leader, Yassir Arafat, out of his country, the PLO set up shop in Lebanon. In 1973 the Lebanese Army attempted to defeat the PLO but the confrontation ended in a standoff. Two years later, a second civil war rocked Lebanon with perhaps ten thousand dead, many wounded, and massive destruction of property. At this time, Syria began efforts to control the makeup of a new government.

The Lebanese political powers rejected their neighbor's attempts and Syrian troops invaded the country in 1976. By the time an uneasy peace was arranged in 1977, Syrian forces had battled with the Palestinians and the Lebanese Army. The settlement failed to resolve the underlying turmoil between domestic factions, or to address the Syrian quest for domination, the role of the Palestinians and the attitude of Israel. The Camp David Agreement of 1977 between Egypt and Israel, while providing a measure of peace and security between those two nations, forged an alliance between the PLO forces in Lebanon and Syria against what they perceived as the common enemies.

Amid the growing divisions within Lebanon, Israel sought to restrict PLO raids by supporting a Lebanese warlord, Major Saad Haddad, whose militia sporadically patrolled the Lebanese border. When a PLO seaborne raid in 1978 caused heavy casualties on an Israeli bus, Israeli soldiers entered Lebanon and inflicted considerable damage on the PLO operatives in the area. Haddad's domain now included a continuous strip of territory in southern Lebanon along the border with Israel. A United Nations Interim Force in Lebanon (UNIFIL) was dispatched to monitor the area.

The Syrian military re-entered Lebanon in 1980 in a further attempt to exert control over the country. The Israeli government restrained itself despite warnings about the role of Syria. But in 1982, Israel launched a full-scale attack. Operation Peace for Galilee, as it was designated, was supposed to create a twenty-five-mile-wide buffer between Lebanon and Israel. Syria offered some resistance but soon backed off and sought a truce through Moscow and Washington. Meanwhile, the Israeli forces had plunged ahead until they besieged Beirut. Only after ten weeks of devastating shelling did the Israelis withdraw, and then only the evacuation of Arafat and the PLO militia brought a cease-fire. When the invaders finally departed, they left behind one unifying element in Lebanon—hatred for Israel.

The hapless Lebanese people had suffered tens of thousands of dead and wounded along with heavy damage to the country. Even worse, however, fragile coalitions between basically opposing factions were fractured. The Iranian uprising banished the Shah and installed the Ayatollah Ruhollah Khomeini, whose followers displayed a murderous face to any opposition and spread a terrorist gospel through Lebanon. Political assassinations rocked the country.

The Iranian revolution exported more than its religious zealotry. It also anointed the United States as the bearer of evil, the Great Satan. The message intoxicated a segment of Lebanese. In April 1983, the campaign to rid Lebanon of Americans took a deadly turn when a bomb was exploded at the U.S. Embassy. Sixty-three people, including nine CIA agents and several dozen Lebanese workers and visitors, died. To protect U.S. interests and because he thought their presence might increase stability, President Reagan sent a

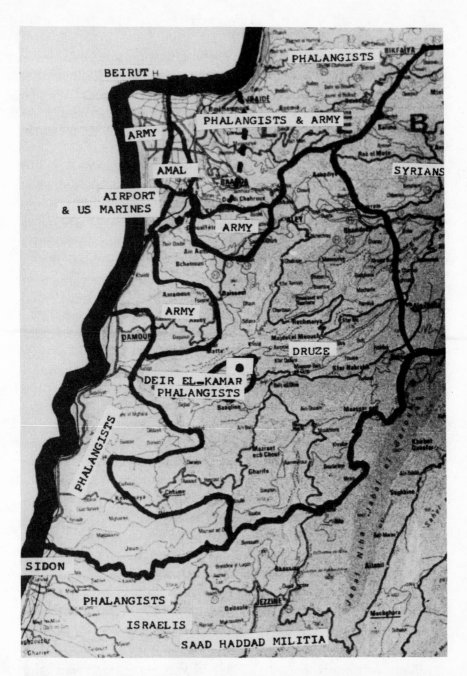

The map partially indicates the partitioning of Lebanon among
various factions while I was a hostage. Within the city of Beirut,
the Druse controlled a small corner and there were neighborhoods
dominated by Hizballah. (Courtesy AP/Wide World Photos)

detachment of U.S. Marines, backed by warships in the Mediterranean, to Beirut. Six months after the assault on the Embassy, a suicide bomber blew up the barracks at the airport, killing 241, crippling another dozen. This was the recent history of the troubled land where I had come to work. Behind it lay centuries of deep divisions.

There is an ancient Arabic proverb that puts this state of affairs in a nutshell: "I and my brothers against my cousin. I and my cousins against the stranger" (or outsider). The credo pervaded Beirut and the AUB hospital. Almost everyone agreed the Palestinians and the Israelis were more or less the "strangers." But beyond that, sorting out the Lebanese themselves, who did what unto whom, required a scorecard laced with small print. The Maronite Christians, a sect descended from a fourth-century, one-eyed hermit monk, arrived in Lebanon in the eighth century as refugees from Syria. Backed by French missionaries the Maronites adopted European ways and as such dominated the country's commercial and educational establishments. Sometimes insisting they were Phoenicians rather than ordinary Arabs, the Maronite Christians disdained the Moslem population. In the form of the right-wing Phalange, the Christians warred on all Moslems. A particular target were the Palestinians who had been expelled from Jordan or who had fled Israel or the West Bank when it was conquered by that country in the 1967 and 1973 wars.

Opposing the Christians were the various native Moslems, who fell into three groups. In a schism that dated back to the seventh century when a dispute arose over the legitimate succession to the founder of Islam, the prophet Muhammad, the followers of the Moslem faith had divided into the Sunni and the Shia branches. The former tend to be better educated and more affluent as well as more secular. Many of them lived in the Bekaa Valley region toward the east. On the other hand, the Shiites, poorer and less schooled, took a more fundamentalist approach to their religion. A majority of the Shiites belong to the sect known as Amal, which means *hope* in Arabic. The extremist minority belongs to Hizballah. The latter draw great support from Iran, dating to the time Ayatollah Khomeini, a Shiite priest, came to power in that land. Among the Lebanese Shiites, Hizballah—the Party of God—were the nation's greatest zealots. Islamic Jihad, the group that claimed credit for snatching Peter Kilburn, was a Hizballah fragment. It is important to draw a distinction. Most Amal supporters were not terrorists, but only wanted peace and justice. Not so Hizballah.

A third and considerably smaller segment of Lebanese Moslems were the Druse, a sect which dated from about the eleventh century and whose religion was cloaked in mystery. Druse women were frozen out of knowledge of the faith while men only began to be instructed when they reached middle age. But the Druse, while limited in number, were known as fierce warriors and overachievers. As the hospital administrator, I looked for a Druse when I needed someone to handle a tough task. For example, when we needed to supply transportation to take a shift of nurses to their homes in East Beirut and bring back their relief through no-man's land during an outbreak of gunfire, I told my assistant to recruit some Druse workers. And they got the job done without incident.

Aside from the believers in their causes or their sects, all of whom fielded their own militias, there were the purely criminal roving gangs intent only on plunder. Roiling the pot further were the Syrians, who occupied part of the Bekaa Valley and northern Lebanon which lay adjacent to their land. And in the extreme south, along the Israeli border, the retired Lebanese army officer, Major Haddad, had arranged his own treaty with the Israelis. They allowed this warlord and his successor to run his private army, which provided a buffer for the Israeli troops who still occupied a strip of southern Lebanon several miles wide.

The hospital staff reflected all of the Lebanese factions. Although they worked together in seemingly complete harmony, I was advised from time to time not to hire a qualified individual because of the person's political or ethnic background. I discovered that the more menial staff members, usually Shiites, were treated with great contempt. For example, the laundry workers labored in an unventilated cesspool building which, because of the soiled materials they cleaned and the unsanitary conditions, made them vulnerable to serious infections. Furthermore, they had to use a single toilet and one rusty faucet for personal hygiene. I was outraged at the conditions and raised hell. In my fury, I confronted the Christian administrator in charge of personnel. He sneered at me, saying, "You're new here. You don't know how we treat those people."

I ripped into him, demanding the laundry staff be treated decently. Our argument grew loud enough for those outside his office to become privy to the debate. Shortly thereafter, my adversary was kidnapped. Whoever did it scared him so much that upon his release he arranged to transfer to a post where he no longer dealt with employees from *any* group.

The Lebanese Army itself was supposed to keep the peace among the warring factions and prevent such ad hoc justice as was meted out to the personnel manager. But as the situation deteriorated, the army became less a force for holding the country together than another group in bloody pursuit of its own agenda. Opposing sides delivered eloquent messages to their enemies via the car bomb, the most notable being the explosions at the U.S. Marine barracks, the U.S. and French embassies and the residence of Sheik Fadlallah, head of Hizballah.

The infamous Green Line separated East Beirut, dominated by the Maronite Christians, from West Beirut, Moslem turf. Crossing the Green Line, a daily requirement for many who worked at the AUB hospital, entailed the risk of snipers hungry to add another notch to their guns, regardless of age or sex. For the most part, only Lebanese Christians regularly crossed the Green Line. On one occasion, Ahmed Nasrallah offered me a tour of the Green Line. Ahmed was like a son to me; he had graduated from Duke University with a master's degree in hospital administration and he seemed to know everyone in Beirut. He drove me right to the "border." The sight reminded me of photographs of Europe after saturation bombing in World War II, a several-blocks-wide belt of rubble. Suddenly a militia man bearing a Kalashnikov rifle stepped into the street in front of us. Ahmed waved a hand at him and we continued our journey. On the way back, the same rifle-toting sentry accosted us and started shouting. Ahmed halted the car and stepped out while the gunman began to berate him. Anxiety rose in my throat. The palaver lasted a few minutes before we resumed our ride. "What the hell was that all about?" I demanded. "Oh, he was just upset because I was not polite, did not stop to chat, when we came through before," explained my guide.

But the Green Line was no joke, as the following tragedy indicates. Only five feet six inches tall, Hajj Omar carried himself with such dignity and strength as to appear six feet six in life. It was Hajj who had met me at the airport on my first visit. He was assumed to have the right of safe passage anywhere. But in April, Hajj drove to East Beirut on an errand. During his return trip, a sniper snuffed out his life with a single bullet to the head. His funeral brought out a huge and tearful delegation from the AUB. The emblem of safety was gone. Among the pallbearers was Dr. Azoury, who so vainly struggled on my behalf as I was being kidnapped.

Still, it was possible to equate Omar's killing to the deadly, random violence that rips the streets of America, where the good and the innocent also fall victim to some deranged individual's murderous act. In spite of such horrors, our attitude was like that of people in the eye of a hurricane. Around us whipped a violent storm but we inhabited an island of tranquility. We didn't speak of the death and destruction that lay no more than a few blocks away, of what had become a way of life for the people of Beirut. We could shut out the noise of firefights and artillery. At AUB we buried a Malcolm Kerr or Hajj Omar and went back to our business. We worried occasionally about the disappeared ones and reminded ourselves to stay away from trouble areas. There was no talk of hostages among us nor in *Monday Morning*, the one English language newspaper, the BBC and Voice of America broadcasts. The troubles in Lebanon had gone on for so long that the citizens behaved as if their extremely circumspect lives were normal. Westerners who worked there, like me, suppressed anxiety and acted as if we were above the battles.

Chapter 2

The Interrogation

As I lay stuffed in the blue van that bright morning of May 28, 1985, I knew that my innocence, or should I say my ignorance, was now thoroughly shattered. There were those out there hell-bent on wreaking their ill will upon Americans. Bile bubbled up into my throat and I fought off an urge to vomit. The van lurched erratically. The transmission whined and slipped in protest as the driver accelerated, cornered, shifted gears up and down, raced his engine then slowed it.

To control my nausea I started a mental clock, attempting to determine how long we were traveling and to imagine our direction. I sensed a veer toward the Avenue de Paris, then another turn, movement along a curve. I guessed we were headed south, toward the suburbs of West Beirut.

We halted abruptly. Maybe we had come to an army or militia checkpoint. Hope surged; if they searched the vehicle I'd be found and released. But we passed without inspection. A cursory look would never have revealed the tiny compartment below the van floor.

After about fifteen minutes, the brakes screeched and we paused. I heard a garage door lift and the van shift into reverse. It backed inside. After the garage door slammed shut, my captors lifted the trap door and maneuvered me into a sitting position, facing the rear of the vehicle. The distinctive whir of a bandsaw and the smell of wood shavings suggested we were in a cabinetmaker's shop. Strangely, my initial fears had lessened. I was still very uncomfortable and damn mad. But I realized that if their intent had been an assassination I would have been dead already.

I sat there for perhaps a quarter of an hour before Mokmoud untied my hands; he removed the gag from my mouth but left the red dress blindfold in place. He climbed out of the van and three other people got in. Someone pulled off the blindfold but warned me in English, "Do not turn around."

I stared at the rear van door while they investigated the contents of my pockets. One of them, at least, spoke fairly good English and the trio began to interrogate me. They demanded an explanation for every scrap of paper taken from my wallet and pockets. Even my credit cards required answers. When they came across one item, their excitement was obvious. A buzz of talk in Arabic ensued, then a question was addressed to me.

"What are these numbers? Is this some kind of code?"

I could not figure what the hell they were talking about. "Show me the paper." It was a piece of yellow, lined paper with a list of ten, four-digit numbers. For a moment, even I was confused. Then I realized what it was. Some evenings, colleagues at the AUB, including Joe Cicippio, would come to my apartment to watch videos. On occasion, I would send Hussein, my unofficial bodyguard, to the store to procure the tapes. Hussein would rent whatever was available from a list of ten movies that I picked out of a brochure and denoted by their numbers rather than titles.

"They're simply listings for videotapes from a catalog," I explained. My kidnappers did not seem wholly convinced but after further discussion they dropped the subject.

"What is your name!" demanded one man.

"David Jacobsen."

"You are CIA. Don't lie!"

"No, I am not CIA."

"You spend an awful lot of time out of the country. You spend more time out of the country and in New York than you do on the job."

"No, you're wrong." I could not imagine what they were driving at.

"Be quiet! Lower your voice!" With the saw humming away in the background I couldn't see how the volume of my replies was a problem. But there was no mistaking the authority of the command.

They began to fire salvos of questions. "Tell us about the finances of the AUB. What is the extent of U.S. government aid? How are people appointed to the faculty?"

As softly as I could, I answered, "My name is David Jacobsen. I am the director of the American University of Beirut Medical Center. I have only been out of Lebanon once since I came here. And that was to attend a conference in San Francisco. As far as the questions about the university I do not know the answers. Ask me about the medical center."

"You lie!" snarled someone. "You are always in New York." Their insistence on my constant presence in New York really puzzled me. Then suddenly I had a revelation. There was kind of a standing joke on the campus about Einer Larson, the university controller. He seemed to be forever traveling abroad. They had to believe I was Einer. There were some resemblances. We both are of Scandinavian heritage and have somewhat similar features. And we wore the clothes associated with Americans. It was all a colossal mistake. They had intended to snatch Einer and grabbed me instead.

The questioning continued. "Who are the other Americans at the university? Are there others?"

I fudged the answer with the vague notion of protecting my associates. "Sure there are other Americans. But I don't know anybody at the university. I'm at the medical center and we don't have any American doctors. They're all gone."

Their attention switched to another discovery, my radio pager. "What is this?"

"It's a device for people to contact me in the hospital or when I am away from my telephone. I'll show you." I turned it on and the pager bleeped its usual start-up noise.

"Shut it off!" they instantly ordered. The sound scared them; perhaps they thought it could serve as a homing device to locate me.

The atmosphere now seemed less charged. I had the feeling they no longer considered me to be a CIA agent. Although I did not turn around I became aware that the person sitting directly behind me was small in stature and wore a religious style garment with off-white sleeves. He seemed in charge of the proceedings. Subsequently, I learned that he was known as "the Hajj," or Hajj Habib. (Hajj is an honorary title conferred on any Moslem who has made the pilgrimage to Mecca.)

A second man, the one who served as translator and actually asked most of the questions, was a man I subsequently discovered called himself Sayid. (As in the case of all of the guards, Sayid was an alias intended to protect him against future prosecution in the event that upon release the hostages might be able to identify their captors.) The third person in the van, who to this point had not spoken, I would find out much later was none other than Imad Mughniya, the leader of Islamic Jihad.

The trio seemed almost sympathetic. "Your head is bleeding a lot. Do you take any medicines?"

"Yes, I have high blood pressure and I take Dyazide for it."

"Your heart pumps well. You have blood all over yourself."

The comment irritated me but I controlled my impulse to snap at them that their pal's smacking me with his gun butt probably had something to do with the blood all over my shirt.

The conversation took a sinister turn. "You are Jewish. You have Jewish name."

That's it. I'm a dead man, I figured. "No, I'm not Jewish. It's a Jewish-sounding name but I am a Christian. I was raised a Lutheran. My parents came to American from Denmark in 1917 and the name has an "e" at the end. I can prove my background. I can say something in Danish." Fortunately, they were satisfied with my response. The truth is I

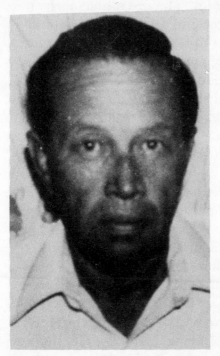

This is the photograph of me taken by my kidnappers, who then gave it to a Beirut newspaper, "to tell the world—no, the universe—that we hold David Jacobsen."
(Courtesy AP/Wide World Photos)

don't know any real Danish other than *Glade Yule*, which I doubt would have passed muster.

The Hajj began to speak Arabic in his soft, low voice while Sayid translated. "We are going to keep you. No harm will come to you. Don't be afraid. You are a good man. You just do exactly as we tell you and don't cause any problems. Don't try to escape and you'll be perfectly all right."

For the first time Mughniya opened his mouth and delivered his message in high-pitched English. "Now we are going to tell the world—no—the universe—that we hold David Jacobsen." On that note he abruptly rose and left.

Sayid translated a few final words from Hajj Habib. "You will be questioned further by others, tomorrow." In fact, I was never interrogated again.

Someone now blindfolded me, using the red dress. I was led from the van a short distance before being taken down a flight of stairs. I entered a chilly room, a basement but with a window through which a morning breeze hinted at the outside world. Any sense of freedom ended with Mokmoud, again my guide, ordering me to lie on the small rug on the floor. He wrapped a chilling chain about my wrists, snapping a padlock on to keep my hands together. He extended the chain to my feet and also locked them together. Mokmoud put a newspaper over my head. I felt him reach into my shirt pocket and remove my eyeglasses. They were never returned to me.

I lay there for several hours with Mokmoud seated in a chair nearby. I knew he spoke some English but he did not utter a word. My nose detected the pungent smell of liquid chemicals, perhaps furniture refinishing materials. My ears picked up the sounds of cars passing the building and the occasional airplane far overhead. Through the thin walls I heard the murmur of voices in other rooms. Time crept by. I felt an urgent need to urinate. I informed Mokmoud and he brought an empty water bottle with a narrow opening. With my hands and feet shackled, peeing into the container was not an easy task. In the long months ahead, I would have ample opportunity to practice and perfect this skill.

Impatience nagged at me. I wanted to take the next step. In my ignorance I wanted them to get on with the operation and get it over with.

By my guess, around two in the afternoon, Mokmoud handed me my lunch, a pita bread sandwich and a Pepsi, obviously bought at a nearby store. By the time I finished gulping down the food and drink, the place seemed to have turned much quieter. The air was heavy with afternoon heat and the stench of kerosene and paint.

Anxiety started to build up within me. I recalled a technique for stress management, which I learned from an American Hospital Association Continuing Education Course and had arranged to be given to employees at the Alhambra Community Hospital in California. I closed my eyes and inhaled deeply. I visualized a lighted globe at my navel. As I silently marked off seconds—one thousand one,

one thousand two,—the globe slowly rose to my head. Then I began to exhale, counting a cadence while the globe descended back to my navel. The exercise forces you to concentrated on the globe while breathing deeply and slowly. It's generally very relaxing.

The remainder of the day passed extremely slowly. I replayed the scene of the kidnapping. Suppose Hussein had been with me. He probably carried a small pistol but against the trio of men he would have been killed. On the other hand, why didn't I have the sense to pivot slightly and push backwards. The two men shoving from behind were both short and slightly built. I stand about six feet, weigh close to 180 pounds. With my regimen of jogging six miles several mornings a week, I was strong enough to apply a lot of leverage. The maneuver could have thrown the pair assaulting me from the rear onto the barbed wire, causing them enough pain to release me. What-if, and why-didn't-I notions were academic, however. The most they accomplished was to eat up the empty minutes.

I thought about my personal affairs. Having worked overseas before, I had the sense to make arrangements that would cover a serious illness, injury or even death by accident. The possibility of being kidnapped, however, had never entered into my planning. My paychecks automatically went to a bank in California. My two sons, Eric, twenty-nine, and Paul, twenty-seven, had power of attorney and any needs for them, or my daughter Diane, twenty-five, could be handled.

I tried to find comfort in my religion. Although, as I informed my captors, I was born into the Lutheran Church I was now more Episcopalian and actively sought to build Christianity into my life. It struck me that no matter what came, so long as I were alive there were two things the kidnappers could never take away: my freedom to think and my power to pray. And I did pray. I asked God to comfort my family when they received the news. I asked Him to protect me, at least to give me peace of mind no matter what lay ahead. And I thanked Him for the fifty-five years of life I had been privileged to lead to this point.

I remember a sermon from my pastor whose brother died in an airplane crash. The minister remarked, "Our fear is not really of death. Instead, we're really most afraid of the way in which we'll die." Or as some wit once noted, "Death is easy, but dying is hard." It was the question of what would happen next that concerned me. And as I faced this fearful unknown, my anger grew with the tick of every minute. What right did these people have to disrupt my life? How dare they cause my family all this grief? And there was Kerrie, the woman I had met while in Saudi Arabia. We had fallen in love and started to plan a future together. Now these thugs had put it all on hold.

Darkness fell. It was perhaps ten o'clock when there was a sudden racket as the garage door opened. I heard a car arrive, its doors open, then bang shut. The footsteps of two men pounded down the stairs to my room. "We are going now," said one in English. "It is only a short drive. You will be o.k."

They unlocked my chains, which clattered to the floor. I stood, stiff and unsteady on my feet after being bound and restrained so many hours. My head still ached from the gun butt blow. Mokmoud now took my arms, folded them across my chest and placed my hands on my elbows. With two-inch brown plastic tape ordinarily used to seal packages, he wrapped my arms and hands in this position. Someone shoved a piece of sheepskin into my mouth and began to tape it in place. I gagged and managed to push the sheepskin out with my tongue. When they finished slapping the tape over my lips and nose I gestured that I couldn't breathe. They adjusted the binding. The blindfold continued to deny me sight.

They walked me up the short flight of stairs to the garage. I was ordered to stand but not turn. I heard the car trunk spring open. I was shoved inside the trunk. As I curled up in the space, my ankles were bound with tape. Someone reassured, "Relax. It's only going to be a five-minute drive." The lid clanged shut. The doors opened and closed to admit passengers; the motor started. I recognized the purr of a Mercedes.

Through the back seat of the automobile I could hear the garbled noises of a walkie-talkie spewing Arabic. My spirits momentarily revived. It seemed apparent that they had kidnapped the wrong guy. Einer was the one they wanted. But if I had really convinced them, was it possible they would now just drive me back to the hospital gate and release me? No, it was too much to hope for, particularly after I remembered Mughniya's ominous promise to inform the world that the group held David Jacobsen.

Once again I tried to construct the route we were taking. At first we were on a smooth, paved road. Then we turned off and bumped over what was probably a dirt lot before returning to a regular street. There were frequent changes of direction, as if the driver knew what I was trying to do and meant to thwart me. It was too much. I surrendered, thoroughly exhausted. My fury and my indignation collapsed. By the grace of God I was still alive but I wept for my children, I cried for myself.

Without warning, the car halted; my heartbeat quickened. A stop could mean freedom, a bullet in the head or just another holding pen. After they opened the trunk, several pairs of hands grabbed my body and lifted me onto my feet. The ties binding my ankles were cut and I was guided down a slight incline. Through my socks I felt soft, sandy soil, as if I were walking through a construction site. Reverting back to my childhood, I was possessed by the absurd fear of stepping on a rusty nail.

After slogging perhaps thirty steps I sensed myself against a wall. Terror gripped me as I was ordered not to move. It could be an execution site. I heard a knock on a door. There were the traditional Arabic greetings, a series of *salaams* with all of the rhetorical flourishes, and my ears picked up the unmistakable sound of a toddler being greeted and kissed.

A hand pushed me inside and I climbed a spiral staircase to the second floor. From behind, I suddenly was shoved into a room. They rapidly heaped further indignities upon me. Someone roughly pulled away my trousers and peeled off my shirt. In my underwear, I was forced to sit on a mat while a new set of chains were attached to my right wrist and right ankle. The chain was secured to a column. A guard advised me I would be all right but followed up with the stern command not to remove my blindfold on pain of instant death. I acknowledged the warning and asked for something to drink. Sayid supplied a plastic bottle with water and an empty container for use as a urinal.

Although it was difficult under the circumstances, I lapsed into a restless sleep. Around 3:00 A.M. I awoke and, without thinking, pulled off that annoying blindfold. Light filtered into my compartment through glass doors leading to a balcony. I saw a guard sleeping on a sofa, then several others on cots. Suddenly, I remembered the warning never to remove the blindfold. I fumbled with it. Fear and hate plus having one hand chained to a column made the task harder but I succeeded without being discovered. Never again did I make such a mistake.

Before dawn, I awakened to the loud sobbing of one of the guards. It was Sayid shedding very real tears. I wondered what had happened. Had he just lost a loved one, a child, parent or spouse? I listened further and realized that Sayid was weeping for Hussein, the martyred son-in-law of the prophet Muhammad, now dead for about 1,300 years. In that moment I realized I had to be a prisoner of Hizballah, the same arch-fundamentalist stock that had swept the Ayatollah Khomeini to power in Iran.

Slowly, I took inventory of the situation. My entire body ached from the chain-restricted, near-fetal posture and from six hours lying on a thin, hard pad on the tiled floor. My hands and feet were swollen, my head still throbbed from Mokmoud's blow. Dressed only in my underwear and socks,

I peered beneath the red blindfold. I actually lay under a wooden shelf and my "living" space measured perhaps six feet by three feet.

There was a wooden partition at my feet and another one by my head. The faint rattle of chains and an occasional garbled mumble from beyond the barrier by my feet indicated the presence of another prisoner. Violent coughing and again the jangle of metal a few inches from my head told me of a third victim who sounded very sick.

In my solitude I thought about what I might be missing. My son Paul was soon to be married. My son Eric and his wife might soon be on the way to my first grandchild. My daughter Diane was now on her own and starting a career. My father was looking forward to his ninety-first birthday. Kerrie obviously would be distraught but at least she would be unknown to the media in hot pursuit of tidbits of information or gossip without regard to the sensitivity of the circumstances.

I cursed against the injustice of the situation. I was no soldier of fortune or Rambo come to Lebanon to shoot up the people. I was the victim of mistaken identification. It wasn't fair.

Silently, I recited the prayer of St. Francis of Assisi: "Lord, make me an instrument of Thy peace; where there is hatred, let me sow love; where there is injury, pardon; where there is doubt, faith; where there is despair, hope; where there is darkness, light; and where there is sadness, joy."

The simple words comforted me, although from what I knew of Hizballah and from what I had already experienced from my captors, even St. Francis himself would have had a tough time making his case. I prayed further for my release. I prayed for the gasping, moaning man in the next cubicle.

My reveries were interrupted by the appearance of Sayid. "Mr. David, how are you feeling? Does your head still hurt? You sure did bleed a lot!"

I had mixed emotions about his solicitude. After all, he

was part of the gang responsible for my injury and my incarceration. But his comments indicated they meant to inflict no further physical harm.

In fact, of all of my captors, Sayid was the most humane. On the other hand he could turn quite nasty. Marty Jenco later told me that Sayid accused him of peeking from below his blindfold. Using both hands, Sayid cuffed Marty on the head so hard that he saw flashes of light. As time passed, Sayid would recall the blows to Jenco, much the way a father reminds a child of a spanking for misbehavior. But as if to atone for the guilt engendered by striking an elderly man of the cloth, Sayid treated Jenco kindly from that day on.

At the time of my kidnapping I managed to get a good look at Sayid. He was about five feet five inches in height, slender in build with a weight of about 125 pounds. He had short black hair, a trim beard, sharp facial features with a small Roman nose, and he tended to strut when he walked. He wore the typical dress of the working-class Lebanese; jeans, a sport shirt and running shoes, all in brands popular in the United States such as Levis, Nike, and Reebok.

Because he spoke better English than anyone else around, Sayid usually served as an interpreter when necessary. Sometimes he would sit by me and talk of his life. He was married, with young children. He was not a stranger to violence. He told me his father had served time for a homicide. I once asked him what his mother would say if she knew what he was up to. He answered she would insist that he release me.

Ordinarily, he plied the trader of barber, but in the depressed economic circumstances of Lebanon, fewer people could afford to pay for grooming. He explained to me that he sought to eke out an existence, serving as a guard for such enterprises as had put me in chains. Sayid told me his salary as a guard was one thousand Lebanese pounds a month. The exchange rate then was about forty to one U.S. dollar, which meant he earned about twenty-five dollars a month for watching over me.

As devout as he was, Sayid rarely mentioned religion to me. I do remember him observing me at prayer once and saying, "We are all cousins. We are all indirectly descended from Abraham. Jesus was a great prophet. But Islam is a seven-hundred-year advance from Christianity."

On that first morning, Sayid checked my chains to make certain I was still bound securely, hand and foot. He reminded me of the rules. "Never take off your blindfold. Be silent, and don't try to escape. You will be safe as long as you obey orders." Switching again from his role as guard, he began to engage in idle chatter: "Your shoes came before you. Even though I was there when we grabbed you, the shoes were so big I thought you must be a giant and it would require two men to guard you. I have decided to give you a name, Clint Eastwood." Later, I learned that he had already dubbed Terry Anderson "Bronson."

Within my first four days of captivity I learned some basic facts about my fellow captives. The room in which I was kept had been divided into three cells. I occupied the middle one; just beyond the floor-to-ceiling wooden barrier by my feet was Terry Anderson, the Associated Press correspondent seized March 16, 1985, about two months before it was my turn. And only inches from my head, behind another thin wall, suffered William Buckley, officially an Embassy political officer but who had headed CIA operations in Beirut. He had been grabbed while in his car exactly a year earlier than Anderson, March 16, 1984.

Other hostages resided in the building. Most of Father Marty Jenco's space consisted of a closet in the hallway that led to the bathroom. His mat extended out from the closet into the corridor and as I was led to the toilet he would growl an objection when my feet kicked the pad.

There were always at least four guards. Apart from Sayid there was Michel, who seemed the squad leader. He was an ugly customer, tall and fairly heavy. One of his eyes turned inward. Several times, he sneaked up on my cubicle, obviously hoping to catch me with my blindfold down. At other

I learned that William Buckley, the former CIA chief in Beirut, kidnapped March 16, 1984, lay just beyond the thin wall of my cell. (Courtesy AP/Wide World Photos)

A comparison of the photo made by the kidnappers of Buckley and his picture on his U.S. Embassy Staff card indicates his physical deterioration while in captivity. (Courtesy AP/Wide World Photos)

moments he would spit water at me and laugh. On one occasion, he announced he had prepared a tasty soup for us—boiled water, an olive pit and a drop of olive oil. As I learned, all of the hostages hated him. Marty Jenco later told me Michel claimed that Jenco's inlays were really radio transmitters and at an appropriate moment he intended to knock them out.

Badr, who had driven the van, was a third member of the team. (He had chosen his *nom de kidnap* in tribute to the Bader Meinhoff Gang, a bunch of West German terrorists who extorted, kidnapped, bombed and killed in pursuit of their extremist political agenda. That Badr viewed them as role models was hardly reassuring.) Roughly the same size as Sayid, he had a mercurial streak. I diagnosed him as a manic-depressive and was terrified of what might happen if one of his extreme moods struck him at a critical moment.

Finally there was Mokmoud. I had also gotten a good look at him during the struggle. He stood much taller than the average Lebanese, coming close to six feet with a slender but muscular physique. His posture indicated a scoliosis, almost to the point of having a hunched back. He was clean shaven, had short hair and wore wire-rim, granny type glasses.

Strangely, the clout to my skull with his gun seemed to have wiped out any hostility toward me. From that point on, he always treated me gently and with civility. Other hostages, however, did not enjoy any dispensations from Mokmoud. He was recently married and he consulted with me— my hospital background was assumed to have conferred medical knowledge—about birth control. My advice did not seem to help much. He soon advised me that his wife was pregnant.

Although I would not classify them as religious fanatics, every one of the guards dutifully prayed five times a day in accord with the custom. They seemed to believe in their cause and the group. Mokmoud remarked once, "It's good to work for a secret organization. No one out there bothers you." Nevertheless, over the months that followed, I became convinced that the chief reason they served in their posts was the twenty-five-dollar monthly salary. Any one of them if offered a job with decent wages would have put away his gun.

Rather than considering the personalities of my keepers during those first days, I became absorbed with the suffering of the hapless William Buckley. It was apparent that he was very sick. I could hear him retching between coughs. He babbled in delirium and I distinctly heard him say to Sayid, "I don't know what has happened to my body. Thirty days ago, I was so strong."

Marty Jenco later remarked that he had heard Buckley in the bathroom, obviously hallucinating, announce, "I'll have my hot cakes with blueberry syrup now."

About six o'clock in the evening of my fourth day in captivity, Sayid came to me and in a weak effort to disguise who was ill said, "My friend is sick. What can I do for him?"

"I understand. He is one of ours," I said. Sayid did not respond. During this period, the guards never directly admitted they held anyone other than me. Presumably, Sayid approached me because he also thought I might have some useful information as a result of my experience as a hospital director.

I did not need any training, however, for my diagnosis. "On the basis of what I hear, you better get him to a hospital or a doctor, or else he is going to die."

"That's not possible," replied Sayid. "You must help. Tell us what we can do here."

I tried to recall everything I had ever learned in first aid courses or heard at medical staff meetings when physicians happened to discuss a case. I suggested to Sayid that the first priorities were reduction of the fever and something to settle the stomach. I spoke of cold compresses, aspirin, yogurt, tea, fluids and even of some prescription medications such as antibiotics. In Lebanon, medicinal drugs obtainable only through authorization by a physician in the United States can easily be bought over the counter at a pharmacy. Among other things, the civil war had wiped out the power of any regulatory agency to enforce laws.

Sayid thanked me for the information and said he would visit a pharmacy and get the medicines. Unfortunately, he either refused to believe speed was essential or else he followed the Arab tradition that places promptness low among the virtues. He sat and watched TV in the guards' quarters while Buckley's condition continued to deteriorate.

Around 10:00 P.M. the gibberish mumbled by Buckley petered out, replaced by an ominous gurgling, the distinct noises of a man in his death throes. Then silence fell. After a few minutes I heard a thud, then feet shuffling as if weighted down by a heavy object. They were removing William Buckley's body.

When the procession passed the blindfolded Jenco in the hallway, he asked where they were headed. Sayid answered, to a hospital. The priest questioned why the patient was silent and the guards admitted the captive was dead. I was told a few hours later that the victim was "in a wonderful place where the sun is shining and the birds are chirping." The description is of the Paradise found in the Koran.

I was furious when I heard Buckley had died. I was angry at the failure of the U.S. government to take effective action for his release. I was enraged by the dilatory behavior of the guards. Their neglect caused him to drown in his own lung fluids. I was sad that he had died alone and that I could not offer him comfort in his last hours. And I was worried that something similar might happen to me.

Buckley's demise really shook up our kidnappers. From a public relations standpoint, it could make them seem even more inhumane. Worse still, they had lost one of their presumed assets and the remaining prisoners might also become infected with a fatal disease.

A few days later, while I lay stretched out on the floor of my cell, a diminutive man was brought in by the guards. He was accompanied by Hajj. He could not tell me his name—he was a prisoner just as I was—but he announced, "I'm a physician and have been asked to examine you." Later, I would learn that he was Elie Hallak, a Lebanese pediatrician, seized apparently because he was Jewish.

"Do you have any health problems?" he asked.

"I feel pretty good," I said. "But, I've been taking Dyazide for hypertension for a number of years. Other than that I have no serious problems." Dr. Hallak checked my heart with his stethoscope and used a standard pressure cuff to measure my blood pressure. It registered high and he ordered a diuretic for me. The prescription, he said, covered ten days.

"Why only a ten-day supply?" I demanded.

"Maybe because that will be all that you will need." Then the Hajj spoke to Hallak in Arabic. The doctor translated for me. "He says your case is cooked and you will be going home soon."

"I don't know how I'll be able to pay you, Doctor."

He laughed and the Hajj immediately wanted to know what the joke was. After Sayid translated, the Hajj replied through Sayid, "Tell him we'll send the bill to Reagan."

Some earlier remarks from the guards also implied imminent release; this was after I mentioned that Paul's wedding was scheduled for early June and I had planned to fly home for the event. I spoke of this to the doctor and he gave me further hope. "You will be home in time for the wedding."

Hallak turned his attention to the conditions of the place. He was appalled at the lack of sanitation. He noted how filthy I and the other inmates were because of restrictions on washing up. He pointed to the garbage and dirt on the floor as sites fertile for bacterial growth. Several prisoners apparently told him of Michel's disgusting habit of spitting at us, of the guards' casual deposits of their phlegm on our floor. Hallak warned that if the place was not cleansed, there was a distinct possibility we'd all sicken and die.

On the following day, the big cleanup began. Michel barked orders to the other two guards and they obeyed without protest. They brought in a hose and washed down the floors and walls with cold water. Our captors got down on their hands and knees and, using disinfectant, scoured with brushes every inch of the ceramic tile. They even gave my feet a thorough scrub.

After a squeegee removed any excess water, new mats and bedding appeared. For the first time we showered, one at a

time. We shared a single—and by the time I got it—very wet towel. And in the bathroom, there was only one toothbrush for the hostages to use. I protested to Sayid. "A single toothbrush is a good way for everyone to become infected." That he understood and on the following day I counted four brushes. Thus I learned that in addition to the man by my feet, Terry Anderson, and Marty Jenco, whose mat I tripped over in the hall, there was a fourth person. It turned out to be the Protestant minister, Ben Weir, who occupied a place down the hall from Jenco.

My situation improved somewhat beyond the rudimentary cleanliness. I was moved into the compartment that formerly held William Buckley. To my surprise, I was handed a Bible to read. Unfortunately, without the glasses snatched by Mokmoud, the print dissolved into a blur. When I explained, Sayid said he would replace my spectacles if I could supply the details for the prescription. I didn't know what to say. He asked me for the focal length, something that Terry Anderson had taught him. I guessed and while I came close with the left eye, I missed badly with the right. Consequently, when I received spectacles from my captors I became a one-eyed reader for the remainder of my stay.

Chapter 3

Company

Two weeks passed slowly. I was not released and there was no indication of any intent to let me go other than the comments from Dr. Hallak and the Hajj when I was examined. This was the first in a never-ending series of raised and then dashed expectations. Cat and mouse was a favorite pastime among all of my abductors, from the Hajj and Mughniya on down to the lowest guard in the pecking order.

To be sure, the Arab mind does not regard time with the same linear intensity of Westerners. They see it as more cyclical. "*Bukrah,*" the guards would say, meaning tomorrow. But the word could signify the day after tomorrow, next week or three months from now. But at the same time, they were well aware of how intensely unhappy we were to be held prisoner for even a day and their careless attitude about time served as one more way to torment us. When they really meant something was about to happen, they cried, "*Bukrah bukrah.*"

Still, life in captivity had improved slightly since the first few days. Right after the big cleanup, Sayid sat at the foot of my cot and inquired, "Mr. David, what would you like to eat? We are going to bring food in for all of us. Would you like a little chicken? A steak? Spaghetti?" And for the next week our main meal at noon improved considerably, along the lines of what Sayid had said. But they soon cut back on our food. For breakfast and lunch it was usually some kind of pita bread sandwich. Yogurt, honey or occasionally some

56

boiled eggs filled the pita. Dinner frequently amounted to a piece of bread and a potato or a chicken noodle soup made from a powder mix. We drank Pepsi or tea, the latter a brew with enough tannic acid to brown the lining of your stomach.

Their public health program allowed us to shower every other day. Sometimes, the guards indulged us with the freedom to perform calisthenics. But usually any exercise was limited by the ever-present chains. In spite of Dr. Hallak's warning, Michel continued to fill his mouth with water and spray us.

Beyond our prison, the battle of Lebanon raged on. Sayid now had more immediate reasons for sorrow. Fragments from a random artillery shell ripped into his wife while she was near the site of my idyll, Summerland. Ironically, she had been rushed to the AUB hospital. He could not describe her wounds but he did say they were severe enough for her to need an emergency tracheotomy. A few days later, one of the other guards informed me that she had died, taking with her an unborn child and leaving the widower with three small kids to raise. Sayid's mother helped to care for the brood since he lacked the cash dowry required for a new wife.

During this first period of confinement, I lived in solitude but I was not alone. I was always conscious of the presence of the other hostages so close by if so invisible. I could hear them padding past on their daily visits to the bathroom—we each were permitted one visit every morning. We could not converse or even exchange a few words. But I drew comfort from knowing of the others. From the small bits of information wheedled out of the guards or remarks dropped by them and the news reports on their TV set I had identified the other Americans.

All of us suffered from the circumstances of our captivity, which consciously or not demeaned us. Bound hand and foot, stripped to our underwear, we were robbed of human dignity. For example, our digestive systems could not always accommodate to the tight restrictions to our cells. One could pee into the bottle but the guards frequently ignored pleas for a trip to the toilet to relieve a bowel demand. Olive oil acts as a laxative with me, and too many foods served to me were laced with it. Diarrhea afflicted me often. Severe cramps racked my body (and those of my associates) while I begged for a few minutes in the toilet. Because of the chains I couldn't get up and move about to ease the stabbing pains in my gut. The agony went on for hours without any response to the appeals. I pounded the floor or the wall but it fell on deaf ears. And I heard the others making similar entreaties.

The torments of those periods nagged at me even when I was not actually suffering from the need to visit the toilet. I would remember the awful moments and began to worry that the diarrhea was about to return. And so I spent a lot of time raising and lowering that golden globe from navel to forehead.

Some of the attitude of our masters was garden variety orneriness. I suspect they also thought their techniques could break our spirit and make us more docile. And often they ignored our needs because of their own pleasures. For example, they became complete couch potatoes when anything of interest appeared on their television set. Their favorite shows were all bootlegged American ones. From my compartment I could hear the sound but couldn't see the flickering images on the tube. One night a segment of "That's Incredible" featured a contortionist who coiled a large python in a two-foot cube box and then squeezed his own body into the twelve-inch opening. As the host John Davidson described the stunt I considered my own fetal posture as equally incredible.

The guards tuned in regularly to the likes of "Dallas," "Falcon Crest," "Knott's Landing," and "Three's Company." Saturday morning, as in the States, they focused on the cartoons ostensibly aimed at kids. Bemused as I had been by Sayid's references to Clint Eastwood and Charles Bronson, whose films suggested the way to solve problems was with

Our hopes were raised after the hijacked TWA Flight 847 came to rest at the Beirut International Airport. The negotiations seemed to include our release. (Courtesy AP/Wide World Photos)

guns, I was even more depressed by the thought that these religious zealots, who lived in an impoverished land ravaged by constant guerilla warfare, formed their bizarre vision of America from the skullduggery and bed-hopping of glitzy soap operas. It was bad enough that American TV beamed false values to the folks at home who at least were in a position to experience reality. But exporting these absurd and essentially evil images to the Third World, whose inhabitants accepted these shows as documentaries, disturbed me. I resolved that if released I would campaign for the networks to dig into their video vaults and share with those abroad some more positive views of America.

The broadcast world became more than a subject for idle speculation, however, when the TV news began to report on the hijack of TWA Flight 847 on June 14, 1985. The airplane had been scheduled to fly from Cairo to Rome. During a stopover in Athens, a pair of Lebanese Shiites either managed to smuggle aboard weapons, or else someone arranged for the guns to be stashed where the Shiites could retrieve them. In any event, the pair commandeered the aircraft and it began to fly back and forth between Algeria and Beirut. The initial demands were for the release of some seven hundred Shiites detained by the Israelis.

The guards themselves were extremely excited by the event and hope welled up among those confined to the cells. The news shows started out talking about negotiations to free the thirty-nine hostages on the plane. That in itself encouraged me because until this moment, the official word from the U.S. government was that it would never negotiate with hijackers or terrorists. Then the figure of Americans at

A Flight 847 hijacker, from the Islamic Jihad which had kidnapped us, pointed his weapon at a photographer. We could not see the TV from our quarters but we could hear the commentary, and the guards filled us in on what was happening. (Courtesy AP/Wide World Photos)

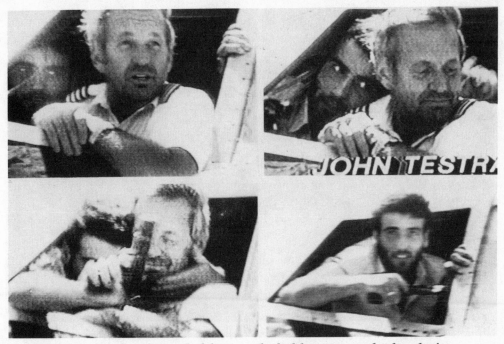

A gunman, who discarded his mask, held a gun to the head of TWA pilot John Testrake at the Beirut airport. The pictures were taken by an ABC News TV crew. (Courtesy AP/Wide World Photos)

stake was raised to forty-six; it seemed certain that the additional group included us.

"Maybe now you can all go home," remarked Sayid to me, buoying my spirits even higher. The news carried comments from alleged authorities. One report said the Amal militia was taking control of the hostages like us as well as those on the plane, but that was sadly untrue. I even broke into a laugh when it was announced that we were all well treated, including being offered menus in both English and Arabic at mealtimes.

Matters seemed to reach a climax with the murder of Robert Stethem, a young navy man on TWA 847. Now it became possible that some sort of military assault might be launched. Although that could free those aboard the air-

Backed by masked associates, the leader, wearing a hood, addressed a rally that supported their efforts to win concessions from the West through the hijacking. (Courtesy AP/Wide World Photos)

plane, or kill and injure some of them, it would end the talks about any swap of prisoners.

The plane finally settled in at the Beirut International Airport. And either late on June 16 or early the following day, Nabih Berri and his Shiite Amal militia took charge. Berri announced, "I am not a go-between. I am a party." While the United States kept claiming it would never negotiate with terrorists, Israel, which had once before traded some prisoners for several of its own soldiers, indicated it was willing to deal, if asked by the American government.

We knew we were in trouble when they stopped talking about forty-six hostages and cut back to a figure of thirty-nine, the number of people still held on the airplane. Indeed, our hopes fell as Berri declared he had no control over the seven hostages who were not aboard TWA 847.

I was crushed when, after a standoff that dragged on for seventeen days, the thirty-nine airplane hostages were released based on assurances by the United States to Syria that Israel would release three hundred Lebanese Shiites held by the Israeli-sponsored militia in south Lebanon.

I could not understand why we had been excluded. Weren't we just as important as the individuals on 847? Nabih Berri, in addition to his role as leader of the Shiite Amal militia, served as Minister of Justice in the shaky Lebanese government. He explained on television that the fate of the other American hostages, meaning us, lay in the hands of Kuwait. I could understand then and now that for political reasons, President Reagan felt obliged to issue a statement in which he declared the United States "gives terrorists no rewards and no guarantees . . . We make no concessions. We make no deals." Berri, however, confirmed that the American government had indeed bargained with the terrorists to free those held on 847. When Secretary of State George Shultz denied it, I believe he lied. From that moment on, I saw the State Department and in particular George Shultz as hostile to my best interests.

The reference to Kuwait as the key to our release was not a total surprise. During the newscasts, there had been some talk about the "Dawa prisoners." Indeed, Sayid once "comforted" me by stating that "you were not kidnapped for any personal reasons, but only to secure the release of our Dawa friends held in Kuwait." And newspapers in the United States had carried reports before the seizure of TWA 847 that the American hostages taken in Beirut were connected with those in Kuwait.

The Dawa members belonged to one of the more fanatical terrorist groups. They literally exploded into the Middle East headlines during 1983. On December 12 of that year, a gang of twenty-one staged a well-planned attack in the tiny, but oil-steeped kingdom of Kuwait. Within the space of ninety minutes the Dawa gang exploded six bombs there. They hoped to so destabilize the land that their fellow Islamic fundamentalists would stage a coup d'état, booting out the Emir and ending Western influence.

The first target, naturally, was the U.S. Embassy compound. The terrorists employed the same technique as was used in Beirut, an explosive-laden truck. But while five Kuwaiti nationals, along with the driver, died, the damage to the Embassy was negligible. A second blast followed at the French Embassy with even less dramatic results; five injured. The third and biggest bomb went off at a major oil refinery. If that installation had been wrecked, the country's economy would have been crippled. The device detonated prematurely, however, and production continued almost unabated. A fourth try misfired at the main water desalinization plant. Again, success would have devastated

Nabih Berri (second from right), leader of the Shiite Amal militia, took charge of negotiations. He made public the ostensible demand of the kidnappers, release of the Dawa prisoners in Kuwait. (Courtesy AP/Wide World Photos)

fresh-water-poor Kuwait. Two lesser attempts at the airport control tower and at the main electrical control center also failed to interrupt service.

The unfortunate driver of the truck aimed at the U.S. Embassy allegedly left some evidence behind in the remains of the vehicle—his thumb. A print from that digit along with the materials from the malfunctioning bombs, supposedly enabled police to quickly identify the Dawa people and arrest them.

A total of twenty-one individuals went on trial. Six received death sentences but three had already escaped the country. Life sentences went to seven conspirators. Another seven were hit with prison terms of from five to fifteen years. One man was acquitted.

Judicial review confirmed all of the sentences but the Emir of Kuwait did not sign the death warrants. Then, after the Dawa made a futile assassination attempt upon the nation's ruler, the executions were placed on hold. The word to the terrorists was that any further attempt to kill the Emir would result in a slow, agonizing death for the Dawa held by Kuwait.

Blocked by the eye-for-an-eye policy of Kuwait, the Dawa champions had opted for another means of pressure. They would seize Americans and use them as pawns to trade for their comrades. But the Kuwaiti government refused to make a deal and the United States was disinclined to throw its weight around. As a consequence, I and my fellow prisoners languished in chains.

A few days later, deliverance literally banged on our door. The Amal militia, fed up with the presence of the Palestinians on their turf, had gone out gunning for them. While stalking the Palestinians through the streets and almost house by house, they were also keeping an eye out for the hostages. The noise reached a crescendo of automatic weapons and grenade launchers. By some odd quirk my imagination created a picture of rank upon rank of British Redcoats from the Revolutionary War marching upright into battle. As the troops neared our place the shooting became deafening. It sounded as if we were in the middle of a full-scale war.

The guards became agitated. They covered me with a flak jacket and told me not to worry, but I sensed desperation. I recalled a happy resolution from before my time in Beirut. The first American seized, in February 1984, less than two months after the Dawa assault in Kuwait, was Frank Regier, a professor at the AUB. He was held with Christian Joubert, a French engineer engaged by an Islamic relief agency. Hands and feet bound, eyes blindfolded, chained to window bars, Regier and Joubert underwent the same sort of captivity as we did. However, three kids hunting birds happened to climb the wall of the house where the two were imprisoned. Through a window they saw the two men sitting on a mattress, with their limbs chained, eyes covered, mouths gagged. When one informed an older brother he notified the neighborhood Amal officials. Nabih Berri ordered his men to raid the place, thereby winning freedom for Regier and Joubert. Berri opposed attacks upon foreigners and if his militia discovered me I would be free.

The firing decreased, momentarily. I kept my disappointment muffled as one of the guards said that the soldiers had turned from our house when only fifty yards or so away and headed in the direction of the Palestinian refugee camps of Shatila and Shabra. Half an hour later, just as I began to abandon hope, the street warfare revived. My keepers removed the twenty-gallon water drums stashed in the bathroom and by the entryway to our quarters. I heard them nervously conferring in whispers. My anxiety picked up the distinctive clicks of weapons being cocked.

Unfamiliar voices from a somewhat lengthy discussion drifted up from downstairs. Silence fell. I could feel the tension of the guards dissipate and they uncocked their guns.

Sayid greeted me with a smile. "Amal security forces were looking for you. But we talked them out of coming upstairs.

It's lucky for you that they didn't because if they did, we would have been forced to kill you."

Twenty feet and some persuasive talk had apparently come between me and either freedom or death. At the moment I was only sorry that the militiamen had not persevered. To be so close and be denied was depressing. How many more chances would I get?

The visit from Amal, however, did bring one great change. One night later, after falling asleep, I was awakened by Michel hurling plastic bags of garbage at me. Annoyed, still drowsy, I lashed out with my feet, landing at least one painful kick. The surly bastard was ready to kill me. Only Sayid's intervention saved me from a bullet.

Michel's unpleasant reveille call arose from a decision that we be moved to new, more secure quarters. I was told to put my urine bottle, water container, plastic bowl and spoon in a plastic bag. I was removed from my cell and made to stand, still blindfolded, in the corridor. But I was not the sole prisoner being transferred. My hand was placed on the shoulder of a man in front of me and I was told to keep it there while we walked.

The two of us were led down the stairs and outside onto that dirt road. Once again, in my stocking feet I worried about nails or broken glass. We walked without incident for maybe one hundred yards and then halted. I heard a door being unlocked and we climbed another staircase, passed down a hallway. We entered a room and received orders to sit on the foam rubber mats. The ubiquitous chains were firmly affixed to my right wrist and ankle. Then the door slammed shut, springing its lock; a padlock also snapped shut.

The room felt very cold. A fan whirred somewhere. Minutes passed without a sound. I decided to chance lifting my blindfold from my right eye. I looked into an eerie green glow, the light emanating from a twenty-five-watt green bulb ordinarily used as a neon light.

Then I remembered I was not alone. I looked over to my

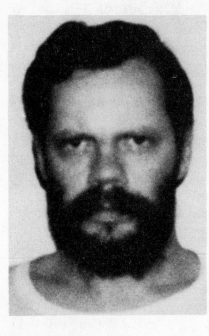

When I first saw Terry Anderson in the dim night light of our joint cell, he, like me, was in his underwear and heavily bearded. (Courtesy AP/Wide World Photos)

right and in the dim illumination saw a short, heavyset, bearded, pale-skinned, dark-haired man wearing, like me, only underwear. He also had worked up the courage to defy the rules and peek. We stared at one another. Then we stretched toward one another, as far as our chains would allow. Our fingers managed to barely touch. He said, "I'm Terry Anderson."

"I'm Dave Jacobsen," I replied. That moment began a comraderie that would be marked by frequent sparks of conflict generated by deep differences of philosophy, politics, and values. But a bond would be forged, too, between two human beings so very much alike in personality and so bound by dire circumstances.

Chapter 4

The Church of the Locked Door

That first night, the two of us, total strangers yet instant intimates, exchanged the stories of our lives. I told Terry all about my career, my broken marriage, my children. I recounted how I had met Kerrie while on the Saudi job and we had found a common interest in religion, sharing a love of Jesus, studying the Bible together. I suspect Terry, a lapsed Roman Catholic and a skeptic of other organized religions, may have found it difficult to appreciate our relationship. Most of those who accept work in Saudi Arabia think in terms of financial rewards and career advancement, or like me they hope to put behind them some unpleasantness. I thought, how wonderful for me that I had found something so different, a spiritual union, as if an angel had been sent to console me in the desert!

I spoke of the joy I discovered jogging in the desert. It was spiritually enthralling to be pounding along and suddenly watch the sun begin to light the morning sky. At such moments I spontaneously broke into prayer. Unfortunately, many of the younger Saudis educated in the West, unlike their elders, ignored the spiritual and pursued material and fleshly pleasures at least as avidly as their American counterparts.

I related to Terry my experiences at the AUB medical

center, detailing incidents and situations that the journalist in him eagerly devoured. I also supplied him with the facts of my kidnapping and first month in isolation.

In turn, Anderson revealed his background, one that was more colorful than mine but I would say considerably more troubled. He had served in the U.S. Marines, done a tour in Vietnam where he received a serious wound in the knee. While recuperating in Japan, he arranged a transfer to the news information section of the Corps. After his discharge, he elected to stay in Japan where he got a job as a reporter and married a Japanese woman. The couple had a daughter.

He matched the stereotype of the foreign correspondent. He worked and he drank with enthusiasm. His career took him to South Korea and South Africa before his assignment to Lebanon. And in that last capacity he spent time with major figures in the Middle East. He believed the only way to do his job properly was through personal observation and verification of facts. That zeal could only put him in harm's way, but Terry still believed in a world where the news gatherers were sacrosanct. He, too, had honestly thought of himself as immune to assault or kidnapping.

In Beirut, where Anderson continued to drink heavily, his marriage began to collapse. He shipped his wife and child, who was ten when I met Terry, back to Japan, and divorce proceedings began. Meanwhile, Anderson fell in love with a Lebanese woman. At the time of his kidnapping, she was already pregnant. One of the things that bothered Terry most was that he felt he had finally started to reconstruct his life and bring stability to it. Now, however, at a crucial point for himself, and for those he loved, particularly his ten-year-old daughter, he was powerless to resolve the remaining issues.

As the local correspondent for the Associated Press, Anderson naturally presented a much more conspicuous image than someone in my shoes. It was the nature of his job to be out in the streets, to seek interviews with those calling the shots. Indeed, only the day before he was grabbed, Terry

70

spent several hours with Sheik Sayyid Muhammad Hussein Fadlallah, the spiritual leader of Hizballah. It is easy to see how agents of Hizballah—Imad Mughniya, for instance, who served as security chief for Sheik Fadlallah—having watched Terry interrogate their revered leader in his bold, forthright manner, might conclude that the journalist was an important figure in his own right, making him a prime target.

While I was still free, the accepted explanation of Terry's capture was that he had been so indiscreet as to play tennis with his fellow American, photographer Don Mell, at a public park, instead of at the protected courts on the AUB campus. It was true, Terry told me, that rather than wait for a court at the AUB he and his companion had used the public court. But he was not seized there. In fact, Don Mell had driven Terry back to his apartment, and they were chatting on the street for a few minutes when the gunmen grabbed Anderson, while Mell stood by helplessly. Obviously, Terry was not simply a victim of circumstances but a well-stalked target who would inevitably have been kidnapped.

Of course, we mulled over our chances for liberation. We reviewed the failed attempt by the Amal militia to find us, wondering whether there was anything we could have done to have helped. Most likely, if we had yelled the guards would have killed us instantly. Still, to have been so close and yet denied, set us off on such fruitless speculations. We also exchanged interpretations on the resolution of the TWA hijack and agreed our government seemed to write us off. He briefed me on our kidnappers. During his tour in the country, Terry had gained considerable knowledge about the various gangs, cliques, and sects. And he never relinquished his role as a reporter during his time in captivity.

In the coming days, our relationship took on new dimensions. At first, we were just so damn glad to have each other that whatever one said the other accepted. We enjoyed one another's company and we traded insights into the local

71

culture and the locutions of our captors. We chuckled as we concluded that in the Arab world, the initials IBM stand for a frustrating fatalism—"*Inshallah*" (God's will), "*Bukrah*" (tomorrow), and "*Mallesh*" (so, what can *we* do about it).

But familiarity bred true respect, wherein one argued if he thought the other wrong. Terry possessed what, in my experience, is a common failing of journalists, an assumption that they are authorities on almost any subject. For example, he tried to tell me how hospitals are managed. He did not have a clue. He had no understanding of how these institutions are organized, the roles of physicians, the functioning of boards, the duties and responsibilities of the chief of staff. Over the years, nothing on the job bugged me more than someone who happened to have seen the latest episode of "Marcus Welby" and then tried to tell me how a hospital operated. The only thing worse was to hear an explanation from a would-be authority like Terry insisting he really knew the drill. Terry, for instance, believed that doctors run a hospital—not hospital administrators—a common misconception of Marcus Welby fans. (I think the day that show went off the air was probably declared a national holiday by all of us hospital administrators!) He had no idea that a doctor's clinical privileges within a hospital are limited and determined by an in-house review board; for example, a family practitioner cannot simply come in and perform neurosurgery. I told Terry he was full of baloney in this particular instance. If we could see the opportunity to "yank a guy's chain," play the devil's advocate no matter how limited our knowledge of a given topic, we would do it. I guess Terry was yanking my chain this time.

Another bone of contention between us was Saudi Arabia, where I had spent a year and dealt with fairly high officials as well as the working stiffs. In contrast, he had spent only a few days there. He made statements about the condition of the Shia peoples in the northeast, near Kuwait, that I was certain were dead wrong. He claimed the Shia in northwest

Saudi Arabia were on the verge of revolt. I knew this just was not the case. I considered his flat assertions to be based on ignorance and a need to establish himself as the omniscient newsman.

He derided Ronald Reagan and I took exception here also. I demanded, "How long since you lived in the United States, Terry?" But that did not squelch him.

We went far beyond the stage of polite, nodding acquaintanceship toward true friendship, where the bond is strengthened because the pair are willing to be honest with one another and admit to their differences.

And indeed we had our differences. I am at heart a religiously oriented, conservative Republican who opposes the values sometimes subsumed under the label of "liberal." For example, I do not accept homosexual behavior as a freedom guaranteed under the U.S. Constitution. There are those who believe it is protected by those clauses in the Constitution that cover private behavior. I don't. It is proscribed in the Bible, and I follow the gospel. Furthermore, I would certainly place limits on freedom of expression when it comes to what I consider pornography. In many cases, one of us would play the role of sophist, taking the opposite side in an argument purely for the sake of keeping the juices flowing. In this case, we had a genuine disagreement on principle.

Anderson's scorn for other religions, in a way, contradicted his other beliefs. He was dubious about any restrictions upon the rights of humans to do what they want, a left-wing Democrat politically. On the other hand, while I was more tolerant of religious credos, so long as they were sincerely held, I do not favor permissiveness. Thus, the stage was set for our frequent, often acrimonious debates. Neither one of us was averse to taking a position without facts to back ourselves up. Sometimes, we became downright angry at one another. He got so upset with me once he warned, "Remember, Jacobsen, I've got a knife."

"Better men than you have tried to stab me in the back," I

answered. There was no real threat, of course. The knife he boasted of was a dull tool for paring garlic. And not for a moment did I ever doubt his sincerity, his integrity or his basic worth as a human being. Terry Anderson is a person I can always respect and whom I count as a friend.

The arguments frequently verged on the ridiculous. Both of us were very angry men. But the real subjects of our ire, the kidnappers, were untouchable. Deep down I think we both realized the bickering had a value; it kept our minds active. Our juices flowed and we avoided the physical and mental symptoms that stem from hyper-suppression of feelings.

After a month, during which time my original blindfold— the child's red dress—became grimy with dirt and sweat, leading to a slight inflammation of the eyes, I received a new covering. Actually, I was directed to make it by tearing strips from a tank top undershirt. That furnished me with a pair of blindfolds, allowing an opportunity to hastily wash a soiled one while wearing the clean cloth over my eyes. Those of us with this type of blindfold quickly learned to line up the threads so that we had some vision that could not be detected by the guards. This was how I came to know the faces of my captors.

In fact, I had a new wardrobe, two sets of underwear and a couple of pairs of socks. The guards, these men whom I am convinced, if so directed, would have murdered me without hesitation, were as modest as young women in a nunnery. Each set of underwear consisted of jockey underpants to be worn beneath a pair of boxer shorts. Later, when another hostage, the fifty-one-year-old priest, Marty Jenco, happened to appear with only his boxers, a shocked Sayid remonstrated, "Oh Father! Shame on you!" A white undershirt and black socks completed our ensemble. I also had my own towel. The problem was that even though I could make an attempt to launder one set of garments, our sunless cell remained damp and nothing ever dried out.

The building in which we were being held was a two-story

affair with both a basement and sub-basement. It appeared to have been planned as some kind of school but the second floor was incomplete. Our room was about twenty by twenty and originally had a large window, but concrete blocks filled the opening. A pair of small ventilation fans high on the wall sucked in outside air. Three rooms on the floor held hostages and there were two bathrooms; one serviced the prisoners, the other the guards. A primitive kitchen with a minimum of appliances provided most of the usually barely palatable food.

Within a few days of our move, Michel, the sadistic guard, suddenly disappeared. He was replaced by Badr, a five feet ten inches tall, heavyset, red-haired and clean-shaven fellow who at first promised to be the most obliging of our captors. But within a few weeks he turned sullen and disagreeable. I nicknamed him "Mafi," meaning "no." Badr supplanted Michel as squad leader and his mercurial nature continued to disturb me. As the head of the unit, Badr would roar off on his motorcycle for shopping. During his absence the atmosphere seemed relaxed. But on his return the level of conversation rose several decibels. We could hear him shouting at the other guards amid increased tension.

On the other hand, Terry was no less combative with Badr than any other of the guards. We were still under threat of death if we removed our blindfolds in the presence of any of the kidnappers but in their absence we were allowed to take them off. In fact, Sayid had instructed us—as I recall, it was in July 1985—that we were allowed to remove the blindfolds when they were out of the room. As soon as we heard the guards start to unlock the padlock, we knew we had to slip the blindfolds back on. The guards never announced themselves; they would just start unlocking the door. We became so conditioned by the threat of death that slipping the blindfolds back on became a reflex. We even did it in our sleep, or rather upon being woken by an unannounced visit from the guards in the middle of the night.

Badr toted what was probably a .357 magnum, a huge

weapon. Anderson, who had caught a glimpse of the pistol, razzed Badr about its size.

"Badr," sneered Terry. "You fire that big gun and it'll knock you on your ass."

Badr took this as something of a slur on his manhood. He shouted at Anderson, in his broken English, "You are wrong. I am very strong. This gun cost me a lot of money and I am not going to give it up." They went at it like a pair of ten-year-olds.

Sayid sat down next to me and said, "This is funny, but pretty soon I will stop it." When he became bored with the exchanges, he told Terry to stop and tactfully cooled Badr off. He made the combatants shake hands, apologize to one another. Then he and Badr left, laughing. In point of fact, Terry was right. That cannon was far too big for Badr and although he never said anything further, Badr, subsequently, packed a scaled-down weapon.

Since Terry had been a U.S. Marine and still took some pride in his military service, the guards indulged their own machismo by challenging him to wrestling matches. He usually lost, for three reasons: Terry was not in great shape as a result of his pre-captivity carousing and our largely sedentary regimen; he labored under the handicap of grappling blindfolded; and because he probably decided not to display his true strength made him a loser. I confined myself to arm wrestling, enjoying some advantage from the leverage of my longer arms. I also was in better shape than Terry. Years earlier I began espousing the principle of sound body, sound mind. And in captivity I complained of my inability to work out. When taken to the toilet I would say, "Hey, I need some exercise," and they'd relent to the extent of permitting me to jog in place for a few minutes. Even while chained by the ankle and hand, I could do push-ups or leg lifts. Sit-ups were beyond me. As a painful joke, the guards once frog-marched us up and down the hall, chortling that we were being given exercise.

Terry told me the story of how, before we were united, he had made the error of offering a bribe to a guard to let him escape. The Hajj was promptly informed. Terry was cuffed on the sides of his head—both ears slapped—for his presumption. He recalled for me the Hajj's warning: "My men are very little but their guns are very big. Don't ever do it again."

I could also be something of a provocateur. Once when Hajj Habib visited us I grabbed his arm and said, "You are now my hostage." Because I kept a smile on my face, he did not take it as anything more than a joke. Indeed, none of the guards, not even Sayid, who knew English quite well, grasped the essence of sarcasm, which is foreign to the language of Arabic. I often masked a put-down with a smile while my comrades understood the uncomplimentary meaning behind the words.

One hot, humid day, we heard a street vendor outside announcing he had *"Bussa"* for sale. *Bussa* combines sherbet, fruit, and nuts to create one of the most delicious ice creams I've ever tasted. I stretched out my chains to the full length, which allowed me to knock on the door to the cell. Terry quickly put on his blindfold; he assumed I would request a guard take me to the toilet. But he also asked me what my problem was.

"I want some ice cream."

"You're crazy," said Terry. "Badr will go nuts. When he hears this, I sure wouldn't want to be in your shoes, if you had any to wear."

Soon, I heard the door being unlocked. A somewhat cranky Badr entered and asked, "What do you want, Mr. David?"

"Badr, I want some *bussa*. I want it now! Go outside and buy some." Badr snorted and said something that was happily unintelligible to me. He slammed the door shut, apparently not pleased.

"David," warned Terry, "Badr could kill you for this."

I chose to play it with bravado. "If I have to die, I would prefer it to be over ice cream and not by accident."

Fifteen minutes passed and the pair of us sat in silence, awaiting Badr's fury. The clumsy mechanical locks unsnapped again and we quickly restored the blindfolds. Badr stood in front of me. "Mr. David, your hand."

I stuck it out, almost cringing from the coming blow. Badr thrust something into my hand, then walked over to Terry and gave him something. As soon as Badr exited, we snatched off our blindfolds and looked at the melting ice cream cones in our hands. Both of us laughed hysterically.

Anderson after a few licks of pleasure remarked, "Do you think the world will ever believe that a crazy American ordered a fanatical terrorist out on a hot summer day to buy ice cream for his hostages and that he actually did it?"

One day, Sayid produced a Bible. Since Mokmoud had taken away my glasses I couldn't read the type. The frame for Terry's glasses was broken but he was near-sighted, unlike me. He could distinguish print, and when we had the Bible he read to me. Among his gifts was a remarkable ability to memorize. He frequently amazed me when, after having read some text, he would rattle off the passages strictly from memory.

We knew there were other hostages in the building. In fact, through the opening in the wall for the turnbuckle to which my chains were attached, I caught glimpses of a man in similar circumstances to mine; he was bound to the same piece of hardware. Although Sayid had brought us a Bible, he would take it away every other day for "someone else." We knew the names of some of the other hostages from the broadcasts at the time TWA 847 was hijacked. From bits and pieces of conversation with our captors we identified those incarcerated in our building as the Rev. Ben Weir and Father Lawrence Martin Jenco, both of whom had also been held at the place where Buckley died.

One day we had a new visitor. Sayid opened the door and introduced us to one of our neighbors, Father Jenco. The guard had been escorting him to the shower when on a whim he decided to permit Jenco to meet us. Actually, our blindfolds prevented us from seeing any more of Marty than his bare feet and legs. On this first meeting we could say nothing more than hello.

Later, when Sayid had stopped by, Terry and I both asked if they would allow Father Jenco and the Reverend Weir to join us for a religious service. Sayid promised to ask permission of his superiors. A couple of days later, without any advance notice, Sayid brought the two clergymen to our room. It was the beginning of a true ecumenical brotherhood.

We were permitted to remove our blindfolds, giving us our first looks at both Ben and Marty. Ben was a slim, sixty-two-year-old, with a white beard and the remnants of short-cropped white hair. Marty was heavier, a dozen years younger, and also suffered from a rapidly receding hairline.

Without any fuss or discussion about which brand of worship should be followed, Ben Weir, the most senior among us, a man who'd spent much of his life succoring the deprived in the Middle East, conducted that first service. I remembered talk in California about the evangelist Amy Semple McPherson and her Church of the Open Door. This, I remarked, in a burst of inspiration, was the Church of the Locked Door.

On a somewhat irregular basis, the services continued during the following weeks. Sometimes Marty Jenco performed a mass and at other times Ben Weir led us. Terry and I participated, regardless of the type of service.

Although he was a lapsed Catholic, Anderson believed the one religion to which he had some connection was the only true one. One morning, upon awakening, Terry remarked to Marty Jenco about a fire-and-brimstone preacher he had heard on the radio during the night while the rest of us were asleep. Anderson ripped into the minister, ridiculing him as a fool and ignoramus.

I'd heard my own share of weird radio evangelists who seemed more interested in reaping bucks than saving souls. But when Terry persisted in ridiculing the man I became curious and asked his name.

"Swindoll," said Anderson.

"Chuck Swindoll?" Terry nodded. Then I lost my cool. I had heard Swindoll preach and lecture. I knew that as a graduate of the Dallas Theological Seminary in Texas, he was a man with impeccable academic credentials. He is held in the highest esteem by educated Protestants. I tore into Terry for his uninformed criticism. We exchanged some harsh words on the subject. My impassioned defense of Swindoll, in the face of Anderson's appraisal, is probably what led Marty Jenco subsequently to describe me as a fundamentalist, which I am most assuredly not.

One day, I happened to be chatting with Sayid while Terry was having his shower. I took it upon myself to inform Sayid that Anderson was a Roman Catholic, and then explained the process of confession. Sayid immediately grasped the hint; he was sensitive enough to see that Terry was a troubled man. We arranged for Father Jenco to hear confession. Afterwards, I returned to the room to find Anderson sitting there with tears streaming down his cheeks. But he wept with relief, not pain.

That moving experience notwithstanding, it is not true that Terry became deeply religious. He retained his skepticism of authority, and anyone who tried to interject Protestant religious doctrine into a discussion outside the precincts of the Church of the Locked Door would certainly be challenged. As a consequence I would needle him after one of our debates, "You're very bright, Terry, but you're not brilliant. You can remember what you read but you don't always understand what it means."

In another bizarre twist, Sayid, now struggling to care for his small children, came to work with his little girl Fatima. He brought her into our room. She screamed, as any kid would, at the sight of a pair of chained, blindfolded men in their underwear. She continued to cry until Sayid finally removed her. Our role as potential babysitters never materialized.

Toward the end of July 1985, the door was opened and the pair of us automatically slipped our blindfolds back on and stood up—we were expected to show respect by rising when visited. Sayid declared, "Mr. David, a friend of yours is here."

"Who is it?" I inquired, since I couldn't see.

Sayid said, "Peek and you shall see."

I lifted the cloth from my right eye and exclaimed, "My God, Tom, what happened to you?"

Our visitor was Tom Sutherland, acting dean of the AUB school of agriculture. "My car was stopped two blocks after we left the airport by two automobiles filled with armed men. They yanked me out of my car, forced me into the back seat of one of their sedans. I saw them shoot out the tires of my car, but at least they didn't harm the driver."

"Where was Mehdi?" I was referring to Tom's regular bodyguard.

"He never showed up at the airport. It was strange since in the past he had always been there waiting to escort me to my office." Again, the circumstances suggested that the kidnapping had been carefully planned.

My shock at seeing Tom was partly because of the change in his appearance from the time I knew him at the AUB. He had been grabbed two weeks after me. They had held him for thirty days somewhere else and during his initial confinement he had lost a lot of weight from his slightly less than six-foot frame. He was also extremely pale. Unlike us, he had been locked up with many other Lebanese hostages in a place near the sports arena. Tom occupied a basement cell he described as a "horse stall." It was so small that the only way to fit in a cot was to angle it at forty-five degrees. He never saw the sun but an electric light burned twenty-four hours a day.

Tom Sutherland, who taught agriculture at the AUB, became a member of our hostage group after he was kidnapped June 9, 1985. (Courtesy AP/Wide World Photos)

He told us that the entire place stank of decaying garbage. Flies and mosquitos infested the area. To add considerable distress, the guards often came late at night and fired their automatic rifles in a nearby corridor. All in all, he considered our quarters somewhat of a palace.

To my regret, Sayid escorted Tom out after our brief conversation and placed him with the two ministers in the adjoining room.

During this period, we became better acquainted with the Hajj, who seemed to be in charge of our kidnappers. He did not live in the building but he visited occasionally. I peeped a couple of times and recognized a resemblance to Sayid, as if they might be kin. The Hajj was about forty, taller, stockier and very neatly groomed; his vestments, which he wore over blue jeans, suggested he might be some sort of junior mullah or religious official. On one occasion while Fatima was on the premises I thought the Hajj had picked her up and kissed the youngster. Certainly, he seemed to have a special relationship with Sayid.

Because the Hajj spoke no English, Sayid always translated when he addressed us. He complained that "The U.S. government refuses to talk directly with us. How can the situation be resolved if the Americans don't know our demands?" We, of course, agreed that the attitude was wrong.

"We are not thieves," he insisted. "You have been kidnapped to be exchanged for our friends in Kuwait." And he apologized, "I am sorry for the conditions requiring your being chained and blindfolded, but I have no alternatives."

Terry and I responded with remarks along the lines, "Release us, and we would be more than happy to relay to our government your demands." When translated, that evoked a laugh. Then we suggested that rather than letting all of us go, why not free a couple, anyone he chose, who would be in a position to carry his message.

"I will think about it," he said. It was the first response to spur hope. Because of the dignity with which he carried himself and the respect shown by his subordinates, I formed an impression of the Hajj as a decent, kindly man. That he had teeth and could bite I would learn later.

There were visitors other than the Hajj. None of them spoke to us. They came to stare, to gawk at the animals. Over and over our guards, including Sayid, tried to tell us that they meant no harm and would protect us. But we knew we were no more than a bunch of high-priced rabbits in a cage.

Terry and I calculated that at least several hundred Lebanese—the families of the guards, people who lived in the building, the ones who came to look—must have known of our identity and location. We speculated, endlessly, how in the Beirut cauldron of informants, spies and warring parties, that sort of activity somehow must attract the notice of the U.S. government or those local forces friendly to it. But apparently there were no visits from anyone intent on our salvation.

Then, one night that summer in 1985 after we had fallen asleep, a commotion in the hallway awakened us. The door to our room unlocked and several people entered, speaking Arabic. Sayid whispered to me. "Great news! You will go home soon. We have caught a Kuwaiti. He is trying to convince us that he is Lebanese. But we know the truth."

After Sayid and his associates left, the silence of our cell was broken by the sobs of a man in the other corner of the room. Terry and I removed our blindfolds and in the pale green night light, gazed on a fat, middle-aged man with a clean-shaven, round face and white hair. His features were not those of the stereotypical Arab. With a towel draped over his head, he wore the uniform of the day, underwear.

We asked his name and he answered, "I am Wadgid Duomoni, the last name is spelled like the song." (He was referring to Dean Martin's hit entitled "Duomoni.") Wadgid claimed his kidnapping was all a horrible mistake. He explained he had been born in Syria but was really Lebanese since he had spent his entire adult life there. He worked for the Kuwaiti government in its West Beirut embassy, however, and while passing through the airport customs, he stupidly pulled out his Kuwaiti diplomatic passport.

Always on the alert, Hizballah agents immediately set in motion the kidnap apparatus. They were truly convinced they now had the big prize who would open the cells for the Dawa prisoners in Kuwait.

After hearing Wadgid's tale of woe, we tried to sleep again. But it was impossible. Not only was the man distraught over being kidnapped but he also suffered from severe claustrophobia. Without surcease, he alternated between sobs and loud expressions of his fears. Furthermore, for some reason he was not bound like us and was therefore able to shuffle about and periodically pound on the door about the injustice visited upon him. The guards became increasingly irritated by Wadgid's behavior, leading to even more commotion.

When morning arrived, Terry was less than charitable toward our new roommate: "I will personally strangle that cry baby if he repeats the anxiety scene tonight."

I summoned Sayid, and when he appeared I said, "If Terry doesn't get Wadgid first, I will finish him off. Either move him out or get some Valium from the pharmacy so he can be sedated tonight."

Sayid dutifully provided me with a five-milligram tablet of Valium. I split it in half and gave the first dose to the patient. It had no effect. I made him down the rest of the Valium but still the drug failed to pacify him for even a moment. Terry and I would have been better off if *we* had swallowed the tranquilizer. The only way we could have shut Wadgid up was to have whacked him on the head with a hammer.

As a last resort, I decided to try to talk him through his terror. He told me the source of his phobia. "As a youngster I was once trapped in an elevator for a long time. Ever since then I have a great fear of being in a dark closed room."

I tried to reason with him. "This room is very safe. We have been here for months. There is always plenty of oxygen to breathe. The walls do not shrink and close in at night."

We went on in this vein for many hours. He seemed to grasp the realities of the situation and his claustrophobia was allayed. As time passed, we actually developed a modest friendship. Every day, he was taken out for prolonged interrogation. He would be asked questions, and given paper and pen to write his detailed answers as a kind of homework.

He told us, "Boy, when I get out, the Emir [ruler of Kuwait] will owe me a big present, like a Mercedes."

Terry and I agreed that in view of how much we had suffered because of Wadgid, the Emir ought to reward us at least as generously!

It was with some regret that I saw him moved into the room of Weir and Jenco. Although Ben Weir said Wadgid talked about me as "his professor who cured him of his phobia and saved his life," sometimes I heard him pounding the door at night as his old fears revived.

Eventually, Wadgid convinced his captors of his real identity; that he was only a Syrian-born, Lebanese resident working for Kuwait. As a hostage he added up to zero value and they let him go. Mokmoud and Fadl drove him to his home. Terry and I were astounded when they told us that upon arrival, Wadgid invited them in for tea and they accepted. This vision of a cozy tête-a-tête between former kidnappers and former hostage boggled our minds. Wadgid supposedly suggested they come visit again. But when they did so a couple of weeks later, he was gone, having been wise enough to skip the country before someone realized he might squeal to the authorities.

Wadgid, however, did do me an enormous favor. During our chats I had given him the telephone number of my son, Eric, in the event he obtained his freedom before me. Wadgid arranged for his son to call Eric and report that I was in good health. This report, in late July 1985, was the first assurance of my condition received by my family.

Eric and Paul, along with John Weir, Ben's son, and aided by Jeremy Levin and his wife Sis, had sought help and information from authorities in Washington. They came away frustrated with the State Department response but slightly encouraged by the attitude of Robert McFarlane, then heading up the office of National Security Adviser. But like me, my family had begun a long cycle of hopeful flickers and bouts of near despair.

The first contact between the Department of State and my family had occurred shortly after midnight on May 28, 1985. My son Eric, having gone to bed, had switched on his telephone answering machine. When the phone rang, he did not get to the receiver until toward the end of the message, ". . . your father has been kidnapped in Beirut, Lebanon this morning at 8:12 A.M. For further information, call the State Department number I've given you after 6:00 A.M. Pacific Standard Time." It was typical of DOS, as Eric would learn, to treat the families of hostages so coldly.

Unwilling to wait, Eric immediately dialed the number left on the tape. He heard the same bureaucratic monotone delivering the message already recorded by his answering device. It was as if the government ran like a small business, with office hours of nine to five. When 6:00 A.M. finally arrived, Eric reached a living person. However, the official had nothing further in the way of information.

The day after the kidnapping, Eric received a letter from DOS via express mail. In part, the message was:

Dear Mr. Jacobsen:

"The Department of State deeply regrets the kidnapping in Lebanon of your father, Mr. David Jacobsen, on May 28, 1985. I want you to know that we will assist you in every way we can to bring about his safe return.

We are acutely aware of the enormous distress such tragic events cause. For this reason, I am enclosing some suggestions intended to help you and your family as you go through this difficult period. The suggestions provided are not definitive and of course should be used at your discretion. We recommend that you contact us if you need further information or assistance. We will certainly call you whenever we have any new information or guidance we think you would want to have.

"We fully share your concerns for your father's safety and will immediately apprise you of all developments."

It was signed by the Director, Citizens Emergency Center.

The letter seemed to promise a vigorous, high-interest attitude toward my welfare and the feelings of my loved ones. But it proved to be a paper promise with nothing to back it up.

The helpful hints offered by the government to families of hostages consisted, first and foremost, of public relations pointers. They were counseled to designate one family member or an attorney or adviser as the media spokesperson so that everyone wouldn't be besieged constantly by requests for interviews. They were advised to pool interviews, in other words hold mini-press conferences, again to reduce the burden of media contacts. If they received any letters from anyone purporting to be in a position to negotiate, they were to handle the letter as little as possible—in the corners only—place it in a plastic bag and mail it to the appropriate State Department official. If private intermediaries approached them with offers to help, they were to contact DOS right away.

The letter stated that the primary responsibility for rescuing the captive family member rested with the government of the country where he or she was kidnapped and/or being held. My daughter Diane recalls how absurd this assertion seemed to her; essentially, Lebanon had no government at that time.

But, for the most part, my children accepted this as advice from experts that was to be carefully followed. The very first day after news of my kidnapping was released, the press began to knock on my childrens' doors, often. The kids hewed to the line from DOS and refused to discuss the situation with the media until the shock had diminished.

Within a few days, the first doubts about the good faith in Washington began. From its letter, one got the impression that DOS would contact the family the moment it learned anything new. Within hours of my kidnapping, an anonymous caller, representing Islamic Jihad, claimed responsibility for the abduction. Did the State Department telephone with the news? No, but the media was quick to inform my children.

This became the script played and replayed for the next four months. DOS refused to comment on any information that it could not immediately verify. If queried about a rumor, the authorities would not even deign to respond.

Hoping to learn more, Eric and Paul made their first trip to Washington for a face-to-face meeting with the appropriate contact in the Citizens Emergency Center. The woman there reported to Eric that she and her colleagues were putting in twelve- and fourteen-hour days, skipping lunch breaks even, while laboring on behalf of me and the other hostages.

That impressed my sons mightily. Then the phone interrupted their conversation and the official answered, "Citizens Emergency Center." She listened to the caller, then said, "There is a very minute chance of precipitation in Israel at this time of the year." Pause. "You are welcome, goodbye." A few minutes later she picked up on another call to identify herself as representing the Citizens Emergency Center. ". . . Yes, the average high temperature is ninety-eight and the low sixty-four . . ."

Several more queries and responses about climatic conditions around the world disillusioned my sons about the efforts on behalf of the hostages. Apparently, they had been referred to the DOS weather-information officer! But they perked up when she introduced a man she said headed the Lebanese Hostage Operation.

Eagerly they plied him with questions. Did they know the specific identification of my kidnappers. "No, not specifically."

"Then do we have *any* idea who they are?"

"It's very difficult to say."

A second man supposedly involved in the hostage situation appeared. Paul asked him, "Do we have any idea what the demands are for my father's release?"

"No."

Eric inquired, "Who is Islamic Jihad?"

"We don't really know for sure. They're a shadowy group with shadowy motives living in a shadowy part of the world. We believe that many small independent groups use that name."

My sons pressed for details. "So each of the hostages may be held by a different group?"

Again, it was a we-don't-know answer. Nor did they provide any information of who led the terrorists. Furthermore, the two men refused to say what was being done to obtain my release. They would not divulge any plans or offer any more information than the basic fact that I had been kidnapped. When my two sons left, deeply dispirited, about all they could say was, "The hostages must be pretty important. They've been assigned to the State Department Weather Bureau."

For four months, the only information my family had about me was the fact that I was kidnapped. They had no idea that I was a hostage, held for something or someone in return. One can easily imagine how grateful they were for that telephone call from Wadgid Duomoni's son.

Chapter 5

The Group

Listening to the noises outside of our building led us to believe that we were very close to the Beirut International Airport. In fact, the sounds of nearby aircraft taking off and landing suggested we might even be occupying a site between the runways! Most obviously, the area drew the attention of gunners. Shells fell in the vicinity daily. Every night, the locals retaliated, hauling a multiple rocket launcher to one corner of our building. For hours on end, the *swish*, *swish*, *swish* signalled the use of lethal rocketry. We guessed the targets were the Palestinian refugee camps. Occasionally, small arms fire thudded and ricocheted off the walls surrounding us.

Toward the end of July, Sayid came to us and announced, "It is getting too dangerous up here. Gather your belongings. We are moving you all downstairs."

Wadgid was still on the premises at this moment but he remained behind in the old rooms. We figured he was either going to be executed or, as subsequently proven, freed. I preceded Terry down to the basement. After they closed the door to my new quarters I lifted my blindfold and to my joy saw Tom Sutherland stretched out on a nearby mat. Terry now joined us. Although we worried about Wadgid's future, we were more concerned about our fellow countrymen, Marty Jenco and Ben Weir. Our Church of the Locked Door had been such a comfort and now it seemed at an end. We feared that the pair had been murdered.

Our new abode below ground level was less comfortable

than the one we had previously enjoyed. The floor remained unfinished, without the usual tiles. The place never dried out, and it was much more difficult to keep ourselves or our pitiful wardrobes clean.

The three of us spent a week fearing for the safety of Weir and Jenco, theorizing about the purposes behind our kidnapping and wondering why our government seemed so reluctant to push for our release.

Sayid appeared one morning and announced, "I have some people here to see you."

"Who?" one of us demanded.

"Guess!" commanded Sayid, as if the entire exercise were some sort of game.

"Ronald Reagan? Walid Jumblatt? [leader of the Druse militia] Nabih Berri? [head of the Amal militia] The Delta Force?" Like kids, we played along.

"Be serious," Sayid said. "I have your friends, Father and Benjamin [which was how the guards always referred to Jenco and Weir, respectively]. They are being moved downstairs and they will occupy the room across the hall from you."

"Sayid, can we talk with them for a while?"

"Sure, why not?" Sayid answered. And so the two clergymen entered. Sayid remained among us as we chatted, making the kind of small talk one might hear at a cocktail party when friends meet after a short separation. But soon we were able to reconvene the Church of the Locked Door. Much of the service was spent in silent prayer and, after half an hour, Sayid became impatient.

"It's time to go."

Almost simultaneously, Terry and I pleaded, "Let them stay with us. We have room."

Tom objected. "There's barely enough space for three men, let alone five. They really should go to the other room. There isn't enough air for all of us and it's not healthy."

Terry argued with Sutherland and when he saw Tom was unpersuaded, Anderson focused on the real decision maker,

Sayid. Fortunately, Sayid liked Terry and, after he listened to him for a few minutes, became convinced it was in everyone's best interest that we remain together.

Now we were five. We had a few things in common. We were all middle-aged or on the verge of senior citizenship. Terry, almost forty, was the youngest; Tom was about fifty-five, as I was; Marty was fifty-one; and Ben was in his early sixties. All of us had spent a fair amount of time living and working outside of the United States. Everyone except Father Jenco had been married and fathered children. Two of us, Anderson and myself, were divorced (Terry's separation was actually in the works when he was taken), but both of us were involved in loving relationships. Tom and Ben had long-standing happy marriages. None of us were bashful about expressing our opinions; even gentle Ben Weir could be quite forceful. Terry and I easily qualified as the most opinionated.

There were, of course, considerable differences. Ben Weir was the kindest of my fellow hostages. He is a thoroughly decent man, without a shred of malice in him. On one occasion, when some bullets struck our building, raising the level of anxiety even above its usual high pitch, I yelled to Sayid, "Give me an AK-47 and I'll shoot back at those bastards if you won't."

In shocked tones, Ben asked, "Why are you so angry, David?"

In another instance Mokmoud provoked an outburst from me. He stalled on bringing us medication to treat our diarrhea. By the time he finally gave it to us, the attack was over. Mindful of how their disregard for Buckley's health had led to his death, I was in no mood to excuse Mokmoud's behavior. He angered me to the point where I loudly berated him. Mokmoud then stormed off, slamming the door. My fists were clenched and I growled, "I'm going to kill that son-of-a-bitch." Again, Ben was appalled by my attitude.

I don't mean to suggest that Ben was timid when it came to demanding his rights or held benign feelings toward those who kidnapped us. But to commit a violent act—or even to consider committing one—upon a fellow human being was simply not part of Ben's character.

Certainly, if any man had a right to a murderous rage against his oppressors it was Weir. When he was moved to our quarters, he told us his story. His horrified wife actually witnessed three men grabbing him outside of their home in Beirut on May 8, 1984 and shoving him into a car. After he had been snatched, the abductors mummified him, wrapping him in that brown plastic packing tape from head to foot. They transported his body to a redoubt in the mountains of the Bekaa Valley. He spent six months in isolation, lying on a soiled foam rubber mattress, shackled to a radiator, the daylight from French doors blotted out as the 120 louvered slats—he methodically counted them—remained shut. During the winter, the temperature dropped precipitously. It was so cold that he could see his breath vaporize. The icy, damp wind bit through the broken windows and a single blanket was inadequate to prevent shivering seizures. During the summer, the place turned into a steam bath.

Father Jenco was also held at this Bekaa Valley location, chained in the kitchen. He later recalled to us how he was so hungry at one point he managed to stretch out and grab an orange to eat. We ribbed him about breaking one of the Ten Commandments: "A Catholic priest ought to know about 'thou shalt not steal'!" And at the time, he received a stern scolding from his captors.

More than a month elapsed before Ben Weir was permitted a shower. He sustained himself through his religious faith and by finding symbols in the bare materials of his surroundings. The three wires hanging from the ceiling served as the hand of God; the exposed hook of a reinforcement rod was the eye of God and a stuffed bird on a shelf embodied the dove sent by Noah to find hope amid chaos. He created an imaginary calendar to number his days.

Like all of us, Ben wore a blindfold throughout his captivity. But, instead of a cloth bandage, he was forced to wear a snorkel mask outfitted with tape to block his vision. (When we first saw Weir and noticed his snorkel mask, we inquired "Where are your flippers?") He was ordered never to remove it. Caught slipping off the blindfold several times, he was made to realize how serious his guards were when one held the muzzle of a pistol against his head and warned, "One more mistake on your part and you're dead." He never committed the error again.

Ben Weir was the fourth American grabbed in 1984. The first, on February 10, 1984, was Frank Regier, freed by the chance discovery. Then it was Jeremy Levin, the Cable News Network reporter, on March 7, 1984. His kidnappers accused Levin of being a CIA agent, then an Israeli spy. Gagged, he was bound in wrapping tape so tightly that he felt the circulation to his fingers and toes vanishing. His kidnappers dumped him on a truck bed, then drove for more than two hours, to the Bekaa Valley. Then they threw him on a pallet with a two-foot-long chain around his wrist.

During his captivity, Levin was slapped around, badly fed, constantly manacled and threatened. In July 1984 he was ordered to read a message on a slip of paper before a video-camera. "I am Jeremy Levin. My life and freedom depends on the life and freedom of the prisoners in Kuwait." The tape was given to U.S. authorities. However, the people in the State Department warned Levin's wife, Sis, that this was top secret.

Becoming increasingly discouraged with unfulfilled promises of action by the American authorities to free her husband, Sis Levin launched her own private efforts with the aid of relatives, friends and among others, the Reverend Jesse Jackson. They picked up intelligence on who was holding Levin and the fact that he had been moved to various locations. Sis Levin's most daring gambit was a visit to Damascus in the company of Landrum Bolling, a university official who enjoyed respect and good connections in Syria. Through Bolling, Sis Levin gained several audiences with Syrian President Hafez Assad's Foreign Minister, Farouk al-Sharaa.

Jeremy Levin, an American correspondent for the Cable News Network, who was kidnapped March 7, 1984, freed himself February 14, 1985, more than two months before they seized me.
(Courtesy AP/Wide World Photos)

Six weeks after she pled her husband's case to Farouk al-Sharraa, Levin discovered he could slip his chain. In his words, "Was it carelessness? Or was it . . . something else?" In any event, he knotted his blankets into a rope, climbed through a window to a balcony, tied one end of the blankets to the railing, and then lowered himself to the ground one floor below. Syrian army soldiers found him hiding under a truck during the night and he became a free man on February 14, 1985.

Without knowing what had supposedly happened to Levin, I often tested the leg binding to see if I could free myself. Based on my experience, I believe the kidnappers deliberately arranged for the reporter to flee. Even the most careless guard could not have been so sloppy as to overlook a shackle that would slide over an ankle.

While Weir and Jenco and Levin were held in the Bekaa Valley, a married couple—Saudis, we surmised—was also held there. Later, they were brought to Beirut and kept in the same building that imprisoned us. We never saw them, but we overheard them speaking in Arabic; it was an intimate conversation, obviously spoken as only husband and wife do. The other evidence that a woman was being held was that toilet paper suddenly appeared in the bathroom. When it was just us men, there was no such luxury. We were expected to wipe ourselves Arab style—with our left (non-eating) hand.

Levin's kidnapping had been followed by that of William Buckley. After the CNN man "escaped," fears that the Syrians in the area might discover the hiding place caused the abductors to shift the hostages. At the new location, and for the first time, about nine months after he had been taken, Ben Weir was aware of the presence of another captive behind a thin partition. He whispered, "I'm Ben Weir, a Protestant minister. Who are you?"

"Lawrence Martin Jenco, a Catholic priest." Marty had only been incarcerated for five weeks, having been kidnapped January 8, 1985. A few days later, they heard from a third inmate, who managed to reveal he was William Buckley.

Marty Jenco, from the Servite order, had done his time as a parish priest and I think suffered burn-out from dealing with the politics and problems of the community. He associated himself with a number of causes, including that of Cesar Chavez and the California grape harvesters. I needled him on the subject. "I don't understand where you got the right to keep me from buying grapes in my supermarket." He talked eloquently about the plight of migrant workers forced to perform painful stoop-labor made necessary by short-handled hoes.

Jenco's social activism must have rankled some of his superiors. I was always asking him what on earth he had done to get the bishop so mad. For the church powers had shipped Jenco about as far from home as possible, to a parish in Perth, Australia. From there, he had worked to aid the poor and underprivileged in Thailand and North Yemen before being transferred to run Catholic Relief Services in Lebanon. Like me, he seemed another case of mistaken identity. Marty had been on the job only a couple of weeks and the kidnappers were really after his civilian predecessor.

The error did not make life easier for him. They accused

him of trying to see their faces and belted him. They smacked him again when he reached for a spoon they claimed he intended to wield as a weapon. He lost about twenty percent of his hearing from open-handed slaps over his ears.

No one, including himself, denied that William Buckley worked for the CIA. There wasn't much else known about him, but after he was captured, Islamic Jihad charged that he was with the CIA and later the U.S. government acknowledged it. I don't think anybody has any definite idea of how Hizballah knew Buckley was station chief in Beirut, but the fact is that most insiders in a country know who the chief CIA man is inside the embassy. What they don't know are the identities of secret agents. Therefore, as soon as Buckley vanished, CIA director William Casey was forced to roll up the entire remaining network of Middle East agents (a great deal of damage to the network had already been done when as many as seven agents were killed in the 1983 bombing of the U.S. Embassy in Beirut) for fear Buckley would be tortured until he revealed all of their identities. As a consequence, intelligence from the Middle East dropped to near zero.

There has been much talk about what Buckley may have revealed when put to the rack by the kidnappers. Although both Ben Weir, Jeremy Levin and to a lesser extent Marty Jenco certainly spent some time in Buckley's immediate vicinity during their captivity, none of them ever heard him being beaten or mistreated. On the other hand, the CIA official may have been isolated from all other hostages for as much as eleven months, and some in the intelligence community (including, as I recall, Ollie North during his testimony at the "Irangate" hearings and Michael Ledeen in his book *Perilous Statecraft*) mention a secret videotape showing him undergoing torture. So far, no tape of this nature has ever been displayed. The only words Buckley spoke directly to the other hostages was his name.

Marty Jenco told us how he heard Buckley slumped in the

bathroom, hallucinating from fever. This was when Marty overheard Buckley saying repeatedly "I think I'll have my hotcakes now ... with blueberry syrup." From all of the symptoms described by Sayid to me and from the noises the dying man made I am reasonably convinced pneumonia or some other lung infection (possibly pulmonary edema from a beating) killed him. It is possible, however, that the treatment meted out to him so battered his body that it was ripe for infection.

As I subsequently learned, his death was only announced six months after I heard his final wheezes. And along with a fuzzy picture of a shrouded body identified as Buckley, Islamic Jihad announced he had been "executed" as revenge for an Israeli raid that killed a PLO official in Tunisia. Islamic Jihad then offered to swap the corpse for Palestinians held in Israel.

I had met Tom Sutherland on the AUB campus but we were little more than nodding acquaintances. Actually, he knew more about me. From his apartment he looked down upon the track where guys like me did their jogging. Stand-

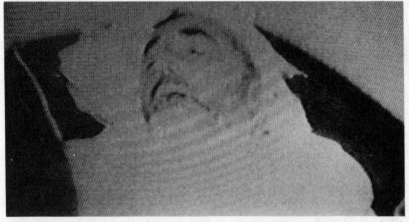

Islamic Jihad released this picture of William Buckley's body months after he actually died of disease. The terrorists claimed they had executed him in reprisal for an Israeli assassination in Tunisia. (Courtesy AP/Wide World Photos)

ing by a window with his double Old Fashion cocktail in the early evening, he had fallen into the habit of timing my laps with a stop watch. Indeed, he had actually watched me work out the morning that I was taken.

Tom, who had taught agriculture in Colorado before coming to Beirut, had the typical academic approach, and it earned him no end of grief. He was intellectually honest to a fault and consequently could never respond to questions from our captors with a simple, straightforward answer. Everything he said required qualification and amplification, which either exasperated the interrogators or heightened their suspicions.

When the first crew plucked him from his car near the airport, the search of his briefcase found letters he had been given in London for delivery to AUB faculty members. The kidnappers sliced open the mail, read the correspondence and then returned the stuff to the case. When Tom arrived at the building where the rest of us were being held, the guards went through his possessions. They discovered the opened letters and immediately accused him of being a spy who read other people's mail. They also asked about a copy of an article on Islam which was in his briefcase. Unfortunately, Tom denied having the article. He apparently did not realize that his wife had put it in his briefcase without his knowledge.

Our masters had grilled Sutherland for a number of days. They had even stuck him in one of the "horse stalls" in an attempt to break his spirit. Whenever our hosts made a comment indicating Sutherland was not what he claimed, the rest of us argued, pleaded and insisted he was not a secret agent but only a typical college professor. Eventually, the kidnappers relaxed and mostly accepted him for what he was.

Tom's wife, who was American, had remained in Beirut and he worried constantly about her and his children. One of our guards took classes at the AUB and he reported to Tom she was alive and well. Unlike me, Tom never had a contingency plan to manage his affairs in the event of a disaster. The Sutherlands owned a house in Ft. Collins, Colorado and a vacation cabin in the mountains. Tom agonized over defaulting on the cabin mortgage. I reassured him that the AUB would continue to pay his salary, supporting his family. I consoled him, "Do you think there is a bank in the United States that would risk the publicity it would get if it foreclosed on the home of a hostage?"

Although we all drew comfort from being together, harmony frequently did not rule the roost. The conditions themselves made for short tempers. Water condensed on the walls, dripping to the floor and eventually wetting down our sleeping mats. Frequently, the Christian forces which controlled the electricity from plants in East Beirut shut down the service to our area. That knocked out the generators feeding current to refrigerators, air conditioners, lights, even water supplies. The basement room took on the quality of a furnace. When we touched the walls we could feel the heat baking the exterior of the building. One time Fadl, still in his good-guy mode, brought in some large pieces of cardboard and fanned us. "Fadl," I said, "You must have a nice mother and father to be so kind." Later, when he became so unresponsive, my colleagues would twit me, "Oh, Fadl, you must have such nice parents."

Each of us received fifteen minutes a day to shower, wash our clothes, empty our urine bottles, draw fresh water and clean our plastic bowls, spoons and cups. The guards became nasty if anyone exceeded the allotted time since, at a minimum, the five of us disturbed their leisure by an hour and a quarter.

Close confinement exposed us to individual quirks. Terry was something of a clean freak and he would wield a broom without regard to the convenience of others. Tom and I complained loudly about the choking clouds of dust he stirred. He also had an annoying habit of pacing at night when he couldn't sleep. Because of our close quarters, the route he followed brought his feet to within a few inches of my head. I requested as cordially as possible that he limit his steps to an area farther away from me. On the other hand, the others frequently found fault with my willingness to express a strong opinion on any issue. Often I issued my judgments just off the top of my head. Terry denounced me as "the most conservative man he had ever met."

Tom suffered from terrible flatulence and he was a trial to us all, particularly one memorable night, January 9, 1986, when he almost asphyxiated us with a single mighty explosion. There was considerable speculation on the Richter scale reading of that blast.

Terry heckled Marty Jenco as "the laziest man on earth." He insisted that when he lent Jenco his self-winding watch it stopped from lack of movement. But the heckling was momentary. Mostly, Anderson deferred to the priest, perhaps as a memory of his altar boy experience. I got on Marty's case on religious grounds. "I don't think you've ever read the Bible," I said.

He was indignant but later he admitted he had not been a student of the Book, reading mainly homilies or Psalms. The Catholic in him and the Protestant in me contested whether one is saved through faith or through good works. It was an ongoing dispute with no hope of resolution. He laughed when I kidded him, "How about asking the Pope to buy us out of here with some indulgences?"

If anything, the enlargement of the group increased the friction between Terry and me. We were like a pair of stallions seeking to establish dominance and we argued until the others wearied of our bickering. On the other hand, Tom, trained in the collegiality of faculty decision-making, annoyed everyone with his effort to make every question a matter for a committee. That led me to say, "Do you want to ask for advice and consent whenever you want to bang on the door to go to the toilet?"

We argued politics, social issues, cultural values, eastern Americans against western ones. Even the most innocent remarks could trigger a truly asinine argument. Placement of a portable fan to relieve the fetid, clammy atmosphere provoked an interminable dispute—should the blower be installed in the back of the room to push air out the door or would it be more effective if located by the entrance to bring new air into our quarters?

Anyone listening to our squabbling, which sometimes degenerated into bitter arguments, might well have assumed that it was only a matter of time before we started to tear at each other's throats. But like a unit of soldiers brought together only by the crush of events and jointly facing death, we bonded most powerfully. I had an advantage. Having been the youngest of five children, I had learned to share. I knew I could not expect to have it my way all the time.

The guards pricked us with remarks such as "Reagan doesn't care about you." They would report stories and quotes in the newspapers critical of the United States and the President. They would spew political rhetoric. Terry Anderson certainly was no fan of Ronald Reagan, but even he ignored their comments. They did manage to irritate everyone by singing an unpleasant ditty, "Death to America." Again, they did not seem to think it was cruel, just a joke among friends. However, we always greeted the song with a chorus of "Shut up! Go outside and sing!"

We plotted subtle and gross revenges. We thought of telling the Hajj that his men, in violation of their religion, were enraptured by the sleazy sexuality of shows like "Dallas" or "Three's Company." Even more dastardly, we considered suggestions that Mokmoud and Fadl, who wrangled often, were really homosexual lovers. In the Fundamentalist core of the Moslem faith that was a sin punishable by death.

We all recognized a common enemy, one far more hateful than the habits or opinions of our associates. And we united with an intent to survive.

Chapter 6

Doing Time

In our basement prison, stripped to our shorts, blindfolded, limited to a diet of poorly cooked subsistence fare, requiring permission to attend to basic personal needs, and under the threat of imminent execution for reasons beyond our control, only one aspect of our previous lives remained a constant: time. There were still sixty seconds to a minute, sixty minutes to the hour, twenty-four hours to every day. And as the days stretched into weeks and months, coping with the burden of time became an obsession.

Everyone recognized time as a potential enemy to survival. When Wadgid Duomoni first joined us, there was a moment when he asked the others how long they had been held. After Ben Weir said thirteen months and Marty Jenco counted more than six, Duomoni clapped both hands over his ears and cried, "I don't want to hear that, I don't want to know."

Getting through the days and nights required strenuous efforts. Exercise served as a primary tool to lift the weight of time. All of us did some form of calisthenics, although Marty Jenco, as I previously stated, was a less-than-enthusiastic participant. At sixty-three, Ben Weir was something of an inspiration. When confined in the Bekaa Valley he would jog in his chains until drenched with sweat. He continued in our new quarters. The rest of us did push-ups, sit-ups or jogged in place.

I even engaged in a routine calculated to strengthen my eyes. I would take a small object like my plastic spoon and hold it at eye level and arm's length, focus on it while I slowly drew the spoon towards me. When it came close enough to the bridge of my nose to become a double image I would repeat the movement. After about twenty-five of these I rotated the spoon in a large circle, sometimes using both eyes, and on other occasions one at a time. In retrospect, the effort probably did nothing to improve my sight. But it gave me the sense of doing something on my own behalf and it devoured some minutes.

Every single day, the group marched around the perimeter of the room for roughly an hour. In our confined space we could only shuffle about in small steps. Anderson, with his aversion to dirt, always wore his socks. The friction tore holes in them but Terry, using a skill learned in his Marine days, repaired the damage with a needle and thread cadged from the guards.

We talked during the first fifteen minutes or so of our hikes, entertaining one another sometimes with educational lectures or imaginary excursions. For example, Tom Sutherland instructed us in genetics and the business of agriculture. He also entertained us with recitations of the poetry of Robert Burns. At the University of Colorado, Tom had been a star performer on Robert Burns Day, appearing at English classes in full kilt to regale the students. He knew all of the Burns works and I particularly enjoyed his rendition of "Ode to a Flea."

Terry conducted a sightseeing tour of Tokyo. He also fascinated us with an imaginative tale of a dragonfly that somehow wound up in East Beirut. There was not a great deal of interest in my explication of how a hospital functions so my modest contribution consisted of softly voiced renditions of show tunes. I had always been fond of musicals and years of listening to recordings had imprinted the words in my mind. My repertoire included everything from *Oklahoma, Carousel, The Sound of Music, My Fair Lady*, up to the most recent show I had seen, *Evita*.

Marty Jenco was particularly enamored of "Over the Rainbow," from *The Wizard of Oz*. He requested it a number of times and if, because of some distraction I forgot the words, he would growl, "Dammit, Dave. Why can't you remember the lyrics." My favorites, however, were the love songs of Jerome Kern—"All the Things You Are," "Smoke Gets in Your Eyes"—which brought reveries of Kerrie, and like Jenco's choice, reinforced hope. "The Impossible Dream," from *The Man of La Mancha*, was another favorite. In addition to these popular tunes, I also comforted myself with Christian praise songs.

There was almost no mention of sex, and not just out of respect for the two ministers. Given our diet and the circumstances, libidos went into hibernation. I do remember, however, one discussion about the possibility of marriage for Catholic priests. Marty Jenco declared he would be the first to volunteer. In a brief discussion of sex, our authority on the netherworld of Beirut, Terry, informed us that the city indeed housed prostitutes with the standard going rate of one hundred dollars.

Usually, we fell silent for most of the morning constitutional. Then it was every man to his own devices. Mine included a wide variety. Sometimes, I yo-yoed that golden ball. Or I lapsed into the Walter Mitty bit, kicking winning field goals, striking out the batter with the bases loaded. I consumed large chunks of time mentally driving the streets of my hometown, Huntington Beach, California. I would "motor" down Beach Boulevard, naming every store on each side of the avenue and rattling off the cross streets, then turn right at the end of the boulevard and head up to Seal Beach to complete a rough rectangle leading back to the starting place. If I made a mistake I forced myself to go back to the beginning. For variety, I drove the freeways, both north and south, silently sounding the exits.

In another minute-burner, I prepared new feasibility studies and budgets for the hospital. I considered how I could translate my job experience into a private business for myself after I was freed. I explored my past, trying to recall events, good and bad. I then analyzed the situations and speculated on how else I might have handled a problem. Naturally, I questioned my decision to take the job in Beirut. But whenever that issue arose, I satisfied myself that I had made the right choice. Indeed, when one of the news broadcasts reported that some man had blown himself up in the medical center lobby, killing and injuring some of the staff, I felt as if I had been wounded. I wanted to be there to protest this invasion of what should be a sanctuary and to aid those with whom I had worked.

After the morning constitutional, we settled down. In the past I had been a spotty Bible reader but now I went through the New Testament from cover to cover. Over my more than seventeen months of confinement, I must have read the Bible a good fifteen times. I spent hours upon hours memorizing passages. Captivity increased my admiration for St. Paul. During my travels, prior to the kidnapping, I had visited many sites mentioned in his journeys. Having been to the place in Rome where he had been chained in a basement under guard and been beaten, starved and faced endless imprisonment, just like us hostages, I was inspired by St. Paul.

I made the Twenty-seventh Psalm a credo for my survival. "The Lord is my light and my salvation. Whom shall I fear?" I would not be frightened by Hizballah. I should fear only that I might lose my values, my faith.

"One thing I have desired of the Lord, that I shall seek: That I may dwell in the house of the Lord all the days of my life." If I resolved to make my cell the house of the Lord, then I could survive the ordeal.

"He would lift me up above my enemies and I would be protected in His pavilion." If I would keep my mouth closed and would only listen, He would set me high on a rock beyond the reach of my enemies.

"Have mercy also upon me, and answer me." I'm not ashamed to say that I cried out for mercy; I begged for freedom.

In my mind I heard the command, "Seek my face." I did and asked God not to forsake me when all others had. I prayed not to be delivered to the will of my enemies and I was not.

As the time dragged by I recalled the thirteenth and fourteenth verses. "I would have lost heart, unless I had believed that I would see the goodness of the Lord in the land of the living. Wait on the Lord; be of good courage. And He shall strengthen your heart; Wait, I say, on the Lord." And so I bided the time.

Because of my ability to draw sustenance from my religion, I think I was better able to withstand the pressure than Terry or Tom, neither of whom enjoyed the intensity of faith that possessed me.

Nevertheless, I believe that our Church of the Locked Door with its orientation towards the infinite essence of God and Christianity helped all of us to deal with the problem of time. Now that we were living together, we conducted services as often as twice a day, alternating between Ben's Protestant offering and Marty's Catholic mass. We took turns saving a piece of the breakfast pita bread to use as the Eucharist. For the morning service it would be fresh and soft but by evening as it dried out the pita turned hard and brittle like a cracker. On one occasion, the donor provided a particularly large chunk. Marty Jenco reminded us, "This is a Eucharist, not a meal." Since no one was in a rush to get out of the parking lot before the traffic jam or hit the first tee before the crowd, these were leisurely services.

Ben Weir, as the eldest, was really our religious leader, with even Jenco deferring to him. I complained, mildly, that under Marty, instead of a hearty Protestant sermon, we got only a five-minute homily. He explained that while he served as a parish priest, members of the congregation would always complain to the bishop about something he said. As a consequence, he trimmed his homilies to the minimum, hoping to avoid controversial remarks.

Terry pulled pieces of tough string from the plastic mats on the floor. He skillfully knotted them to serve as rosaries for Marty Jenco, me, and himself.

During the day it was not uncommon for one of us to become stressed. We established a rule that if anyone became upset, all of us would walk and talk with him until he felt some relief. All of us experienced the terrors of the hour of the wolf, those fright-filled minutes ordinarily experienced by many in the darkest hours of the early morning. But with no sunlight and in our debased, infantalized circumstances, the wolf could call night or day, any time.

It was not all somber reflection. I pretended to read the tea leaves after our breakfast cup of tea. "I see a vision of San Francisco Bay. There is a 747 landing at the airport and look who is deplaning . . ." None of us believed in crystal balls or tea leaves, but Marty Jenco told me he savored my readings because they were always upbeat.

There were practical jokes. Tom Sutherland had oily skin and he rapidly went through the allotment of tissues, all the while accusing us of wasting them. He argued they should be rationed. I managed to cache some and while he was taking his shower, I slipped them underneath his pad. When we started our morning constitutional, and he lifted his mat I needled, "Hey, Tom, what's this about the Kleenex? You're hoarding and you're saying we're using them up?" He became flustered until everyone started to laugh.

Sutherland and I engaged in mock basketball, aiming a wad of paper at the refuse basket. But there was not enough room for active sports. We managed to fold some paper into airplanes and hurled them about.

After lunch we napped; sleep, if one can manage to get it, serves as the most effective way to withdraw. One valuable soporific was provided when Tom tried to teach French to Terry. It was so boring that it would put Marty and I out almost instantly. When nap time arrived we often requested they start the language lesson.

Terry, with his manual dexterity, provided us with unique tools for fun and games. Our captors had given us a few books, some colored pens, and bits of paper for scribbling. Terry ripped blank pages from the books to add to our few sheets of paper, carefully tore the sheets into squares, and then used the pens to create a deck of cards. The games of Hearts were vicious. It was one more acceptable way of discharging hostility without risking retaliation from the real enemies. We played partners and sometimes went three against one. Marty would become furious with Tom when Sutherland ignored a plot to drop the spade queen on the designated fall guy. In his mild way, Tom would say, "I forgot," making Jenco even more irate.

To spice the diversion, occasionally we'd stack the deck on an unwitting player and draw giggles of satisfaction from his discomfort. Undoubtedly, psychologists could infer some deep-seated needs for making one of the group the butt of a joke. But the urge to dump on an individual was spread about evenly among us. Sooner or later it became every person's turn to take his lumps.

Evidently, we were enjoying ourselves too much. The guards discovered us at play and, perhaps instructed by the Hajj, took away our cards on the grounds that such frivolous pursuits went against their religion. Undaunted, Anderson now hoarded scraps of aluminum from the wrappers of the processed cheese served at some meals. He manufactured a complete set of chess pieces and a plastic mat became the board. When our keepers confiscated the chess equipment we protested that this was an ancient and honorable pastime. The appeal went before a mullah for a decision. He ruled that such activity consumed time that would be better spent in religious study and contemplation.

However, by some quirk, a guard challenged Anderson to a game of Arabic checkers. Not allowed to look at his opponent's face, Terry could only peek below his blindfold at the bottle cap pieces. In five minutes Terry whipped his opponent who then bolted from the cell, taking the game with him.

Denied pastimes that employed pieces, we spent hour upon hour in mental games. Twenty Questions was a favorite, and the traditional query "Is it bigger than a breadbox?"

still rings in my ears. Then we dredged up conundrums from memory. For days we sought the answer to the old mind boggler about the two missionaries and three cannibals trying to cross the river in a three-person canoe, without the missionaries on land ever being outnumbered by the maneaters.

Tears of laughter ran down our cheeks when we hit on the notion of a handy phrase book to be used when traveling in areas subject to hostage-taking. With the aid of Sayid, whose sense of humor was among his graces, we came up with a series of one liners:

"Akbar khali-kili haftir lotfan"—Thank you for showing me your marvelous gun.

"Fekr cabul cardan davat paeh gush divar"—I am delighted to accept your kind invitation to lie down on the floor with my arms above my head and my legs apart.

"Auto arraregh davateman mano sespaheh-hast"—It is exceptionally kind of you to allow me to travel in the trunk of your car.

Comparing notes, we agreed that far and above all other vehicles, hostages preferred the trunk of the Mercedes. It was carpeted, best insulated against exhaust fumes and the most roomy for a human body.

We put together the essentials for a hostage kit. It would include Preparation H, giant size toenail clippers that could also be used to cut hair, needles and thread, a standard three-piece suit of undershirt, jockey and boxer shorts. There was some argument over whether lomotil tablets or Pepto Bismol would be more valuable.

These jokes may strike an outsider as one more case of "you-had-to-be-there" humor, but we desperately needed any excuse for a laugh. The essential coping mechanism of humor is denied to individuals kept in solitary confinement. I do not know whether our kidnappers realized it, but putting us together where we could indulge our senses of the comedic was crucial to our mental well-being.

Around 11:00 P.M. the guards would shout "lights out." But before turning them off they would ask if there was anything we wanted. Marty Jenco usually responded, "Call me a taxi." I would request, "How about an F-15 fighter-bomber." Or, "I'll take a fully loaded M-16." Sometimes I called for wine or beer and once I even suggested, "Find a wife for me." They would laugh and then it was time to try to fall asleep.

When one blessedly dropped off—no small task under the circumstances—one more day had passed.

Throughout our days of captivity, Marty Jenco and I kept separate calendars to mark the passage of time. Anderson made succinct diary notations on scraps of paper he squirreled away in a hollowed-out spot in his foam rubber mattress. We all felt responsible for preserving his diary and it was agreed that should one of us be released, he should try and take it with him.

Ecclesiastes says, "To everything there is a season, and a time to every purpose under heaven. There is a time to be born, to love, to kill, and to die." Our time for an ordeal had come. Still, although we had lost our physical freedom, we retained our sense of time. It was an anchor to sanity, held our memory and nourished our hope. Time continued to serve as the manager of our lives. It enabled us to arrange the days and nights despite the absence of freedom.

To retain sanity, one must know the date, time and place. The rational person holds onto time in order not to escape from the self. Hostages, POWs and incarcerated criminals intuitively share an understanding of the importance of keeping track of time—with one vital distinction. The convict numbers the days down, marking them off until the end of his sentence. The POW or hostage counts the days up, accumulating them from the date of captivity.

We looked upon time as both a chasm to cross each day and our one constant connection with external reality.

Chapter 7

Freedom for One

There was a universal fear among us that time would run out and no one would ever now what happened to us. To notice blood in the toilet after a bowel movement, as I did, aroused a nagging fear of a bleeding ulcer or stomach cancer. Detected and treated early, these diseases might be cured. But without recourse to any medical attention, a serious ailment could worsen. And after death, one's body would join others dumped in a shallow grave or discarded on a garbage heap. It was not death that worried us but that we would sicken, suffer and then disappear without any notice to loved ones. They would be condemned to nourish a futile hope interminably.

I feel that those who learn that they are fatally stricken go through a four- or five-stage reaction to the news and that the five of us went through a similar process in reverse. Instead of progressing from anger and denial to acceptance, we went from acceptance to anger and denial. For the hostage or kidnapping victim, the initial reaction of acceptance comes quickly after the first reflex moments of resistance. They have the guns and there's not a damn thing you can do to change the situation. I surrendered the moment Mokmoud put his gun against the head of Dr. Azoury. And after Mokmoud slammed the butt on my head I knew better than to struggle. Surrounded by armed men, bound, gagged and blindfolded, you come to accept the role of captive and hostage.

After the first shock of confinement, which may include

beatings and deprivations, you open negotiations. First you try to bargain with the guards. You promise a reward if they will only let you go. That is of course futile and in the case of Terry Anderson earned him a beating. Then you offer yourself deals—behave nicely and they will relent. Since you get nowhere with these, you open a dialogue with God. You vow to be a better person. If God, or anybody, will intercede on your behalf, you will wholeheartedly enter His or their service. You will sin no more and devote yourself to virtue. All you ask is to go home. The first two stages are valuable to survival because they protect the hostage against truly irrational acts, like attempting to overpower the guards or trying suicide.

A third stage follows in which you perceive the whole business as a colossal mistake. Not only have your good-faith promises failed to move either earthly or heavenly forces, but it is clear that your captors have taken the wrong person hostage. In my case they were looking for Einer Larson. In Marty Jenco's situation, they thought he was the previous head of the Roman Catholic charities. Terry Anderson could beef that he was merely a reporter, not someone who took sides. Indeed, he had long been sympathetic to the causes of the oppressed. Ben Weir had spent thirty years in the country helping the very sort of people who now abused him so badly. And Tom Sutherland was apolitical; just a fellow trying to teach the local people how to improve their agricultural production. Our entire quintet could see themselves as motivated by unselfish, humanitarian urges. The reaction adds up to a kind of denial.

The fourth stage may be the most critical. As time stretches out, the appalling open-endedness yawns ahead. This is an infinite sentence to a life of indignities, pain, and reduction to a sub-animal existence. Totally frustrated, you can become depressed, physically, emotionally, and spiritually. Individually, we all went through periods of the three "H's," haplessness, helplessness, and hopelessness. Fortunately, we never simultaneously hit bottom. There were always three or four others to buoy up the downcast.

The final phase, one we unanimously shared, was anger. Ordinarily it is the first mood experienced by one told he is dying from a disease. The injustice of the situation was overwhelming. There was an almost irresistible urge to lash out. Instead of adopting the Christian stance of turn-the-other-cheek, you opt for an Old Testament view—I'm going to kill the evil sons of bitches and under the circumstances that won't be a sin. They do have all the guns, however. Reason controls the angry impulses. But the hot coals of a suppressed fury await an opportunity to burst into action.

There was a moment, for example, when during one of our passages to the toilet, Terry and I, as usual, peeked downward under our blindfolds. In a moment of laziness, the guard, instead of escorting us portal to portal, had allowed us to walk by ourselves. We both noticed a snubnose, silver revolver carelessly left on a chair. We discussed the circumstances. Both of us thought it might be possible to grab it and come up firing. But we also realized that it might be nothing more than a ploy to trap us. The weapon might be empty and the guards only having a bit of sadistic fun. I let the opportunity pass but the chance of making a break, engaging in bloody violence, remained an idea whose time I prayed would come.

Meanwhile, the flame of hope, while very faint at times, flickered among us. We drew comfort from the stern insistence of the jailers that we remain blindfolded in their presence. That reassured us that we were some day expected to be freed and when that happened they wanted to avoid identification.

I played a kind of game with Marty Jenco. I would announce to him, "It came to me last night. We're all going home next Sunday." He would smile in delight. When the day passed, I would say, "Oops, I got the wrong Sunday. It's one week from now." Another imaginative plan called for me to smuggle out a letter to the Internal Revenue Service pointing out that I had failed to pay my 1984 income tax (the IRS did send a warning letter to Jesse Turner, kidnapped in January 1986, calling him to task for failing to file his 1985 return) and did not plan to submit any more returns. After all, the IRS was the one government agency that always got its man, so to speak. Didn't they lock up Al Capone and a whole string of big shots? I would volunteer to serve my time at the federal penitentiary in Lompoc, California, near my home. Those little games were child's play but somehow they helped us keep our spirits up.

The food continued to be a problem: there was either not enough or else what they served bordered on the inedible. As if in response to our complaints of insufficiency, the guards showed up one day with a huge portion of a local dish they called "*kibby niya*." Both Ben Weir and Marty Jenco politely abstained. But Terry and I were famished and we eagerly fell upon the dish, which is raw ground lamb flavored with herbs. The two of us gobbled up second portions, packing away the amounts intended for Weir and Jenco.

Within a few hours we paid the price of food poisoning for our gluttony. For several days, spasms in the gut doubled us over. We would pound on the door pleading for one more trip to the toilet to relieve the excruciating pangs. Subsequently, the guards served us a broth flavored by hooves discarded by a butcher shop, and which they retrieved from the street. Nor were our appetites whetted one night by a delicacy that featured the head of a sheep complete with eyeballs.

Another piece of creative writing for us became *The Hostage Cookbook*. "Hint of Chicken" described a dish of rice in which a chicken walked across the grain. The only residue was the fowl's droppings.

While we struggled to fill our hours and amuse ourselves, an event occurred in July 1985 that tested our fragile alliance to its utmost. The Hajj arrived and following the customary salutations, speaking through Sayid, said, "We have decided to try your suggestion. We will allow one of you to go home and carry a message to the American government about our demands."

Their message was in essence the same one that had been delivered on two previous occasions: once through Jeremy Levin when he escaped—or was permitted to escape—in February 1985, and once when they hijacked TWA Flight 847 in June of the same year. They wanted to initiate talks leading to an exchange of the Western hostages for the Dawa prisoners held in Kuwait.

It was great and stunning news. But there was an even more breathtaking kicker. "You will select the best person to plead your cause back home. Let me know and he will be released."

In that single sentence, our little union exploded. Everyone wanted to go home. Everyone could make a case for himself. I saw instantly how divisive and cruel the order from the Hajj could be.

Our captors withdrew, leaving us to begin an acrimonious debate, with far more at stake than a political campaign. Terry immediately said, "Let's do it democratically. It should be through a vote. Let's have secret ballots but the decision must be unanimous."

One of the most important lessons I had learned as a hospital administrator was to calculate the consequences of a certain solution would be after a dispute was resolved. In this instance, everyone wanted to go home but only one would make it. There would be four left and we would all have to live together. It was vital to anticipate the feelings of those who stayed behind.

"Before rushing into a vote," I counseled, "we should talk about this. No matter what the Hajj said, *they* are going to actually make the decision. It's a mistake for us to play the game. This could all be a cruel hoax, leaving us only frustrated with nasty feelings toward one another."

Tom Sutherland agreed with me. But Ben Weir, Marty Jenco and Terry refused to discuss the relationships and emotions that would be engendered by making this a con-

117

test. They called for a vote and outnumbered us three to two. The two clergymen declared themselves ineligible and nominated Terry. Tom put up my name. The balloting began and we probably voted ten times. The count remained the same; three for Anderson, two for Jacobsen.

Finally, Tom and I caucused. We decided that to continue the election would only make matters worse. We would both cast our ballots for Terry. This was to be the final vote. Anderson opened the slips of paper and announced, "One for Terry, two for Terry, three for Terry, four for Terry." His expression slowly turned to pain. The final vote was for me. He had changed his vote! I genuinely felt his sorrow. He wanted so desperately to go home and I think he really believed he could get the rest of us out through his efforts.

We went back to the polls. This time it was unanimous for Anderson. Sayid stopped by our cell and asked who had been chosen. "It's me, unanimously," answered a jubilant Anderson.

Several days passed while we waited for the Hajj to return. Finally, he arrived and after we made our expected obeisance, he unexpectedly began to speak to Ben Weir in Arabic. During his many years in the Middle East, Ben had picked up the language and as he listened to the Hajj, we heard him cry out, "Oh no, no no!" Hearts jumped into mouths. Had our death sentences been pronounced?

We clamored for a translation and Ben broke down. "It's me. I am the one who is being released."

Terry lost his aplomb. "No, no!" he shouted, almost echoing Ben. "I'm supposed to go home! I was the one elected!"

The Hajj, talking through Sayid now, said, "No. You are a bad man. You will stay."

Anderson was beside himself. He turned to me. "Dave," he demanded. "Talk to him. Tell him that I was chosen unanimously. Tell him I am the best person to bring their message to the government."

I did manage to stammer some sort of argument in favor of Terry to the Hajj, the gist of which was "Hajj, we voted that it

be Anderson." But I knew it didn't matter. Nothin
say would change a decision by Hizballah. The onl\
even tried in a half-hearted way was because of sym
Terry's shattered expectations.

As I anticipated, the Hajj refused to consider wha
say. After he and the guards departed, Anderson t\
me in fury. "Dammit, Dave. You didn't defend
didn't fight for me."

Now I lit into him. "You wouldn't listen to me wh
you that they would make the selection. You're be\
who can't stand to be told he can't have what he w
all want to go home but it's going to be their decisi\
time out."

He responded with further angry words. Bot
clenched our fists and the argument threatened to
violent. Our compatriots tried to calm us down. Ac
was Terry who defused the situation. He banged on
and demanded to visit the bathroom. In his absenc\
expressed concern over his emotional state.

The charged atmosphere dissipated somewhat \
return of Sayid. He had the task of making Weir m
sentable to the world. Reverting to his professio\
barbered Ben's hair and trimmed his beard. Then
lowed him to luxuriate in a long, hot shower.

An hour passed and it was the moment of farewel\
prayed together. Temporarily, good fellowship war\
room. Individually, we embraced our departing co
Ben whispered in my ear, "Keep them alive, David.'

And then he was gone. It was a night mixed with th
one man and the antagonism that remained from
fated election. The affair poisoned my relationsh\
Terry for months.

About an hour after Weir was removed from th\
Sayid returned to describe the ultimate scene. He
they had driven the minister to the AUB campus ent\
few feet from where I had been kidnapped. After B
ordered to get out of the car, the vehicle parked

Ben Weir received his freedom at this gate to the AUB campus.

distance away. The Hizballah men observed the freed man's
joy and watched him put himself safely in the hands of the
university police.

Now it was our turn to wait to see if Weir's mission would
produce the desired results. Several days passed and an obviously disturbed Hajj returned to scold us. Why had there still
been no public disclosure of Weir's release? Why hadn't the
American government, having been informed of the kidnappers' demands, opened negotiations? The Hajj had come to
the wrong place for his answers. We had no explanation for
the news delay nor the behavior of U.S. officials. Fearful of
his displeasure, we made excuses. "They probably wanted to
be extra careful moving him from the AUB campus in West
Beirut to the Embassy in East Beirut. And in Washington
they most likely need full confirmation that it is Ben Weir."

He left, unmollified. It occurred to me that he answered to
higher authorities. Having presented our idea of a messenger
to his superiors, he was now taking the heat for what appeared to be a failed strategy. Hizballah, we assumed, like
the PLO and other Arab organizations, operated through
a small executive committee, of which Hajj was a key
member.

In fact, the State Department committed an enormous blunder in handling Ben Weir. Flown from Beirut to West Germany and then back to the United States, the authorities callously refused for twenty-four hours to allow his wife and son a chance to meet with the husband and father who had been a hostage for sixteen months. The behavior of the government people was either simple stupidity or small-minded pique. Weir's wife is a strong-willed, plain-speaking woman. She had already annoyed the bureaucrats with some justifiable bitterness about the government's unwillingness to make efforts to free her spouse. She and her son had exchanged some angry words with Secretary of State George Shultz.

At first, apparently, Ben cooperated amiably in the debriefing. But when prevented from seeing his family, he turned recalcitrant, an attitude reinforced by the way his wife had been treated. He now took the position that he would do nothing on behalf of the government. (After my release, both the FBI and CIA expressed their anger and disappointment over Ben's refusal to help.)

Ben Weir was actually freed on Saturday night, September 14, 1985. Not until four days later, on September 18, did President Reagan announce his release. It was explained that the word had been held up because of hopes that the remaining hostages would also be emancipated. It is utterly incomprehensible, given the information that Ben carried, that there could have been any question of the rest of us being voluntarily liberated. The official U.S. government statement reported that Weir had indeed carried a message from his captors but the details went undisclosed. A day later, at his own press conference, Ben explained to the newspeople that the hostages were being held to ransom the Dawa prisoners in Kuwait.

As much as we hoped that Ben might serve the ends of Hizballah and open up negotiations for our freedom, we also thought he might provide the information necessary for a quick rescue by the Delta Force, a special military assault

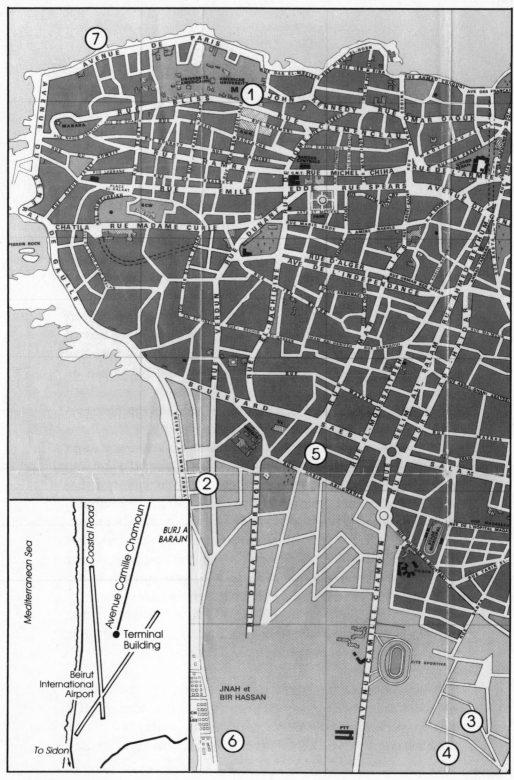

This map of Beirut shows the areas where we were held. The inset shows the Beirut International Airport site. Our location fell inside the trajectories of planes using the runways.

DOWNTOWN BEIRUT

1—Kidnapping location

2—Interrogation, first day

3—First place of captivity; where Buckley died

4—Second place of captivity; held in room with Anderson; Weir released from here

5—Third place of captivity; Jenco released from here

6—Last place of captivity

7—Point of release

team. We had put together our own intelligence on our whereabouts, to which Weir was of course privy. The deafening thunder of jet aircraft positioned us close to the airport. We counted the seconds that elapsed from the time we heard a jet start down one runway until it lifted off at full throttle—six seconds. Then there were the takeoffs from a different direction and runway, eight seconds. We had noted the daily flyovers by a pair of Israeli fighter planes, their sonic booms announcing their arrival. Undoubtedly, they made aerial photographs that could have been scanned for clues to our location. How many uncompleted schoolhouses could there have been in close proximity to the airport? Could not the geniuses of precision bombing have plotted our times for jet takeoffs and calculated our location? Even though the CIA network had been ruined by the capture of William Buckley, there must have been someone among all of the competing forces in the city who, given the facts known to Weir, could have pinpointed the place of our imprisonment.

We stayed in this site for twenty-nine days after Ben Weir's deliverance. Throughout this period I waited with great anticipation, yearning for shots and shouts, for the blessed sound of concussion grenades stunning our captors, for the quick steps of the Delta Force commandos charging up and down the stairs, for the sight of heavily armed troopers battering down our door. But nothing happened. Weir refused to cooperate. He was not only hostile to the U.S. authorities but also he demurred on the grounds of "not wanting to encourage military action." He also feared that brute force would only end with our deaths. We remained hidden in our little redoubt.

Ben Weir had no right to decide whether or not the U.S. leaders should launch a raid to rescue us. He lacked the knowledge or experience to determine the riskiness of such an attack. Furthermore, it was *our* freedom and *our* lives that were at stake. When I learned upon my debriefing in Wiesbaden, West Germany immediately after my release

The behavior of U.S. officials so angered Ben Weir and his family that he refused to cooperate with them after being debriefed. However, he has continued to work for the freedom of those still held in Lebanon.

that Ben had refused to supply the intelligence necessary for a strike on our behalf, I was furious. Later, as I began to understand his reasons, my anger subsided and I was simply upset. After all, he was held for sixteen months and then kept away from his wife and family for a full twenty-four hours upon his return to the United States. Although it was not his decision as to what strategy should be pursued in attempting to gain our freedom, I can understand the experiences that influenced his decision and I must respect his aversion to violence.

I had always been prepared for an opportunity to send a note to my family. When the Hajj proposed it, I already had one ready. All I needed to add was the current date with the addendum that I was still alive. The contents were straightforward. I addressed it to Eric and his wife Cathy, Paul and his wife Lori, and to Diane:

"Greetings in the Lord's name to everyone and especially Kerrie, Dad and my family. Pastor Ben Weir is being released tonight. If I and the other hostages are to be released, the seventeen men held by the Kuwaiti government must be released. That is the only condition for my release.

Please contact all the politicians—your representative and Senators Wilson and Cranston. Telephone, write to them, pester them. Have others write letters. My release is dependent upon public pressure on the U.S. government. Believe me, those who believe in quiet diplomacy would change their philosophy after a day of captivity.

I am being well treated. There is no torture or physical abuse.

I am with Tom Sutherland, Father Lawrence Jenco and Terry Anderson. We have church services twice a day. Also plenty of time for exercise.

My dearest family, I love you very much. Please love one another. Take care of Kerrie and provide for her needs. She is very special to me and her bringing me to the Lord has made it possible for me to survive.

God bless all of you. Please reassure Dad that I will be home soon. Encourage him to write his book. In regards to money, the AUB should be sending you my monthly salary. The first check should have been for May. If they are not doing it, contact them in New York.

Please don't worry about me. My captors are kind to us and want us to go home, but they demand that their friends be released from Kuwait. Please impress this on the U.S. government officials. Again, have faith in God and pray for me and the safe release of my fellow prisoners.

I have only a few minutes to write this letter, so my thoughts are not organized. Remember that I love you very much. Help one another in every way possible. May God bless you and keep you. May His face shine upon you and give you peace. May God hold you in the palm of His hand until we meet again.

Again, it is vital to tell the government of the conditions of my release. Be forceful with them. If the United States can exchange prisoners with Russia we certainly can be exchanged for the seventeen prisoners in Kuwait.

If you have problems with the AUB New York, telephone Joe Cicippio of the AUB in Beirut. He is my friend and he will help you.

Oh, time is short to write. I think of you constantly. I am in the best spirits possible under the circumstances. My health is good.

> God bless you.
> All my love,
> *Dad*

Late one night in September, Sayid and company aroused us from our sleep. We were handed some clothes, told to dress quickly. "You are going home," said Sayid. Bewildered by the sudden change in events, we fumbled for our effects and again cheerfully followed instructions.

They loaded all four of us into a van and drove through the city streets. Presumably, it was dark; we wore our blindfolds so it was impossible to know for sure. The guards seemed on edge, fearful of running into an unexpected military checkpoint. The trip took perhaps thirty minutes, replete with stops, starts, U-turns, lefts and rights.

When we halted, we were taken inside a building and instructed to put a hand on the shoulder of the hostage in front as we climbed stairs. They ordered us to move swiftly

Our "penthouse" apartment was in this neighborhood, a southern suburb of Beirut near the Kuwaiti Embassy.

and we fairly ran up six flights. We climbed out on a rooftop, breathing in the clear, cool night air. They led us, single file to a wall, guided us to get atop it. "Jump!" commanded Sayid. From beneath the strip over my eyes I could see a narrow gap between two buildings and a slightly higher ledge on the adjacent structure. Each of us leaped across without any difficulty. We were then led inside to a kind of penthouse apartment.

This was our new jail. As so often, we had been cruelly deceived with a false claim of imminent release. The hope of liberation by the Delta Force also collapsed with our transfer to this site.

Our latest quarters were roughly twenty by twenty. Steel shutters blocked any vision through the windows. The bathroom lay down a corridor that ran between a living room and dining room used by the guards. There were two other bedrooms on the floor, one used by the gunmen and the other by, as we learned later, three French hostages.

After we settled in and were reduced to living in our underwear again, I became convinced that my best hope for freedom lay in an escape. I watched for an opportunity. When Sayid gave us our occasional haircuts, he sat us in a chair. During one moment when he was absent I removed a metal rung from the back of the chair. I explained to my companions, "I think I could pry loose that sheet metal that covers the sliding doors to the terrace." The others were aghast at the notion. Both Tom and Terry worried that the sound of my popping out the rivet fasteners would summon the guards. I managed to loosen some rivets but could not pry enough aluminum away from the frame for a human to slip through. Figuring on the metal piece as a tool for some future use, I wrapped the chair rung in my spare underwear and stuck it in my plastic bag.

Still, I stayed alert for an opportunity. During one of the periodic sieges of diarrhea, I rapped on the door asking to use the bathroom. The guard on duty was named Abu Ali. He spoke very little English but he knew enough to answer, "Later."

"No," I insisted. "I have to go now."

"Later." But as I continued to hammer away, he relented and unlocked the door to explain to me, "You wait. Mokmoud, he in toilet."

I quickly grasped the situation. There were always three guards assigned to watch us. At least that was the number visible on our floor. One of them was frequently out buying supplies. With Mokmoud attending to his own needs, temporarily out of circulation, that left only Abu Ali, who was considerably smaller than me, to bar the way to the stairs. And whoever was detailed to escort us did not tote a gun.

I started down the corridor as Ali backed up. I think he sensed that I might have a notion to go on the attack. "No, no, Mr. David," said the retreating Ali. I hesitated. I had to decide, should I lunge for his throat? Could I strangle him before he managed to yell and alert the others? Could I kill a man with my bare hands? Should I just grab him, knock him aside and then try to find his weapon? Who should I shoot first, Ali or Mokmoud? Would it be faster to run down the stairs or take the elevator down the six floors? I paused just long enough for him to dash into one of the guards' rooms and retrieve a pistol.

I smiled at him. "Okay, I'll just go in the toilet." That ended the incident. He never reported me, apparently because he could have been reprimanded for failing to follow the appropriate procedures. The incident, which probably lasted about thirty seconds, made me realize I needed to do some homework before I attempted an escape.

Chapter 8

**The Cast
of Characters
Expands**

The dreary routine of living in darkness depressed me. Earlier, Terry and I had been given two brief moments in the sun. The first time, we were taken to a window and allowed to lower our blindfolds for a few minutes to gaze on bottle-brush trees and eucalyptuses. The scene bore a vague resemblance to my California memories. Later, we enjoyed a brief exercise period in an enclosed patio while the sun shone down on us. But our eyes remained covered throughout. Those were the only exposures to sunlight during my entire incarceration.

In fact, I became almost obsessed with our isolation from the great outdoors and cried out to the guard, "Tell me, Mokmoud, is there still a sun, moon and stars!"

A few nights later, Mokmoud herded us all into the room ordinarily occupied by his colleagues. I felt fresh air blowing on us, like a cold drink for long-parched throats. Mokmoud said, "Mr. David, we have a wonderful surprise." He took me by the hand and led me outside on the roof, told me to sit down, and after moving out of the range of my vision, instructed me to lower my blindfold. I looked up into a silent, clear, moonlit night with thousands of stars twinkling. One by one Mokmoud had brought out my companions and we sat there one at a time dumbstruck at this first celestial panorama in so many months. As I wallowed in nature's awesome spectacle, which we usually take for granted, mankind contributed its own delicate touch in the form of a purple flare fired by one of the warring parties. Slowly, the violet fire descended, illuminating the horizon. And as the final light of the flare died away, the silence ended. For the purpose of man's addition to the nighttime beauty had been to display targets. The artillerymen shattered the quiet with exploding shells. Quickly I was returned to our quarters.

When Mokmoud took us all for our moonlit night excursion, I was terrified that the real purpose might be a room search. On my return I found nothing disturbed, but now I squeezed my metal rod into the space between the sheet metal and door frame where if it were discovered, no one could accuse any of us of possessing it.

The gift of a few minutes in the moonlight hardly compensated for having robbed us of our right to indulge in the heavenly splendors whenever the urge came upon us. Nevertheless, the moment was a kind of rebirth. Sagging spirits revived.

We badly needed such momentary boosts. The close, continued confinement exacted a toll on normal compassion and forbearance. Carping and criticism of one another became a way of life. On one occasion, while Tom occupied the bathroom, Terry and Marty groused about what they perceived as Sutherland's total adaptation to captivity. As his friend, I defended Tom. When he returned to the room, he accidentally bumped into Jenco. Words followed and then matters threatened to get completely out of hand with a fistfight. When I tried to intervene, I was told to butt out, that it was none of my business.

At that moment, a guard arrived for my trip to the shower. I left with some misgivings but when I returned all was calm. Somehow the differences were at least temporarily resolved and my three companions were circling the room.

When we were alone and able to remove our blindfolds I said, "You know, the acoustics in this building are strange. While I was in the bathroom, I could hear everything said in this room." They looked sheepishly at me. They did not realize, immediately, that I could not hear a blessed sound while in the toilet.

Although tempers flared quickly, they cooled even more rapidly. No one needed to apologize. We understood how our situation created enormous tension and how an emotional blow-up was a safety valve. My intent was to trick them into a truce and at the same time warn them to be careful. Our basic resource was one another. We could not afford to actually fight.

In these first weeks occupying the penthouse, we learned the identity of the occupants who shared the floor. There were hints that they were French because occasionally we caught snatches of conversation through the walls and recognized the language. And in the course of Tom Sutherland's lessons in that tongue to Terry, he asked our keepers if they could bring him a book in French. The request was met so promptly the book must have been on the premises. Because we habitually received our bathroom privileges after them and the place was always such an untidy mess, we joked they must be French.

On one of my trips to the can, I passed by the entrance to the adjoining room. The guards had left the solid wooden door ajar and I glimpsed three men in their underwear, obviously hostages. When I returned to my associates I gave them the news. Terry then visited the bathroom. In their laziness, the sentries let him go unescorted. He brought back more specific information. "The guys next door are French. One of them spoke to me in English and said 'I'm Marcel Carton. The others are Michel Seurat and Jean-Paul Kauffman.' He asked me 'Are you Terry Anderson, the journalist?'" Terry added he only had time to answer "Yes," before the guards halted the conversation.

We developed resentments against the French group. The

French diplomat Marcel Carton, kidnapped March 22, 1985 with colleague Marcel Fontaine, occupied a nearby room. This picture of him is from a videotaped message conveying demands by the kidnappers. Carton and Fontaine were released in May of 1988. (Courtesy AP/Wide World Photos)

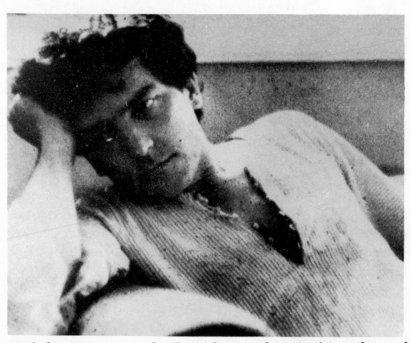

Michel Seurat, a researcher from the French center for studies and research of the contemporary Middle East, was taken May 22, 1985 and apparently died of cancer later that year in a room with other French hostages. (Courtesy AP/Wide World Photos)

Jean-Paul Kauffmann, a French journalist, shared the quarters of Carton and Seurat. This photo of him was made during a video tape by Islamic Jihad. Kauffmann also went free in May, 1988.

guards seemed to indulge them more than us. They were given far more time for their bathroom privileges in the morning while we were chided for dallying during our limited periods. It became something of a point of honor for me to challenge my keepers when they tried to enforce the fifteen-minute rule on me.

The slovenly habits of our fellow hostages became more directly disagreeable when we abruptly switched rooms. In the fashion of tidy Americans we had done our best to sanitize and improve our quarters. Our protests to the guards had brought a heater fan to dry out the foam rubber mattresses, which had begun to rot and stink like moldy straw. Petitions about poor ventilation led to the installation of a door with bars in place of the solid wooden one. This change improved air circulation but it also humiliated us with its obvious reminder of our prisoner status. Still, we swept the place, picked up the rubbish and tried to keep ourselves clean. The walls were in fairy decent shape, partly because we took pains to maintain them.

Now we were not only evicted but also housed in a pigpen. On closer inspection, however, the condition of the place was at least partially due to an apparently serious illness of one of the men. Along with the scraps of bread and orange peels on and under the mats, we discovered the apparatus for intravenous solutions, used syringes, an empty plastic blood container—Type O from my hospital, the American University of Beirut Medical Center. And in the waste basket lay bloody bandages.

We had learned earlier, through an unrelated piece of business involving our diet, that a doctor, presumably Dr. Hallak, must have been on the premises. At one point, our bread ration had been cut in half. Given the small amounts of food supplied, the shortage of bread left us hungry. We griped about the reduction and demanded restoration of the original supplies. "What's the problem, are you running out of money for food?" I grumbled to Sayid. "Look in my wallet. I had some money in it and you can use it to buy bread."

The cutback dragged on with Terry venturing another explanation. "Maybe the Christians cut off delivery of flour to West Beirut." That was a standard tactic in the war of nerves between the two sections of the city.

After a number of days, however, one of the guards let slip the real reason. "The doctor said that you are all getting too fat." Pressed for more information, our keepers advised us that the physician had seen us on our walks to the bathroom and noticed we were all putting on weight. For health reasons he suggested fewer calories through bread. Actually, it was less a matter of adding pounds than it was replacing muscle tissue with fat because of a diet high in carbohydrates and low in protein.

We soon learned more about the physician. A long, unmailed letter in the pocket of a pair of trousers hanging on a makeshift clothesline disclosed his identity and the details of why he had been summoned to our jail. The four of us huddled together and silently read the missive. Written in English, it revealed an articulate, compassionate, and thoughtful man. It was addressed to his wife.

The author described with brilliant insight the civil war that racked Lebanon. An especially poignant section spoke

Parisians in May 1986 carried placards with photographs of their countrymen held hostage in Beirut. More than a dozen French citizens were kidnapped. (Courtesy AP/Wide World Photos)

about a young fighter whom we deduced must be his son and whom he labeled even more of a hostage than he. The letter specifically related how he had been brought to our location to treat a sick Frenchman, after having been held at another location with five or six friends, all of whom were Jewish.

The doctor then reviewed his desperate efforts on behalf of the patient. He referred to his pediatric training and the difficulty of arriving at a diagnosis without the availability of critical clinical tests. He spoke of a desire to confirm his belief in the nature of the illness but mentioned the need for a definitive workup through my hospital. Sadly, the kidnappers refused to permit such an examination.

The letter, which was in the form of a day-by-day account, seemed more like a diary. Above all, the author stated and reiterated his love for his wife. At the end of every day's section appeared the Arabic word, *"katkout,"* meaning little chick or bird. Accompanying the signature was a stick cartoon of a tiny bird. We all felt some discomfort at reading such intimate and eloquent words of endearment.

Subsequently, we were further disconcerted when Badr bounded into the room, obviously in a manic state. He pronounced himself Dr. Badr and said he would take our blood pressure. He then slipped the usual cuff on our arms and inflated it. But he had no stethoscope for an actual reading. Badr was trying to be funny but the result was purely ugly. The cuff and stethoscope are basic items in a physician's gear. It seemed unlikely that a doctor would abandon them. The implication did not bode well for "little bird." After my release, I met with Marcel Carton. Ironically, the kidnappers outfitted him with the remnants of my prison wardrobe. He knew it was mine because the garments bore the initials DPJ. Carton informed me that after the patient, Marcel Seurat, died of cancer, Dr. Hallak supposedly was given the option of remaining with the Frenchmen. However, he chose to return to the company of several other Lebanese Jews being held. "The doctor was taken out of our room," said Carton. "A few

Marcel Carton, one of the Frenchmen imprisoned in an adjoining room, received his freedom in May 1988 and celebrated with his daughter Simone Elkhoury. (Courtesy AP/Wide World Photos)

minutes later, we heard a gunshot. We assume that he had been executed."

Ominously, the third of the French trio, Jean-Paul Kauffman, was handed both Dr. Hallak's stethoscope and his clothing. For my own part, I contacted the pediatrician's wife, Rachel, to tell her of my knowledge of her husband. Although she clings to the hope that he is still alive, and there have been some reports that he survives, the evidence indicates otherwise. His murder would be one more testament to the savagery that lies just beneath the surface courtesy exhibited by the hostage-takers.

We vigorously protested the conditions of the room to which we had been transferred, pointing out the cracks in the wall paint, the dirt on all surfaces, and the wet floors, after nighttime condensation sent water coursing down the walls. We demanded another heater along with rags to wipe up the place. We tried to take the edge off with a joke that unless improvements were made, we'd no longer pay any rent.

The Hajj, perhaps remembering the fate of William Buckley and certainly aware that a dead hostage had no value, heeded our complaints. The guards appeared with buckets of hot water, detergent and antiseptic, and ordered us to scrub the walls and floor. When we completed the cleanup, they brought a ladder, paint, and brushes. After a few minutes of work covering the surfaces with a pale green wash, they tired of the labor. Ordered to finish the work, we complied. Aside from making our quarters habitable, the task passed time. When we were done, they allowed us hot showers as a reward for our efforts.

Another petition to the Hajj also paid off. During one of his periodic visits, we persuaded him that our survival demanded more than food for our body. We needed sustenance for our minds or we would die. He contributed a marvelous little library. The books included The Bible, Charlotte Bronte's *Wuthering Heights*, George Orwell's *1984*, selections from the works of Charles Dickens and William Shakespeare, a world history text, and Homer's *Odyssey*, among others.

Merwin Peak's *Titus Groan* from *The Gormenghast Trilogy*, with its extravagant fantasy, provided a welcome note of escapism. All of us found special meaning in *The Plague* by Albert Camus because its depiction of Algeria during the 1940s mirrored our experiences in Beirut. Marty Jenco had problems sleeping at night after delving into *Alfred Hitchcock's Favorite Ghost Stories*.

A source of constant argument centered on Marcia Stigam's *Money Market*. This six-hundred-page tome with its academic description of financial machinations triggered some noisy disputes between Anderson and me, reflecting our different political orientations. The fact is, neither of us knew what he was talking about, but that never kept either one of us from voicing an opinion!

We also profited from reading Nikki Keddi's *Iran: Its Religion, Its Culture and Its Politics*. The book contained perhaps ten essays edited by a UCLA professor, and they offered insights into the thinking of the people behind Hizballah. Another book with special meaning was Gary Sick's *All Fall Down*, an account of the U.S. Embassy staff taken hostage in Iran in 1979. And then there was Robin Wright's *Sacred Rage*. Wright was a correspondent whom Terry knew, and her book purported to cover Middle East politics. Anderson denigrated her expertise, suggesting she spent much of her time interviewing other journalists. After pouring over *Sacred Rage*, he pronounced, as if addressing her, "You're a really lousy reporter. That's not the way things happened."

The library donated by the Hajj smacked of a college student's required reading for courses. I wondered who among our captors might have spent some time in the States.

The most welcome addition to our little home, however, was a radio, supplied after great entreaties to the Hajj. For several hours a day, the guards permitted us to listen to a seven-band Sony portable. Our primary interest, of course, was the news broadcasts. Radio Monte Carlo, in English, provided us with the most information, but we also followed events and programs over the BBC and the Voice of America.

We delighted in Alistair Cooke's "Letters Back Home" over the BBC, a kind of chatty recounting of events in the United States. I became a devoted fan of Garrison Keillor's "Prairie Home Companion" aired Saturday evenings on the Voice of America. Keillor's denizens of Lake Wobegone made us laugh in our dismal circumstances and the humor helped us ward off melancholy.

But there was also the bad news. Whenever the subject of hostages came up, the spokesman for our country reiterated the policy of "no negotiation with terrorists." It was particularly depressing to hear the sentiments quoted by President Ronald Reagan. That always provoked an intemperate outburst by Terry about that "Teflon President." I automatically defended Reagan and we would be off on another loud confrontation.

On a typical hot humid day, behind a double-locked door, with three armed guards on the premises, with the fans laboring in an ineffective effort to cool and dry our room, we squatted on the damp mattress pads in our underwear and sought consolation on the radio. Turning the dial, we came across the voice of Henry Kissinger, former National Security Adviser and Secretary of State under President Richard Nixon.

In his gravelly voice, Kissinger declared, "I could advise the President of numerous ways to secure the freedom of the American hostages in Lebanon, but the fact is they will have to use their own resources to gain their freedom."

I was dumbfounded, then outraged. "*What* resources, Henry?" I screamed. To my associates I said, "His comments are proof that some people are educated beyond their intelligence."

I commented that we would have to give Reagan credit for never having employed Kissinger in any official capacity. And we all knew the talk about Kissinger profiting from his U.S. government connections after he returned to private life.

Kissinger reportedly had once remarked that he would not expect the government to bargain with terrorists even if he were abducted. We wondered how long he would have retained that detachment when fed our diet and forced to live in his underwear while his well-armed captors humiliated him with daily indignities.

Chapter 9

Enter Terry Waite

Brooding over Kissinger's off-hand dismissal of us, I scoffed to myself about his reference to "our resources." Chained, locked up in cells, weakened by inadequate food, guarded by armed men who would kill if challenged, it was preposterous to assume we had any resources.

But then I suddenly thought of something we could do for ourselves. To the others I said, "Let's say thank you, Henry. Why don't we write an open letter to President Reagan and have the Hajj give it to the media?"

At first, the reaction was disbelief. The others were deeply discouraged by Kissinger's statement. My idea was rejected as ridiculous. "It won't work" and "It's a waste of time" were the most charitable comments.

I persisted, pointing out that the open letter was an old and often effective political technique. I argued that as a hospital executive I was as much a politician as an administrator and I knew the authorities would have to respond to an open letter. If our captors went for the idea, the letter would appear in every newspaper in the United States and be shown on the TV news programs. At the very least it would make millions of people conscious there were American hostages and at best it might force some efforts to free us.

Once everyone was convinced that a letter might help, the text became a matter of controversy. After all, it was a committee effort. And whoever heard of a group project in which the principals readily agreed to the wording of a statement?

143

Terry thought the letter should be in his handwriting. He felt that would persuade people it was genuine. The penmanship seemed unimportant to me. We went back and forth over what we would say and we expanded the list of recipients.

Finally, we reached a consensus and drafted the letter. The one to Ronald Reagan read as follows:

8 Nov. 1985

Mr. President:

"We are appealing to you for action. We have read and heard over the past months of your refusal to negotiate with our captors, and your rationale for it. We understand it, but do not agree. You negotiated over the hostages from the TWA plane, and such negotiations have been held repeatedly and successfully by other countries—Israel, Egypt, El Salvador and the Soviet Union. You, and they, did so because you believed that saving the lives of innocent hostages should be the primary goal. We are asking the same consideration. There is no alternative. Our kidnappers say they have no connection with Syria, Iran or local Shiite leaders, and will not give in to pressure from them, so no one knows their identity. They say they will not be moved, and are growing impatient. You have tried other routes, but have not won the release of a single hostage in more than eighteen months. We have no chance of escaping, and our captors say if any attempt is made to rescue us, they and we will all die.

They believe they have shown by unilaterally releasing Pastor Ben Weir that their intentions are good. They do not wish to harm us, and want to bring this to a rapid and peaceful conclusion. But they say, you have so far given no indication, public or private, that you are willing to negotiate. Mr. President, how long do you suppose these people will wait? We are told William Buckley is dead. Father Lawrence Martin Jenco has been a hostage ten months, Terry Anderson eight months, David Jacobsen six months, Thomas Sutherland five months. The conditions of our captivity are deteriorating again, as is our physical and mental health.

We are kept in a small, damp—[here the kidnappers blacked out the words 'windowless cell']—twenty-four hours a day,

144

8 Nov 85

Mr. President

We are appealing to you for action. We have read and reread over the past months of your refusal to negotiate with our captors, and your rationale for it. We understand it, but do not agree. You negotiated over the captives from the TWA plane, and such negotiations have been held repeatedly and successfully by other countries — Israel, Egypt, El Salvador and the Soviet Union. You, and I see because you believed that saving the lives of innocent hostages should be the primary goal. We are willing for the same consideration. There is no reason. Our kidnappers say they have no connection with Syria, Iran or local Shiite leaders, and will not give in to pressure from them, since no one knows their identity. They say they will not be moved, and are growing impatient. You have tried other routes,

We are kept in a small, dark, Bay, without proper exercise, sanitation, fresh air, or a balanced diet. We have only intermittent access to outside news. It is difficult to remain cheerful and optimistic when we see no sign anywhere of progress toward our release.

Mr. Reagan, we thank you for the efforts we have heard through these long months, but your "quiet diplomacy" is not working. We know of your distaste for bargaining with terrorists. As you know the consequences your continued refusal will have for us? It is in your power to help us home for Christmas. Will you not have mercy on us and our families and do so?

May God be with you

Terry Anderson

Fr. Lawrence Martin Jenco, O.S.M.

David Jacobsen

145

without proper exercise, sanitation, fresh air or balanced diet. We have only intermittent access to outside news. It is difficult to remain cheerful and optimistic when we see no sign anywhere of progress toward our release.

Mr. Reagan, we thank you for the efforts you have made through these long months, but your 'quiet diplomacy' is not working. We know of your dislike for bargaining with terrorists. Do you know the consequences your continued refusal will have for us? It is in your power to have us home by Christmas. Will you not have mercy on us and our families and do so? May God be with you."

And beneath that wish appeared our four signatures.

We had marshalled all of the arguments in favor of negotiation, pointing out the precedents and the hostage-trading done by a disparate group of countries. We noted that the current policies had produced no results and there were signs our kidnappers would act in good faith. We indicated as best we could the extent of our suffering and we appealed to the President's sense of fairness and his compassion. We agreed that we had left nothing out.

Over the BBC we had heard the Archbishop of Canterbury, Robert Runcie, express a desire to aid in our release. Therefore, we penned a personal and confidential letter to him, requesting his help.

Through the Voice of America we had learned that two members of Congress, Robert Dornan from my home state of California and George O'Brien of Illinois, reminded their fellow legislators, daily, of the plight of the U.S. hostages. We wrote a thank-you note to Dornan and O'Brien. In it, we stated, "They [our captors] say they are not subject to pressure from Syria, Iran or Lebanese leaders, since no one knows who they are or where we are. President Reagan's efforts on our behalf have accomplished nothing—they have not won release of a single hostage from this group in nearly two years . . . Our release can be very rapid, our captors say. We ask you, your fellow Congressmen and members of the U.S. Senate to try to persuade President Reagan to take the only

To the AP + all news media,   8 Nov 85   1:00 PM.

We have just been told that someone has claimed that Islamic Jihad has killed all of us. Obviously this is not true. Our captors say it was an attempt by the U.S. government to spoil negotiations.

Father Lawrence Martin Jenco

Terry Anderson

David Jacobsen

Thomas Sutherland

Along with the missive to the President, we scrawled a brief note to the Associated Press and the rest of the media saying that, in spite of rumors, we were still among the living. (Courtesy AP/Wide World Photos)

course available to win our release, and to take it quickly."

At Terry Anderson's suggestion, we prepared a fourth missive for the Associated Press asking the wire service to make certain the government did not censor or restrict the letters.

Once we finished our writing, we asked for a meeting with the Hajj. Coincidentally, he had decided to visit us because of a rumor that we had all been executed. He told us the rumor was most upsetting and asked us to write to the media and our families informing one and all we remained among the living.

Reports of our deaths plagued our families and friends. My son, Eric, was awakened at 2:30 A.M. one morning by a telephone call from Peggy Say, Terry Anderson's sister. She informed him of a report out of Beirut that an anonymous caller to a Western news agency that has asked not to be identified, announced that all the American hostages would be executed in less than two hours and that a subsequent call would reveal where the bodies could be found. Peggy had already contacted the State Department, which could not confirm the information.

Struggling to collect his sleep-muddled wits and to digest the devastating information from Peggy Say, Eric could not even pray. His thoughts were interrupted by the jangling of the phone. He quickly answered, seeking more news. The voice identified himself as a reporter for the Chicago *Tribune*. The newsman, after ascertaining that Eric had heard the rumor, asked, "I was wondering, how does the possible death of your father make you feel?" Eric hung up. The *Tribune* call runs a dead heat with one Eric received right after I was grabbed. A reporter from the Orange County *Register* reached him on the telephone and asked for some quotes. When he politely demurred, she turned abusive. "We're going to run a story about your father whether you comment or not. Don't you have anything nice to say about him?" He slammed down the receiver.

The deadline for the executions passed without any notification or explanation. Meanwhile, the telephone calls from reporters flooded the line. Eric had switched on his answering machine and was monitoring his calls. It was frustrating and he recalls shouting for them to stop tying up the line.

Around 7:00 A.M. Peggy Say called. "They got the call," she said. "They were told to go to an abandoned, bombed-out factory, but when some Lebanese policemen got there, they searched the building and didn't find any bodies."

To add to the distress of the families, the Orange County *Pilot* carried a front-page story that morning, November 7, 1985, with the headline, "Beirut hostages reportedly slain." Only by reading midway into the piece did the account cite the information given to Peggy Say that no bodies had been found.

This was the sort of material that disturbed the Hajj. When we explained to him the potential value of our open letter to the White House, he listened carefully. Perhaps spooked by the Weir experience, he reacted cautiously and refused to commit himself. He did agree to consider the matter and reply soon.

In any event, we eagerly accepted the invitation to write to the news organizations and our kin. The letter concerning the premature reports of our deaths was short. Addressed "To the AP and all news media," it simply said: "We have been told that someone has claimed that Islamic Jihad has killed all of us. Obviously, this is not true. Our captors say it was an attempt by the U.S. government to spoil negotiations."

The last sentence, we hoped, might help forestall any negative steps by the bozo brigade in the State Department, if our open letter plan was accepted. We wanted to make it clear who was blocking negotiations.

The Hajj decided to go along with our idea of the open letter to President Reagan. When he departed, he carried off with him all of our letters. He returned the next day with the wonderful news that everything had been delivered to the Associated Press in Beirut. That ensured that no bureaucrat in the White House or State Department could bury our open letter to the President. (According to accounts from the AP, a young man tossed the package of letters at the feet of a guard at the wire service offices, instructing him to deliver it.)

To my family I sent the following:

Dear Eric, Cathy, Paul, Lori and Diane:
   There is so much to say and so little time to do it. You are constantly in my thoughts and my prayers. I love all of you very much and long for the day that we will be together again.
   Trust in the Lord, we will be together soon. My situation is difficult, but you know my strength and determination, and I shall survive."

I then gave some instructions for handling my finances and buying Christmas presents. I spelled out my circumstances as much as I could.

My situation is not the best, nor is it the worst. I am in a small windowless room with Tom Sutherland, Father Jenco and Terry Anderson. We are no longer in chains, which is a relief. The care is minimal, the food marginal . . . Exercise is limited by the size of the room. We do some sit-ups, push-ups and walking in circles. We are provided with medicines when requested. Our captors have not physically abused or tortured us. At times the boredom becomes overwhelming. Father Jenco conducts service twice a day and there is plenty of time to read the Bible.

I hear of your trips to Washington, DC to meet the President and the Vice-President. We are aware of the President's position on not negotiating with terrorists and can understand the rationale for that position, but it doesn't work, nor is he consistent. Negotiations for the hostages in the TWA airplane incident are well known in Lebanon . . .

The conditions for our release are simple. Ben Weir has made them known to the U.S. government and the general public. The release of the *four* of us is within the power of President Reagan and can be accomplished *immediately*. Our captors want to talk, but my government apparently refuses. They, the captors, approve the International Red Cross as intermediaries.

President Reagan could authorize negotiations for TWA, why not for us? America and Russia exchange spies (criminals) all the time. Why can't we be exchanged? Ask him . . .

Our captors want a fast resolution to the problem. They are frustrated by the U.S. government's refusal to talk. Negotiations would not be difficult if the U.S. government officials did not become overly concerned with minor details. In fact, if one group were to be released unilaterally, we would be released unconditionally and immediately. Face-to-face negotiations would not even be necessary. Have faith!

Please release the contents of this letter, except parts you might consider too personal, to the *Los Angeles Times* and

the *Orange County Register*. Please reassure m
bless everyone. I love you.

I had written out this letter beforehand, in o
something ready to send on a moment's notice i
an open letter was accepted by the kidnapper
sheet as a postscript.

We are alive! We were told yesterday, someone c
be Islamic Jihad telephoned the news media and s;
the American hostages had been shot and killed.
Apparently, someone wants to disrupt the pos
talks concerning our release. Our captors believ
American government is trying to disrupt any an
tiations for our release.
I cry for the hurt that the false report has given
Please keep the faith. I shall survive!

My family received my letter via the State D
which kept the original for forensic purposes. I l
ately repeated much of what was in the open le
more way of insuring that the conditions for
would be made public. I also wanted to encourag
dren in their efforts and give them ammunitio
arguments.
Back in our cells, we captives could only m
fearful of shattered expectations, and wait for som
on our behalf. We shouted with exultation when
reports led with accounts of our open letter to the
Its publication actually came only one day after t
tale of our alleged murders appeared.
A backhanded thanks went to dear Henry Kiss
we had resources—we had the power to think, the
the media. These were heady moments and we so
stations covered by our seven-channel radio, looki
ther reports on the story.
To our intense dissatisfaction, White House s|

Larry Speakes responded, "The President's policy has not changed and will not change."

Then, over the BBC came a message of hope. The first item carried the voice of a man named Terry Waite. He said he was a representative of the Anglican Church and wanted to come to Lebanon to help free the American hostages. From the news broadcasts we learned something of Waite's background. Working through the Church, he had long been involved in aiding those in need. Even more promising, Terry Waite had already gained valuable experience, having previously bargained with authorities in Libya and Iran for the release of British businessmen taken hostage.

After the BBC program, the parishioners of the Church of the Locked Door held a prayer session marked by strong devotion. For the first time we believed we had a champion, someone willing to put himself on the line for us. To be sure, we were puzzled and disappointed that our homeland seemed to be so unconcerned. It had volunteered nothing. Our would-be savior was an Englishman none of us had ever heard of before, but at least he cared about us even if the Department of State did not.

Neither the Associated Press, which had employed Terry Anderson and benefitted from his coverage in an area of high personal risk, nor the AUB, which had invited me to Beirut, seemed to have made any significant effort on our behalf. Some students and staff of the AUB went on strike briefly to protest my kidnapping. The Dean of the School of Medicine spoke with officials of Amal who looked for me. But the university never took any formal action. And I have found no evidence of any efforts by the Associated Press. Neither AUB or AP, so far as I can ascertain, applied any pressure to the U.S. authorities.

On the other hand, I did learn of two individuals who, strictly on their own, had tried to help. A remarkable man named Ray Barnet, an ordained minister from Canada, operated an organization known as Friends of the West to relieve the hapless victims of disasters in the Middle East. Barnet

also participated in the release of missionaries taken captive in Africa and a group of Soviet Pentacostals who took refuge in the U.S. Embassy in Moscow. Through his contacts, Barnet sought to reach our kidnappers, hoping that his humanitarian approach might convince them to strike an arrangement with him.

The other active paladin was Hussein Nasrallah, my erstwhile bodyguard. Following my disappearance, Hussein took to tramping Beirut's meanest streets, accosting anyone he knew in search of clues of my whereabouts. He continued to poke and probe until his brother, my assistant Ahmed Nasrallah, received a telephone call. Leaving no room for doubt, the voice at the other end advised Ahmed that unless Hussein immediately ceased his hunt, he would receive a bullet through his head. Ahmed managed to persuade Hussein to abandon his investigation.

On his next visit to us, the Hajj inquired whether we had heard Terry Waite volunteer his services. When we said we had, the Hajj replied that although he wanted to talk with Waite, the enterprise would be dangerous for both of them. Waite, undoubtedly, would be followed. The slightest indication that hostile elements had gleaned clues to our location could prove, in his euphemistic language, a major problem for everyone, meaning a lot of people including us could wind up dead.

The air left our balloon rapidly. All of the good intentions would go for naught because nobody had thought the scheme through. If ever necessity fathered an inspiration, this was the moment. A way out struck me.

"Hajj, there is a means to negotiate with Waite without the risk of discovery. You could communicate with him by two-way radio. You give us two frequencies and we will write to Waite instructing him to bring a radio with him. He can stay in a place like Terry Anderson's apartment near the waterfront while you drive around Beirut in your Mercedes, talking to him through the two-way radio. You will be safe and so will Waite."

The Hajj, as was his custom, took time to mull the suggestion over and then gave a noncommittal response. "I will return in a couple of days and tell you whether this is possible."

One can imagine our jubilation when he reappeared with the go-ahead for the plan. He supplied the radio frequencies and instructed us to write the letter to Waite with the details about the radio and where he should stay.

Our note directed Waite to contact Robert Fisk, a British journalist pal of Anderson's, who could arrange for our envoy to gain access to the apartment. Obtaining an adequate radio was not an easy matter for Terry Waite. He had very little money himself and the Church was in no position to supply the equipment. On a chance visit to the London offices of the Associated Press, Waite mentioned the problem. On his own, a staffer offered Waite the use of a piece of rather primitive equipment. If the CIA or its British Equivalent MI6 was aware of Waite's involvement, neither organization stepped forward with the kind of sophisticated electronics that would have made communications so much easier.

Now a news broadcast announced that Terry Waite was on his way to Lebanon to see what could be done to gain our freedom. Optimism surged among us. We greedily pursued every tidbit of news of his progress and activities through the available media.

Matters obviously were moving at a brisk pace as Sayid arrived one evening bearing clothes. He told us to dress quickly for a photo session. The cameraman took individual Polaroid shots while each of us held up a copy of an issue of the *Wall Street Journal* with Terry Waite's name printed in large block letters atop the page. We also posed for a group picture.

The Polaroid and the newspaper had been supplied by Waite. He timed the interval between handing over these items and the return of the photographs. The swiftness of the action proved to him that he was dealing with the appropriate people, that we were together and not held far away.

Waite's two-way radio, even when not subject to break-up of voice transmissions, was useful only as a means of opening negotiations. The process required face-to-face encounters. But both sides were very concerned about leaks or worse, discovery of the sites for any meetings. There were groups who could see a profit to themselves in disrupting the negotiations, compromising or even physically assaulting the parties involved.

Still, our captors continued to pursue their end of Waite's mission with sincerity. The Hajj proposed a way for Waite to meet with representatives of the kidnappers. "Mr. David," he instructed me, "Write a letter to Dr. Adnan Mroueh and ask him to serve as an intermediary." Dr. Mroueh had been a friend of a physician at the AUB and when approached by the kidnappers requested some proof I was still alive, hence the letter. As an afterthought, the Hajj asked Tom Sutherland to put his signature on the letter also, since he too was affiliated with the AUB.

Waite moved out of Terry Anderson's flat to a hotel where radio transmissions suffered less interference. Standing six feet seven inches, he naturally towered over the locals. He traveled under the protection of Walid Jumblatt, leader of the Druse, who could claim something of a neutral status.

All of this cloak-and-dagger stuff only heightened our anticipation of a satisfactory resolution. Even the guards expressed happiness at the imminent end of the ordeal. Soon it would be Christmas and we envisioned a spectacular gift for us—freedom. Certainly, our kidnappers could appreciate how the world would bless them for their generosity during the season of good fellowship.

Christmas Eve arrived with us still penned up.

Nevertheless, the Church of the Locked Door celebrated the birth of Christ with hosannahs of thanksgiving at our imminent deliverance. We tuned up our radio, ready for more Christmas cheer. We listened to the voice of Terry

Waite himself. "I am sorry that I must leave Lebanon without the American hostages. There is more work to be done, but I will return for them as soon as possible."

Shocked, appalled, frightened, despondent—take your pick; all of these sentiments drowned our tender hopes. The only balm for our discomfort came from Waite's promise to come back.

We spent Christmas Day, 1985, in a collective funk. Our church service was brief and uncharacteristically muted. We felt alone, deserted by our country and its officials. We fell so far down that no one even attempted to commiserate with anyone else. Silence ruled our room. For me, it was back to the golden ball and a desperate search for comfort through the Bible.

The unlocking of the cell door broke the spell of quietude. Reflexively, we adjusted our blindfolds. Footsteps into the room announced the arrival of several guards. My nose twitched; something was burning. Then there was the sound of an object being placed on the floor.

Sayid spoke. "Look at what Robert [a part-time guard] and I have brought for you. It is okay to peek." Slowly we slipped the covering from one of our eyes. In the center of the room was a birthday cake with flaming candles. And as we stared, Sayid and Robert sang, "Happy birthday, Jesus."

Chapter 10

No Way Out

Whatever solace we drew from Waite's assertion that he would return on our behalf, the weeks following his departure were marked by depression. Tempers shortened. There were daily arguments, petty but bitter. Desperately, we tried to heal ourselves with more intensive exercise programs.

The failure of Waite's mission renewed fears for our safety. Ahmed Nasrallah, through his contacts, pressed for word that I was alive and well. His lobbying with influential Shiites was strong enough to convince the kidnappers of the desirability of a communication from me. I wrote a brief note to Ahmed telling him I was well and that I appreciated his concern for my well-being. If a functionary at the AUB, a Western-supported institution, knew how to reach our abductors and influence them, it seems appallingly strange that the mighty U.S. government continued to claim it did not know who held us or how to open a dialogue with them.

Because of Ahmed's campaign for me, I was granted the privilege of writing another letter to my family. ". . . I want to reassure you that I am well and optimistic for my early release. Heard on radio that UCLA won in the Rose Bowl. God bless Coach Donahue. Please telephone my dear friends the Mohlers. Tell them I want to sing the UCLA fight song at their front door, but that I am delayed . . ."

That the privilege of writing a letter home was mine alone caused some resentment among the others. However, the fact that I could inform everyone we were okay outweighed any temporary bad feelings.

With the collapse of—or at best the delay in—Terry Waite's mission, I broached a sensitive subject. "I think we had better be prepared to escape if nothing happens in negotiations soon." These words stopped any conversation. Although the idea naturally flitted across everyone's mind more than occasionally, it was something we had never really discussed.

Marty Jenco responded first. "I don't want to hear anything more about escaping."

"Dammit, Father, if no one is negotiating for our release I don't see sitting here and rotting to death. What about you, Tom?" He was usually my ally when the four of us disagreed. But this time he only shrugged his shoulders.

"Terry, how about you?" Anderson was the feistiest of our crew and his Vietnam experiences made him no stranger to the sort of action required for an escape.

"It's not for me," said Terry, to my surprise. "I won't try it."

"Ever?"

"No, never!"

"For God's sake, Terry. You were a U.S. Marine. What's wrong with you! Have you lost all your courage?"

I defied the clear majority. "I don't care what you guys will or won't do. But I'm telling you, I am going to be ready and able, if and when an opportunity comes. Terry, teach me the Marine Corps method for silencing a guard."

He was reluctant but said, "Okay. Just don't expect me to get killed along with you. I'll show you how to break someone's neck and then you can practice."

Terry began to school me in how to throttle a man with a swift, forearm blow from the back and then almost simultaneously knock him down to immobilize him. We practiced the maneuver for days until I felt comfortable with the technique. A serendipitous pleasure for both of us was the mock physical combat. In fact, we both drew a secret delight from smacking one another very hard during my training.

I embarked on my own private physical fitness program, assigning myself six hundred push-ups and six hundred sit-ups a day. I needed to be strong enough to overcome anyone with my bare hands and have the endurance to outrun pursuit.

Helpfully, Terry pointed out flaws in my escape plan. Did I have any idea of how to find my way out of the slums of Beirut to safety? With all of the gangs of armed men in the streets, I could easily be killed as just another interloper. I said I'd either take my chances or the others could join me once I was free and we'd have enough weapons to control our building. There was no enthusiasm for that proposal.

Anderson warned me that I probably could get by the first guard, but what would I do when I met another one too far away for my sneak attack, on a different floor or even in the street. I countered that by then I would have possession of a weapon and do whatever was necessary.

His questions raised a significant issue. I supposed I might render unconscious the first sentry I encountered. But if I started shooting, the odds were I would have to kill the enemy. Escape thus probably involved homicide. From my childhood I had been taught the Sixth Commandment: Thou Shalt Not Kill. It did not seem to provide for exceptions, certainly not in the case of seeking one's freedom as opposed to self-defense. Furthermore, I had been enjoined by Christianity to turn the other cheek.

Obtaining freedom by my own efforts challenged my religious beliefs. How could I reconcile my faith with the taking of another man's life? I would kill some poor Shiite who actually thought he was rather kind to me, someone who was thoughtful enough to bring me a cake on Christmas Day when my spirits had hit bottom.

I anguished over the dilemma, searching the Bible for direction. In my memories of the Old Testament, in spite of its Sixth Commandment, I recalled its stern emphasis upon righteous justice, the eye-for-an-eye retribution. And in the New Testament, so saturated with commandments to love, the obligation to scourge the wicked still appeared. Some moments I prayed for forgiveness for even harboring the terrible thought of committing a murder. But then I looked at myself in fetters, worse off than most animals and possibly doomed to death in this condition at some future date.

Did I ever resolve the conflict within me? The truth is that I could never permanently settle the issue. So long as I was a prisoner, I considered escape an option. When and if an opportunity came, I would have to make my decision based on whether my freedom was worth a possible breach in my beliefs. Until that moment, the dispute was academic. One more aspect of my life was reduced to a waiting game.

Early in February 1986 we received an unexpected treat. When Waite had come to Beirut in December, he toted with him letters and telexes for all of us from the outside world. Our kidnappers delayed delivery of the mail for nearly two months, less, I think, out of innate cruelty than the typical Arab insouciance about time. To them it did not matter how long it took for the news from the folks back home to reach us. The important thing was that we did receive the mail.

It was an odd bag of items for men starved for word of their loved ones. Terry Anderson came close to weeping as he showed us a photograph of his ten-year-old daughter Gabrielle taken at Disneyland and one of his newborn child. But the picture bore no identification, leaving him wondering whether he had fathered a son or daughter. Although Terry hungered for information about his family, his only letter was from a fellow journalist who claimed to know him. Terry was puzzled, "I can't recall ever meeting this guy, but he sure writes like I'm his best friend. The only problem is, who is he?"

An equally unknown Catholic sister from Australia sent Marty Jenco a card. On it she mentioned Psalm 102 with the comment that it was the Hostage Psalm. We quickly opened our Bible to scan the text. It reads: "Hear my prayer, O Lord, and let my cry come to You. Do not hide Your face from me in the day of my trouble. Incline Your ear to me. In the day that I call, answer me speedily . . . For He looked down from the height of His Sanctuary. From heaven, the Lord viewed the earth, to hear the groaning of the prisoner, to loose those appointed to death."

The psalm, which certainly applied to us, is also considered a prayer for the afflicted.

Jenco received a letter from one of his nephews and Marty shared with us details about the life of the author.

My stuff included a telex from all three of my kids and a note from my sister, Doris. Nine months had elapsed since I had any word on my family. I read and re-read the notes, savoring the tidbits of information about their lives during my absence.

We were all so caught up in our mail that we failed to notice Tom Sutherland, glumly sitting there. He had received nothing and the more we glowed with delight, the deeper was his sadness. Terry Anderson noticed the discrepancy first. He leaped to his feet and battered the door with his fists. "Bring Tom's mail to him. I know you have something for him too. Stop being such goddamn jerks!"

Sayid and an associate entered our quarters. "Quiet down," he commanded. "What's the problem?"

Terry shouted, "It's not fair. You talk of justice, so why are you hurting Tom! We know that you must have mail for him also. Don't lie to us. Give him his mail or else you take ours back."

"Right," chimed in Marty Jenco. "Here's my letters," and he proffered them to Sayid.

"I'm with you, Terry," I said. I held out my telex and letter to Sayid.

Sayid was nearly tongue-tied. He stammered, "My leaders have left orders that Mr. Tom is not to get his mail." Sayid and his companion left, bearing with them our telexes, cards and letters. Through the walls we heard them jabbering at one another in Arabic. Sayid returned and with him he carried a telex from Sutherland's children and a letter from his wife, as well as all of the items we handed him. It was one of our better moments, when we united to support one man singled out for mistreatment.

161

Our captors apparently never quite relinquished their suspicion that Sutherland was something more than a simple academician. Their doubts about him, aroused first by the contents of his briefcase, continued partly because of Tom's pedagogical training. When asked a question he answered as if he had something to hide, always qualifying his responses. In the minds of the kidnappers he was being evasive. In truth, the man was simply being honest. A direct yes or no struck him as an oversimplification, something that went against his nature.

We argued hard whenever any of the guards even hinted that Sutherland had sinister connections. There had been a time when Sayid and the Hajj suddenly announced they were removing Sutherland from our little group. We protested vigorously; Marty actually burst into tears. They relented and allowed Tom to remain. We joked that if he were a typical CIA agent our country was in deeper trouble than anyone knew.

Tom suffered from a disease common to hostages, hemorrhoids. He requested Preparation H suppositories. The heat melted the first batch into a gooey mess before Sutherland could apply the medicine. Tom told the guards to keep the next box in a freezer. When Sutherland asked for his suppositories while in the toilet, I teased Abu Ali, the guard on duty, "Hey, Ali. You think this guy is CIA? You think he could pass their requirement to eat live rats? No way. He even has to have his Preparation H frozen."

For all of our efforts, the kidnappers kept probing at Tom, looking for ways to compromise him. One day, they pulled him out of our quarters for more than two hours. When he returned, he was a frightened man. We asked what happened.

"I can't tell you. They warned me not to discuss the matter."

"We're all in this together, friend. What affects you involves us. So you had better tell us," I said.

Somewhat fearfully, he told us in whispers about his session with the Hajj. "They showed me this long handwritten report by William Buckley. They said his script was not legible enough and they wanted me to copy it so the memorandum could be easily read. I don't know what they were talking about. I had absolutely no problem reading Buckley's handwriting,"

"What did Buckley say?"

Sutherland searched his memory; you never got a swift answer from him. "It was very lengthy, maybe forty or fifty pages. He admitted he served as the CIA station chief and detailed his daily activities in the American Embassy in West Beirut. Most of his job seemed to be acting as a liaison with the Lebanese intelligence agency. Much of the report covered the routine clerical matters. He did remark on some operations, like warning Amin Gemayel of an assassination attempt. [Indeed, the Lebanese president's brother Bashir had previously perished in just such a political killing.] But Buckley said nobody paid much attention to murder plots in Lebanon. They went with the territory."

Tom emphasized that one thing he did not come across in Buckley's document were identifications of CIA agents in the Middle East. Buckley may have been beaten and tortured for information but, on the bases of this account, he had not surrendered any real secrets, names, or information on CIA tactics and strategy. Subsequently, U.S. representatives dealing with Iranians were advised that Tehran possessed a huge, several-hundred-pages-long confession authored by Buckley in which he divulged hundreds of names. Based on what Tom saw and judging from developments in the Middle East, that item was pure bluff and a slur on a man who died in the service of his government.

Sutherland's dilemma was a difficult one for us to solve. He summed it up. "If I make a copy, then it will sound like my handwritten confession that I am CIA. If I refuse God knows what they will do to me."

We worked out an approach that would enable Sutherland to satisfy the demands of the kidnappers and still shield him from an accusation that he served as an intelligence agent. He carefully copied the text but wherever Buckley employed the first person "I" or "we," Tom inserted the phrase, "the original author said." Our keepers accepted his handwork without comment and the notion of Sutherland as a spy lost more currency. We also fended off queries intended to reveal that Sutherland had consulted with us. When the guards asked us where we thought Tom was spending his days apart from us, the answers were, "You took him to the beach for some sun," or "Isn't he at a soccer game?"

The strange alternation between acts of decency, like delivering messages or mail, and cold, calculated cruelty continued. Without any warning or for any visible reason, the radio was removed in March 1986 and the books were taken away two months later. The literature had allowed us to flee our miserable surroundings. The broadcasts, particularly the news, kept us in contact with the outside world. The deprivation of these resources devastated us.

At first, Terry's anger boiled over into a tantrum in which he beat on the door, yelling, "Bring back the radio! Why have you taken it away? Bring it back! Enough is enough! We want the news. We are not animals and we are not criminals. Do you hear me? Bring me the goddamn radio!"

The guards ignored him and they dismissed the more gentle requests from the rest of us. We turned to each other and sought to discover the reasons for this apparent punishment. We had not violated the rules about use of the radio. We had done everything asked of us.

Much later, after my release, I learned that both Terry Anderson's father and his brother Rick had died about this time. Rick Anderson had actually recorded a heart-gripping appeal to the kidnappers, begging them to release his brother before Rick died. I could entertain the charitable notion that the Hajj, having heard of the deaths, decreed the radio should be silenced in an effort to avoid so much pain for Terry that he would not survive. On the other hand, why was it then necessary to also take our books? What I do realize is that those who held us had the capacity to engage in bloody brutality while simultaneously demonstrating streaks of kindness. The dual nature, the exercise of such diametrically opposed behavior, is one more reason why dealing with these people is so difficult.

Anderson switched from his futile attempt to bully the authorities and went on a hunger strike. At first, the guards tried to coax him to take some food. When he refused for several days, they adopted the position that it was less work for them. They stopped bringing him anything to eat. The fast lasted for about a week before our entreaties and his own good sense led Terry to abandon the tactic. Passive disobedience works when those with the guns accept certain restrictions upon themselves. It's a total flop in the face of an enemy willing to use the vilest, most debased tactics upon the oppressed.

A new face appeared on the scene. The bolts on the door rattled open and in stepped a short, stocky man with what I call the "Iranian look,"—short black hair and beard. He wore blue jeans, a sport shirt and loafers with a Levi's tag.

"Hi guys. How are you? My name is Ali. I am a friend of the Hajj and he wants me to help you. You should know that I am not one of the people who kidnapped you. I am only here to see that you're treated properly. And I'll carry any messages you have directly to the Hajj."

In unison we gave him the first message. "Let us go home."

He smiled while we looked him over further. His opening salutation was so inappropriate under our circumstances that we enjoyed a few giggles at his expense after he left. He had a partial grasp of colloquial American speech, indicating time spent in the States.

We welcomed him as a break in the dreary routine and because he brought with him figs, fresh oranges, bananas, and a carton of cigarettes. We gladly fell on the fruit but told him to take the butts elsewhere. We informed Ali that Marty

Jenco was the only one of us who had been a smoker and if he ever took up the habit again in our company, we would cheerfully break both his arms and all of his fingers.

Ali chatted with us, supplying his own version of news from the outside world. He filled us in on the unstable political situation of the Philippines, where Ferdinand Marcos struggled to hang on to power. He recounted, with some pleasure, the difficulties the Americans were having with the space program, and the latest "crimes" perpetrated by the Israelis, such as the bombing of a Lebanese village where two children were among the dead. For sports fans he supplied results from the World Cup. He even told us that there were negotiations underway for our release. In this area, however, he offered no details.

Ali thought himself much smarter than he really was. None of us bought his rap that he was our "friend." He occasionally boosted our low protein diet with some tasty fried chicken. He arranged for our books to be restored, but not the missing radio. When asked why he had persuaded the Hajj to allow us the reading matter he answered, "I convinced the Hajj that you were all behaving and that you really needed the books for psychological reasons. You help me and I will help you."

From the first ludicrous "Hi guys" we saw him for what he was, an informant seeking our confidence. The help he desired from us was in the form of reports on our guards, how they treated us and how devoted they were to their duties. None of us felt inclined to serve as a fink for Ali. When he inquired what I thought of Badr, who had disappeared, I did say, "Keep him away. The last thing we need around here is a maniac like him." And we never saw Badr again.

In one conversation with him, I remarked that every time I left the United States, my alma mater, UCLA, finished with a winning football season. In fact, we'd even whipped the mighty University of Michigan squad twice in a single season, knocking them over the second time in the Rose Bowl on New Year's Day.

"Oh, yes," answered Ali. "My Wolverines had a bad year." He fell silent, looking stricken. It was most unlikely that someone from the Middle East, who had never spent time on the Ann Arbor campus of Michigan, would possessively refer to the nickname of the school—"my Wolverines." I pressed him about his days as a Wolverine and he tried desperately to convince me that he attended either the University of Oklahoma or the University of Florida. Later, I would seek to discover his true identity, and learn that his name was Hassan Musawi.

Whoever he was, Ali was definitely not on our side. Anything he said about negotiations on our behalf was calculated only to con us. He never offered a shred of evidence to back up his accounts. And I was soon to learn, painfully, just how good a buddy he was.

Chapter 11

Perils and Portents

It was lunchtime on an April day in 1986. The door unlocked and we adjusted the blindfolds to hide the sight of Sayid. We readied our eating utensils. "I have a surprise for you," he said. And along with our food he presented each of us with a white flower for Easter. It was a small touch but it enthralled us because we were so walled off from the blooming, buzzing confusion of Nature.

The pleasure of the moment, however, vanished as an atmosphere of tension emanated from the guards and raised our level of anxiety. In bits and pieces we learned of the raid by U.S. aircraft upon Libya in retaliation for a series of terrorist attacks that culminated in the bombing of a West German disco patronized by U.S. troops. The assault revived the possibility of a commando-type attack on our behalf.

What we did not know about immediately was the revenge sought by Libya's dictator, Muhmar Khadafy. His agents hunted for victims upon whom they would wreak vengeance. They found their prey in the hands of a Lebanese gang. In one of the most barbaric acts of modern times, Libya paid the gunmen several million dollars for the AUB librarian Peter Kilburn and three Britons—Alec Collett, kidnapped less than a month earlier, and two others, Leigh Douglas and Philip Padfield, taken in December 1984. Those who sold the three Englishmen could have been a separate Hizballah bunch or an entirely independent outfit only out to profit by exploiting the agendas of the conflicting inter-

168

In April of 1986, terrorists released this photograph of a hanged
man whom they said was British journalist Alec Collett, "executed" in retaliation for Britain's cooperation with a U.S. air raid
on Libya. I was told that the kidnappers sold Collett to Libya's
Muhmar Khadafy for his revenge on the attack. (Courtesy AP/Wide
World Photos)

ests. All four were executed by Khadafi in retaliation for the air strike against Libya. The Englishmen were murdered to demonstrate the dictator's displeasure at Great Britain for permitting some U.S. planes to use airfields there to launch the strike.

In the wake of the raid on Libya, Sayid drew me aside and casually asked what did I think I was worth. I gave the standard smart-ass medical school evaluation. "After you boil down my carcass, about three dollars in chemicals."

"No, no, Mr. David. How much alive?"

I figured he was thinking in terms of a ransom. "Oh, maybe half a million."

Sayid smiled. "No, it is more like seven and a half million." He would not supply any basis for his estimate. As usual, the kidnappers kept their information close to the vest. Later, I learned from Oliver North that Khadafi had tendered a bid of $10 million for our quartet. When the people in Washington were advised, they faced the problem of how to protect us. The decision by Ronald Reagan was to put forth a pre-emptive figure, one that Khadafi would not top. So, $30 million became a price circulated through a neutral African leader in the Middle East. Dividing the number by four, Sayid arrived at my seven and a half million worth. It worked out to no sale, since much higher stakes appear to govern our captors' prices for Americans.

The roller coaster dips and climbs accelerated. Ali, proclaiming his friendship, grandly declared we soon would be set free. In preparation for the great event, he instructed us to change our appearances. With a straight face he issued the bizarre orders that Marty and I would have to shave our beards, while our companions Terry and Tom received orders to sprout facial hair.

Jenco and I objected. Both of us had grown accustomed to our beards. Not only did they provide warmth on cold nights and a softer place for our cheeks when lying down, but also there was only a single, disposable razor for the four of us to share over a period of months.

Tom Sutherland also protested. He hated long hair and face fur. To keep himself trim when Sayid could not exercise his tonsorial skills, Tom actually cut his hair with a finger nail clipper. Terry, with his habitual disdain for authority, disliked the new regulations on principle.

We spent considerable time among ourselves trying to discern what lay behind this new order. The best answer seemed that they were about to transfer us to a new location. By altering our appearance, they would reduce the possibilities of someone recognizing us in the streets and raising an alarm.

A month passed and it all proved one more fuss without substance. We ignored the instructions and the guards made no effort to enforce them. Indeed, Sayid trimmed my full, bushy growth into a neater shorter beard while Tom and Terry scraped their cheeks clean with the same dull blade.

The only change in the daily regimen was the installation of a small table with four plastic stools. Sitting down at a table for our daily rice and canned vegetables in a sauce of dehydrated tomato soup and olive oil flavored by raw garlic cloves, added a touch of dignity to our lives.

Ali gave us fresh hope in June 1986. "You are going home soon and we want to give all of you new clothes and shoes."

Even the guards seemed to believe in our imminent deliverance. Sayid bubbled, "Great news and I am so happy that you are going home." Even the surly Fadl turned half-pleasant. Their wages notwithstanding, the keepers also appeared tired of the ordeal and wanted it to end. Fadl was assigned the task of determining our sizes. He carefully applied a tape measure.

All signs augured a favorable outcome. Within a few days, they supplied us with new, cheap Italian shoes, stockings, wash-and-wear pants and cotton shirts. Except for mine, the trousers fitted poorly. Terry Anderson, through his skill with a needle and thread, served as a tailor, sewing hems in the cuffs. We agreed he had earned another merit badge. The guards were cheerful. One night we were permitted an extra shower and allowed to keep our fine clothes in the cell. We talked of what we would all do as soon as we tasted freedom. Tom Sutherland, whose wife still worked at the AUB, said, "I am going back to the university. I'll stay there to recuperate. It will only take a few good meals to get my body working again and then I'll get back on the job."

The rest of us laughed at him. "You're nuts," declared Marty Jenco. We all intended to flee Lebanon as quickly as possible. Anderson believed he would receive a sabbatical from the Associated Press and return to college to obtain a Masters degree in journalism.

I kidded Jenco. "This time your Bishop will send you so far away to such an unknown place you'll never get in trouble or be heard from again." I knew I would go back to California and roam the world no more.

We should have known better. We should have been prepared for the moment when the guards reappeared and snatched away all of those fine new garments. We surrounded Sayid and demanded an explanation, but we didn't get one. "Some stumbling blocks have developed in negotiations," is all he said. Most likely, his superiors simply did not reveal to him the specifics. He did not explain the substance of the talks or the sticking points. "We think that they can be resolved quickly. So we are taking your clothes, so they can be kept clean. We want you to look nice when you go home."

Every time we crashed we went through that same period when we could barely tolerate one another. Political arguments about who in the government was doing what and why quickly degenerated into personal invective. All our anger surfaced in attempts to hurt one another. Lost in the welter of disappointment and despair was the faint hope that rather than an abominable ploy to destroy our morale, Sayid had been truthful when he said that a hitch had developed in the continuing negotiations. When we paused between bouts of castigating each another, we preferred to believe someone indeed was working to save us. And the best bet lay with

Terry Waite, seeking to fulfil his Christmas Eve promise to return.

It seemed as if the sudden downturn also goaded our captors into renewed savagery. There were verbal tongue lashings for alleged infractions of the rules. Tom Sutherland, wearing his blindfold, was standing against the wall in the hall with his arms over his head. He heard the chimes denoting the time on a BBC broadcast from the radio used by the guards. Out of habit and his own singular penchant for accuracy, he peeked at his watch to see if it matched the BBC. A guard caught him in the act. A storm of vituperation followed as if sneaking a look at the time proved he were a CIA master spy. We feared for his safety.

Marty Jenco saved the day. The priest was sitting in the hall with a dentist, who had been summoned to deal with Jenco's pain from a decayed tooth. The dentist, incidentally, refused to work on a blindfolded patient, declaring, "I don't care if you do see me." He had just extracted the bad tooth and Jenco, hearing the commotion about Tom, acted as if he had fainted. The guards forgot about Sutherland and rushed to succor Marty. In the process, they returned Tom to our cell and their anger abated.

When we were all alone, Marty wheeled on Sutherland. "You are impossible! Why risk dying just to make sure you have the correct time!" Tom did not reply; he just smiled.

At least Sutherland had done something to trigger the fury of the guards, even if the offense was trivial. I, on the other hand, was minding my own business when I was escorted from the cell one night to a room at the other end of the apartment. A voice I did not recognize ordered me to face the wall, hands above my head. I complied. I felt something cold and metallic press against my neck. There was no mistaking the touch of a gun muzzle. The voice hissed, "You dead!"

It was the close of another long, tiresome, depressing day. There was no adrenalin available in my system. I was too damn tired to care, to fear, or to think. To my surprise, I heard myself growl, "This is Tuesday night and I have a lot of things still to do. Tomorrow there is a full schedule of activities. Come back Thursday, after lunch, to kill me."

The gunman must have been even more astonished than I. He walked off, leaving me standing alone.

Undoubtedly, he was a friend or relative of a kidnap crew member who showed up for some posturing. I cannot believe he had the authority to perform a spontaneous execution. As we had reassured ourselves on countless occasions, a dead hostage was worthless. Still, he could have been a crazy or a true believer carried away with the power of the moment. Several minutes later, after I re-enacted the scene in my mind, I started to tremble. Ali saw my agitated state and came over. "What's wrong? Why are you shaking? Are you crying? Relax, everything is all right."

I never informed the guards, Ali, or the Hajj of the incident. It would have been my word against that of a fellow who might have influential friends or kin. There were enough enemies out there without adding another.

Sometime during the second week of July, when I had endured about fourteen months of captivity, they brought me into the room where the guards spent their days. Ali and Sayid invited me to take a seat by the window. I could feel the warm glow of the sun streaming through the thin curtains designed to block our prying eyes. I smelled the chicken on Ali's plate. Sayid suggested I might like some and they treated me to a few delicious bites.

The two of them bantered with me about inconsequential matters. It was on this occasion that Ali asked me what I thought of Badr and I answered, "He is crazy." From past experience I knew that my jailers could be very devious. If they had some purpose behind this session, it would eventually be revealed. But it was a waste of time for me to look for an explanation.

Ali finished his food and his tone changed to total seriousness. With all of the sincerity he could muster he said, "I want you to be able to go home. I want you to give us the

174

script for a video, now." Apparently, my initial effort as author of an open letter had satisfied the house critics. Ali provided some general instructions. I was to say how bad conditions were, and that our situation could worsen. I was to express my strong desires for the American government to negotiate. He said he wanted the precise wording to be mine in order to signal its authenticity.

I wrote out a message and after Ali scrutinized it, he approved. I was returned to our cell. Several days dragged by and then about 9:00 P.M., as we began to wind down for another night of restless sleep, Ali burst into the room. "Wonderful news, you're all going home. Quick now, get dressed. There is a bus waiting for you downstairs for your journey. I am so happy for you all."

The guards distributed our new clothes and shoes. Terry, Marty, and I wasted no time donning our getaway garb. But Tom Sutherland wandered around still in his underwear. Asked what the holdup was, he answered, "I want my own shoes, my shirt and my briefcase. And it's not negotiable."

We were flabbergasted. On the verge of freedom and the man refused to go because he couldn't wear his own stuff? "What the hell is so special about your belongings!" was probably the politest comment from any of us.

He stubbornly insisted, "Those shoes and the shirt are special to me. I paid a good price for them and they are comfortable. The briefcase contains my address book and a miniature 35 mm camera I've used for years. These things are mine and I want them returned. The kidnappers say they are not thieves. Let them prove it now."

None of us had patience for this sort of thing. He was told either to hurry up or he would be left behind. Tom, reluctantly, readied himself. We sat there, like passengers in a departure lounge fretting about the schedule. An hour elapsed before the Hajj and Ali appeared. We would go one at a time because the elevator was so small.

They led me out first and I began to praise the Lord silently for my deliverance. We entered the room where Ali had instructed me to provide the script. The blow fell. "Sorry, David. Only Father Jenco is being released. But I promise, you'll be the very next to leave. Just have patience. All will be okay. Right now, we'd like you to make a video using your statement, so why don't you review it."

I forced myself to concentrate on the paper. Then I was guided to still another room and seated at a small table. Tom Sutherland entered and our captors directed him to sit facing a corner. Then Terry Anderson arrived. When we had been left alone I informed them only Marty was leaving. Like me, they were somewhat inured to disappointments but still it was bitter news. All of the preparations, the new clothes and then actually walking out of our locked room, yet we were denied freedom.

Sayid joined us. "Try to smile and look pleasant, Mr. David. We want you to look nice on television." He adjusted the collar on my shirt, combed my hair and beard. When he was satisfied with my appearance, he instructed me to keep my eyes tightly shut. I complied while he removed my blindfold.

Almost immediately, the heat of flood lights struck me. Someone commanded, "Open your eyes! Look directly into the lens!"

I saw first the camera and then the stranger behind it. Only about five feet tall, the young man wore spectacles with strips of yellow tape stuck to the halves of each of the lenses. A white smock hung over his blue jeans. Oddest of all he had the shape of a pear; the visible round half from waist up tapered off to a tiny head.

When ordered, I began to read the statement. I identified myself to viewers and expressed our happiness that our colleague had been freed. But I added "Our captors tell me this is the very last sign of their good will. Our release will be by death if the government doesn't negotiate right now. It seems that by not negotiating the American government does not really care about us."

I continued. "I feel like one of General Custer's men or one of the men at the Alamo, waiting for help to arrive. You

On July 26, 1986, this video tape of me reading a script prepared with my captors was shown on TV stations. (Courtesy AP/Wide World Photos)

know the end of their stories. Pray that ours will have a happier ending." I mentioned that Terry Anderson, Tom Sutherland, and I would only be released if the American authorities met demands by the kidnappers. I said I did not know what the conditions were but that Marty Jenco bore instructions for the government. In fact, the issue remained the Dawa prisoners. I remarked that it might be true that "our government has been less than candid and perhaps even lied to our families."

My voice cracked when I related, as I had been instructed, that William Buckley had been "executed" because of Washington's refusal to bargain with his kidnappers. I knew Buckley died of illness, not directly at the hands of Islamic Jihad. But I had no choice about using the word "executed" and in a sense it was true because he would still be alive were it not for the conditions to which they subjected him. In point of fact, when Islamic Jihad announced the death of Buckley the

Lt. Col. William Higgins of the
U.S. Marines, who was with an
observer group attached to the
United Nations Peacekeeping
Force in south Lebanon, was
kidnapped by terrorists.
(*Courtesy AP/Wide World Photos*)

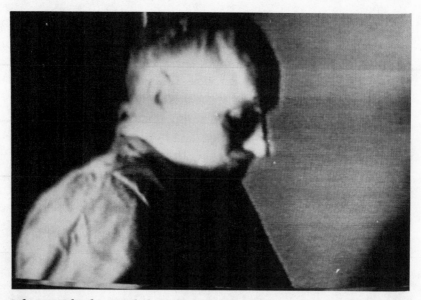

Islamic Jihad issued this photograph with a claim that they had
hung Higgins, although some investigators believe he died from
other causes. (*Courtesy AP/Wide World Photos*)

previous October, it had blamed his killing upon charges of U.S. complicity in an Israeli air attack against the PLO's offices in Tunisia.

Claiming a natural death as an execution was a standard ploy. In March, the kidnappers told the world they had murdered Michel Seurat, who died of cancer next door to us, because of the French government's perfidy in turning a pair of anti-Iraqi agents over to the Baghdad regime of Saddam Hussein. Much later they would declare they hanged Col. William Higgins, a U.S. officer serving with the United Nations forces in Southern Lebanon, when he in fact probably died of asphyxiation from an improperly applied gag while being transported in a car trunk.

I followed the approved script very closely but, for some inexplicable reason, I chose to ad-lib while on the subject of Buckley. During one of our conversations, one of my companions had remarked that poor William Buckley was married. Somebody claimed to have seen a family photo which included his daughters. And so I slipped into my recitation an expression of sympathy to the widow and daughters of Buckley. I finished my little act and no one commented immediately upon my improvisation.

Meanwhile, back in our old room, Marty Jenco had learned for the first time that he alone was to be freed. Given a few minutes by himself, Father Jenco prayed for all of us and in his joy performed the only push-up he ever did while in captivity.

To prepare for the trip, they bound and gagged Marty, winding the reliable packing tape about him until, like Ben Weir when he had first been kidnapped, he resembled a mummy. Ever thoughtful of his charge's comfort, Sayid, just before applying the gag said, "Father, you have a long journey ahead. I want you to relax. We don't have any Valium but we have something just as good, Dyazide." With that he forced the two tablets into Marty's mouth and taped his mouth shut before the priest could protest. Sayid, in his ignorance, had fed Jenco a diuretic instead of a tranquilizer, about the

Marty Jenco donned his priestly vestments after his release. (Courtesy AP/Wide World Photos)

worst possible thing for a man going on a long drive with no chance to pee.

Marty did travel in the small elevator. He was taken down to the street and then placed in a car trunk. The vehicle sped on for hours while Jenco writhed from the pressure on his bladder. When they finally halted, far away from Beirut, in the wilderness of the Bekaa Valley, the escorts gently lifted the bound man from his compartment.

Two men held him erect while a third patiently cut away the wrappings. The blindfold remained undisturbed. When Jenco at last stood, shakily, on his own two feet, he felt something forced into his hand.

"What is this?" asked Marty.

"Peek, see for yourself," giggled a voice.

The good Father saw a wad of Lebanese paper money. "What is this for?" he queried in bewilderment.

"That's for the taxi that you have asked for at night." And his captors melted away while Jenco plunged into the darkness until he bumped into some Lebanese kids who summoned the police.

It was July 26, 1986.

Chapter 12

New Moves

While Marty Jenco drew his first free breaths in eighteen long months, the three of us returned to our quarters. Sullenly, we surrendered our new clothes and surveyed our home. It was a mess. During the short time Jenco waited there as the only captive, several guards on the scene had discarded their cigarette butts on the floor. Someone had dumped all of our personal belongings on the floor, leaving stuff strewn about.

The solid wooden door that provided some privacy remained open; the barred one locked. Half-heartedly we attempted to reorganize the place. But after poking about for a short time, we were too depressed to continue. We turned off our light and tried to sleep.

Our captors, however, had been observing us until we dozed off. In the morning, Ali led a lengthy interrogation. "What were you looking for? You spent a lot of time going through Jenco's things."

Somewhat amazed, we answered, "You guys and Jenco made a mess of the place. You scattered things all over the room. We simply tried to collect what belonged to each of us. What the hell's wrong with that?"

"C'mon, guys. I know you were searching for something," persisted Ali.

"Listen, if you think we've got something hidden in here, be our guest. Go ahead, search the place." We turned away from him and he stomped out.

Far more depressing was the reaction to the videotape that

I had made. Marty Jenco had turned it over to the Syrian authorities after they assumed custody of him. The people in Damascus did not release it for four hours. Both the Syrians and the American representatives considered the video to be, in the words of ABC's Barry Dunsmore, "a classic piece of propaganda." My video, aired on July 26 and 27, did not win rave reviews in the United States. An editorial in the New York *Times* described it as a "crude attempt" to set the families of the hostages against the government's policy. John Scali, as the spokesman for the U.S. government, declared, "There will be no negotiations with kidnappers."

We turned to religion for solace. During the next few days, services of the Church of the Locked Door were the most intense of any during my confinement. The tiny congregation vowed never to lose hope. I swore, "They will not destroy me. I will live to be freed and to testify against them someday, even if that day lies thirty years in the future."

Terry denounced Ali as a miserable bastard. He vented his spleen on the State Department and the President. He went so far as to throw in negative comments about the media, which from the snatches of broadcasts we overheard appeared unconcerned with our plight.

Tom Sutherland served as the voice of moderation. "Anger does not help any of us," he counseled. "Relax. Let's get our things in order and wait for a better day." Even he, however, labored against the weight of growing discouragement.

The spirits of our guards also dropped. They too had enough. Mokmoud and his wife were expecting their first child in September. His home was in south Lebanon and he wanted to be there. Fadl too showed increasing disinterest in the job and longed to join his family. He and Mokmoud squabbled angrily, to the point where others were forced to intervene. The substance of their quarrels was who would get days off. Abu Ali also yearned to spend more time with his wife and youngster.

Only Sayid seemed unconcerned. His mother and children lived close enough for him to visit with them regularly. He genuinely liked us as men to whom he could talk. We offered more intellectual stimulation than his peers. We chatted with him about world events, Lebanese politics, spoke of our travels, helped him with his English. Within a few days, Sayid carried a TV set and then a VCR into our room to show us the news reports on Marty Jenco following his release. The joy of watching the Father in his freedom temporarily acted as a balm to our sore spirits. Sayid furnished a running commentary, like a doting, but chiding parent. When Jenco appeared in a white safari suit with a shirt on backward to resemble an over-size clerical collar, Sayid chided him. "Oh Father. Why aren't you wearing the nice clothes we bought for you?" We could have supplied several reasons but did not.

"Look," continued Sayid. "Father is smoking cigarettes." Captivity without butts had cured Marty's addiction and we had told him if he ever took up the habit again, we'd punish him. But at this point we didn't care.

Once again we nourished a dream of exploding concussion grenades and a quick burst of small arms fire as a U.S. raiding party broke into our unfortified redoubt. As with Ben Weir, we had been able to plot our location with Marty Jenco sufficiently to hope that experts could pinpoint the precise site. From what we observed there was minimum security around the building. (For instance, I never saw any evidence of explosives in place for the eventuality of an attack.) Once again, nothing happened.

A week elapsed, and another show and tell session began. Unfortunately, this time I was to be at center stage. The disaster began with the guards toting a television set and VCR into the room I shared with Anderson and Sutherland. The guards did not smile when one remarked that I would find the tape very interesting.

It was a U.S. network news program. Because they were still keeping a news blackout for us, we could not hear the audio from the anchorman. My face filled the screen and I realized that we were watching the tape made at the time of Marty Jenco's release.

The anchorman's face appeared briefly in a small box in the upper right hand corner of the screen. Then in the lower left hand section there appeared a picture of William Buckley with the caption, "CIA". While I silently mouthed my statement, words in script began to float down the screen from the anchorman's face. The words traveled over my face and then approached Buckley's image. With growing apprehension I read the inscription, *Coded message*. Just before the inscription reached Buckley's picture, it changed to *Bachelor*.

I knew instantly that the scene and the commentary covered my regrets to Buckley's non-existent wife and children. To this day, I cannot figure what kind of coded message I could possibly make through an erroneous reference to his family. But I suspected the Hajj and his clique would believe the worst of me. For I was well aware that Arabs tend to think of the U.S. media as the voice of authority.

I turned to Terry. "I am in big trouble."

He was outraged. "That's the most irresponsible speculation I have ever seen in all of my years of journalism."

"If I ever get out of here alive," I vowed, "something awful is going to happen to that bastard."

Anderson counseled against violence. "You want to kill him now and that's understandable. What you must never do is mention his name publicly. If you accuse him by name, he'll defend himself. He will have access to TV and you won't. Most people will accept his version. The other thing he could do is simply ignore your charges and in time everyone would forget."

I interrupted Anderson. "I want that man's head."

"Calm down, David. I know my peers. If you mention the incident frequently without divulging his identity, other journalists will put pressure on him. Whenever he goes into a bar or shows up at some social event, a reporter will make a crack that there's the guy whose irresponsible remarks nearly caused the death of an innocent person. Journalists

don't forget and we can be vicious. Believe me, David. Reporters will make him suffer."

"Okay, Terry. I trust you and if I am ever freed, I"ll follow
your advice." And I have not openly accused the anchorman
I believe put me in jeopardy. He knows who he is. I have
requested a copy of the tape of the broadcast from the appropriate network but have not received an answer. So much for
the willingness of that organization to cooperate when it is
part of the news.

I am aware that this was not the only instance of an
accusation about a coded message. I have seen a tape in
which ABC's John McWethy, doing a voice-over, added fuel
to the fire with the question, "Was Jacobsen's comment a
mistake or a coded message?" But that version did not show
my face and carry the overprinted words.

The fact is that Terry was wrong. If anyone snubbed or
castigated the anchorman whose off-the-wall theory endangered my life, it has escaped my notice.

As the McWethy broadcast indicates, the anchorman was
not the only one to falsely finger me for allegedly tricking
my captors. One thing is certain, the offenders never acknowledged or apologized for the error which eventually
would bring me much pain.

My main gripe is that U.S. television news seldom digs
into a story in depth. Everything gets compacted into the
thirty- to sixty-second sound bites aimed to grab a perceived
short attention span among viewers. The newscasters shoot
from the lip, then hurry off in search of the next sensation
without the slightest awareness of the possible consequences of their words. In the news business—this includes
the newspapers but particularly the electronic media—the
competition is such that everyone fears getting scooped.
That leads to copycats; wild tales are repeated until they
become established as facts by dint of being oft told.

Many Americans, to their credit, have developed a certain
amount of skepticism about the media because of the ob-

vious stretch for sensation. But what the U.S. press and public does not realize is that in the Middle East, the American media is reputed to report the gospel truth. Listeners and readers over there do not understand the degree of speculation in our press. They skip right by words like "allegedly," "reportedly," "supposedly," or "rumored" and accept what's printed or broadcast as hard facts. The only exception is the statement of a Western political figure. Here, there is an almost direct opposite; nothing our diplomats and officials say is credited as truly authentic.

Most immediately, my emotions were pure anger followed by high anxiety. To be absolutely powerless, to be innocent but judged guilty without any opportunity to offer a defense, that's a prescription bound to create a sense of terror. Living under this weight was agony. The passage of time did not alleviate the feeling. I understood the Arabic concept of time. They have no compulsion to react immediately. I was certain something awful would happen; I just didn't know when and I could only hope it was not my execution.

Days passed while I lived in dread of the inevitable confrontation with Ali and the Hajj over the interpretation of my unscripted condolences. So far the Hajj had not demonstrated to me any capacity for violence, but only a fool could ignore the history of torture and murders perpetrated in the name of Islamic Jihad.

I thought my moment had come when nine days after Marty Jenco left our ranks, Ali and the Hajj paid us another night visit. As they hurried into our room, Ali ordered, "Get dressed, quickly. You are going home at last!" Of the three of us, I was easily the happiest. I was going to escape retribution for my indiscretion and be free. The guards themselves were enthralled. They slapped us on the back, even hugged us as we scurried about preparing ourselves.

The Hajj and Ali went to the adjacent room where they delivered similar good news to the Frenchmen. We heard the excited conversation of Marcel Carton and Jean-Paul Kauffman, the two survivors of the original trio. In a display of good feeling, Terry Anderson thumped on the wall the beat of "The Star Spangled Banner." From their side, the Frenchmen responded with a triumphant banging of their anthem, "The Marseilles."

We abandoned our protective skepticism. There was no doubt. We were about to start the long journey home. We thanked the Lord for our deliverance in a brief and final Church of the Locked Door service.

There were no delays when they came for us. Tom Sutherland wasted no time squabbling over the absence of his own clothes. Single file, we marched to the elevator and descended with three guards—so much for the sham on the night of Jenco's release when we were told the elevator could not contain us all.

Outside, still blindfolded, we trudged by a row of parked cars to a van. We huddled in the back with Mokmoud and Fadl. I felt Mokmoud suddenly pull off my wristwatch. "You guys say you're not thieves. Give it back," I whispered. He handed it over. Warned to remain silent, there was no further conversation. The only strain was to contain the joy bubbling up within.

The vehicle halted after fifteen minutes and a garage door rolled up. The van pulled into a building; the engine switched off and someone slid open the van door. A vaguely familiar voice declared, "You will be staying here for a few days only and you are not to make any trouble. My superior officers have given me permission to kill you if any rules are broken. You will be locked in cells equipped with miniature cameras and electronic listening devices. If you do or say anything in violation of the rules, you will be seen or heard and severely punished. Behave, and you will live to be free." I realized the speaker was Imad Mughniya trying to alter his voice and conceal his identity.

Although he referred to his "superior officers," Mughniya was the boss of all bosses in the hostage operations. The Hajj took his orders from Mughniya, who, incidentally, also was entitled to the honorific since he too had made the pilgrimage to Mecca.

My spirits sank precipitously. To be held even for a few more days might expose me to the wrath of the Hajj and his cohorts. I meekly followed orders as they helped us out of the van and guided us through rooms and corridors. Someone advised, "Now, you must go down a spiral staircase, into the basement. Do not touch the hand rails or something awful will happen."

Gingerly, I wound my way into the depths and after the final step entered a long corridor. We stepped across a threshold alongside a heavy metal door and proceeded another twenty feet further before the guards shoved us into a small room. As they locked the door before leaving, they crushed us. "This is bad. We are sorry."

It had all been a sham, just a con to get us on our best behavior and give them the least trouble. Certainly, none of us even thought of yelling for help while in the street or van because we were convinced liberation was at hand.

The charades continued for several days. Our "new" escorts spoke in either falsetto voices or guttural ones but we realized it was the same old crew. Sayid captained the squad and the familiar Mokmoud, Fadl, and Abu Ali were still on duty.

When our guards described the situation as "bad" they spoke correctly. Not only weren't we freed, but in comparison we had moved from a four-star hotel into a sewer. The three of us occupied a tiny space, what had once been two rooms, six feet by six feet, with a ceiling under six feet high. Three full-size men squeezed into an area where a pair of mattresses covered the entire floor of what had been one room and the third pad ate up half the space in the other. Tom and I bunked on the two mattresses in one room while Terry slept in the other half of the "suite."

When I attempted to stand, my head hit the ceiling, which was three or four inches too low. It forced me to hunch over so uncomfortably that I abandoned tries to pull myself fully erect. I spent most of my waking hours either prone or sitting. And after about two weeks when I lifted myself up to peer through the six-inch transom of the door, I fainted from the unaccustomed position. When I regained consciousness, Tom was rubbing his knee. My total, dead weight had fallen upon his leg, giving him pain for weeks.

White tiles about twenty centimeters square finished the walls and floor and unpainted plaster covered the ceiling. A six-inch ventilating van installed in the lower left hand corner of the thick metal door pushed at the fetid air. To summon a guard we pressed a buzzer button located near the door handle. We quickly discerned that the warning about miniature cameras and electronic listening devices was pure fiction.

The only light in the room sifted from the hallway through the transom. In these faint rays we read the only literature permitted, the Bible. Incandescent and fluorescent bulbs provided illumination but when a power outage forced the use of a gas-fed generator, the radio hanging in the corridor emitted a ghastly squeal. The radio wasn't there for our information and edification. Apparently, its purpose was to drown out exterior noises whenever the ordinary hum of the building's normal electrical power failed to provide an acoustic screen. The system worked, until the radio batteries died. Then, when the generator went on stream, we could pick up the unmistakable sound of the ocean and high-speed automobile traffic. Terry, who had driven through much of Beirut, figured we were being held on the Coastal Road, near the airport.

It became obvious that there had never been any intention of releasing us. This was to be our home for an indefinite period. Indeed, we picked up clues that we were not the only people being held here. Through the fan opening in the door bottom, we counted the feet that passed on morning trips to the bathroom. We shared our observations from our own moments outside our cell and figured out that our floor consisted of a ten-cell block. We occupied numbers 2 and 3. We added up minute scraps of overheard conversations between guards and captives to identify some others among the ten or eleven our floor held.

Cell number 1 housed an Englishman. Tom Sutherland, of Scottish descent, acted as our expert on dialect and accent from that part of the world. We knew of a Briton and an Irishman held hostages but Tom could not decide whether our next-door guest was the journalist John McCarthy or AUB Professor of English Brian Keenan. McCarthy was kidnapped April 17, 1986; Keenan was taken six days earlier, but he was released in the autumn of 1990. McCarthy is still being held as of this writing.

Somewhere down the hall, in the vicinity of cell 4 or 5, lived a man with an Oriental background. We could hear him faintly repeating the words, "pee pee," and "yah yah," referring to his most pressing bodily needs.

We listened for indications of our French associates but could find no hints they were on hand. Perhaps the kidnappers housed them on a floor above us.

To our dismay, Sayid, the most congenial of the guards, disappeared without warning. When we asked what happened to him, his colleagues remained silent. Sayid had been the most responsive to us and in more than a year of his company we had forged something of a mutual trust. The gloom thickened. We speculated on whether something terrible had befallen him or worse, our kidnappers had canned him because he was too nice.

During the second week of September 1986, I overheard the news on the guards' TV. Two more Americans apparently had been kidnapped. One was Frank Reed from the International School in Beirut and the other my friend from the AUB, Joe Cicippio. The news account noted that Cicippio had been badly beaten when snatched. That evening, sneaking a look through the transom when I heard footsteps, I caught a glimpse of a bloody, bandaged head. I guessed it was Cicippio. And when I asked one of the guards if Joe were seriously injured, he reassured me that my friend was in good health.

Joe held the dual posts of comptroller for the AUB Medical Center and assistant comptroller for the AUB itself. When I arrived in Lebanon for my new job, Joe was one of the two Americans still working at the hospital. The other was Gladys Mouro, the director of nursing. Both of them became good friends of mine.

Cicippio had considerable experience in the Middle East. Although he had been in Beirut less than a year, he had worked in Saudi Arabia for about a decade. Before that he had been a banker in Pennsylvania and active in Republican politics.

Kind and gentle, Joe was known in the hospital for a near excess of concern for the feelings and welfare of the employees. He did the little things, such as making certain Philippino nurses returning home for vacation would receive their pay in U.S. dollars and purchasing airplane tickets for them to keep delays to a minimum on a long trip.

Many evenings, Joe would come to my apartment to watch a video, rented through the catalog list that initially bothered my kidnappers. Joe would drop into an easy chair and, almost before the titles finished, I would hear his cannonlike snores. He would loll forward, then snap his head back up before starting to slouch over again. When the film would end I would awaken him. He would always claim he had not slept, that it was a great picture. Then he'd leave for his own apartment building a short distance off. Once home, he would always call, not because of fears of kidnapping but because of the more apparent (to us) threat of robbery or burglary.

He had been married twice and although he was devoted to his kids, both of his marriages had ended in divorce. One day, a beautiful young Druse employee, Jumana, asked to see me privately. In my office she went directly to the point. "We all love Joe Cicippio, but he's making a pest of himself. He's in love with Miss Mouro and constantly bothers her. He

Joe Cicippio, the AUB controller, spent many evenings in this chair in my apartment where he dozed off while watching films on the VCR.

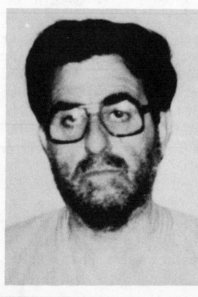

After two weeks in captivity, late in September of 1986, Joe Cicippio, in this photo released by the kidnappers, already was full bearded, his face drawn from stress. (Courtesy AP/Wide World Photos)

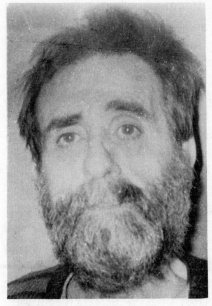

The picture of Joe Cicippio, distributed by Islamic Jihad in March, 1990 as he finished three and a half years in captivity, shows the ravages of his ordeal. (Courtesy AP/Wide World Photos)

sends huge bouquets of flowers almost daily, telephones her at night. The trouble is, she is not interested in him. She does not want to make an official complaint but the situation is becoming very difficult."

I immediately went to see Gladys. "I understand Joe has a terminal case of puppy love for you and you have a terminal case of rejection for him." She smiled and filled me in on the details of Joe's Don Quixote-like pursuit. She confirmed that she did not reciprocate his feelings. I promised to solve the problem.

First, I approached my assistant Ahmed Nasrallah. I explained the situation and instructed, "If you want to keep your job, you better find a nice lady for Joe immediately. He is a very lonely man."

Then I summoned Joe. I gently explained that his one-sided courtship was making life difficult. The technique was never going to overwhelm the object of his affections and people were starting to snicker behind his back. I firmly advised him that he was an adult, not a lovesick adolescent.

He was to leave Gladys alone. It was not an angry confrontation but more in the nature of counseling between friends. Joe agreed to stop pestering Gladys.

Meanwhile, Ahmed was actively on the case. A few days later, he informed me that a blind date he arranged for Joe had worked to perfection. Joe had now fallen in love with Elhem, a lovely Shiite Moslem woman who had never been married. Indeed, Cicippio shortly confirmed to me that he had indeed been smitten and he laughed about his unrequited passion for Gladys.

One Sunday, Joe invited me to accompany him on a visit to Elhem and her family. I begged off because of some pressing work. On the following Monday, Mouro and her staff greeted me with the news that Joe and Elhem, in the local fashion, had pledged themselves to one another in a ceremony conducted by a mullah. The rite resembled a wedding but the couple were not to live together until a second ceremony several months later. I also learned that, following the local culture, Joe had pledged a dowry, a very large one in fact. I kidded Gladys that she had passed up an opportunity to become a wealthy woman.

Joe and Elhem were officially married in July. By that time, however, I was a guest of Islamic Jihad and unable to attend. Still, the future for a devoted couple who found one another in troubled times seemed bright. Islamic Jihad also shattered their dreams, though, when he was kidnapped in September 1986. What I have learned from others who were held with Joe is that he has unfailingly maintained his gentle disposition and was well-liked by the guards. As of this writing, he is still a hostage.

On September 19, 1986, about six weeks after the showing of my video that allegedly contained a coded message, I was awakened very early in the morning by Mokmoud. He directed me to follow him. And as we left the cell, he said, "I am sorry." My heart started to race. My stomach tightened. Were they now going to take their revenge for what I'd said about Buckley? I could have only a few more minutes of life before they put a bullet in my brain. It was all so sudden. Time had stretched interminably in front of me, now my life could end before I even realized what was happening. I felt my blood freeze, numbness gripped my limbs, a whirl of ghastly images tumbled through my mind.

Mokmoud brought me to a room near the guards' quarters. Even though my eyes were covered I calculated there were six people present. From under the lower edge of the blindfold I saw Ali sitting at a table. There was none of the "Hi guys" tone in his voice as he ordered me to sit. My butt hardly touched the seat before white flashes ripped through my head as a pair of open hands cuffed me across my ears. Another blow thumped the side of my head. I toppled onto my back. Someone yanked me back upright in time for another series of painful head slaps, some with open hands, others with closed fists.

A hubbub of voices in Arabic assailed me. "Why is this happening?" I stammered to Ali.

"You have embarrassed us," said Ali, "by sending a coded message in the video given to Father Jenco."

"No, no," I protested. "It was all a mistake. I really thought Buckley had a family. It wasn't a secret message."

Someone screamed at me in Arabic. I did not understand. A fist to the cheek knocked me on my backside. My feet were grabbed and forced between the strap and the stock of an automatic rifle. The assailant twisted the weapon until my feet were painfully and tightly bound. Then he lifted my legs well into the air until only my head and shoulders touched the floor.

It seemed as if everyone now took a whack at my body. Those who could not reach me rained a jumble of curses upon me.

"Ali, why don't you help me!" I begged.

"Shut up," he shouted and he himself struck me. Ali, some guards I did not recognize, the Hajj and Mughniya, they beat a tattoo with rubber hoses on the soles of my feet and my toes. My tormentors turned their attention to my legs, to my genitals, my stomach and back. I writhed in agony. I flashed a memory of a beating victim brought to the emergency room at a hospital where I had worked. He lasted several days in intensive care before a painful death from internal bleeding.

At first I choked off my sobs, resolved to show stoicism in the face of barbarity. Then I realized that might only inflame them. I began to cry out, to moan, "Dammit, stop! Oh my God, please stop! For mercy's sake, use a gun; end the torture." I was half in earnest. If this was to be my life from now on, it would be better if it ended.

"Get it over with," I pleaded.

And then the beating stopped; it was maybe ten minutes of excruciating cruelty that seemed to last a decade. I lay there gasping, sore in every part of my body. I ached and sharp, stabbing sensations assaulted me all over. Ali whispered, "Relax, the boys were only having fun."

Except for Ali, the Hajj and Mughniya, I think the others, including the fellow who wrapped my feet in his rifle strap, were all strangers. The efficiency and effectiveness of their attack indicated they were all well practiced in the sadistic arts. I cannot believe the guards who had been with me for more than a year could have participated so enthusiastically in the assault.

I now hated an American, too, the network anchorman who had reported my "coded message." Until that morning, I had disliked him as a person with a potential to create mischief. Now my body bore scars from his reckless speculation.

My tormentors were not finished with me. I had scarcely regained my breath before I was commanded to stand and jog in place. Undoubtedly, they extracted one last taste of vicious pleasure as I hopped about on my battered feet and toes for five minutes, wincing in pain.

Their blood lust sated, I was told to sit quietly. Ali said, "Now you will write a letter and there will be no mistakes this time." He issued instructions on the matters to be covered. The theme was that while we hostages were being ignored by our government and the American people, Daniloff in Moscow was receiving the utmost political and public attention.

I was mystified. I had no idea what he was talking about. "Who is this Daniloff? What did he do?"

"You know who he is," insisted Ali.

I blew off a bit of steam. "How the hell can I possibly know who he is! You people have isolated me from the world for months. You took away our radio. I'm not telepathic." The small expression of indignation had less to do with Ali's assumption of my omniscience than with my anger for the earlier mistreatment.

He relented and filled me in on the Daniloff affair. In August 1986, FBI agents arrested one Gennadi Zakharov, a Soviet citizen employed by the United Nations in New York, and charged him with espionage. Subsequently, the KGB retaliated and seized journalist Nicholas Daniloff in Moscow for allegedly obtaining proscribed information. Obviously, the Soviets intended to trade their captive for Zakharov. The U.S. government, from President Reagan down through the State Department and the media, objected furiously to the transparent stratagem. But there was no getting away from the fact that the Americans were negotiating with the Russians for Daniloff. And following about two weeks in a KGB jail, he now lived comfortably in the U.S. Embassy while officials worked out the details for his release.

After supplying the facts and the theme, Ali left me alone with pen and paper. I scribbled out a statement that compared the situation of Daniloff to ours. I noted that he had been held only a short time while we had been locked up for more than a year. I asked if we were not also Americans. I argued that negotiating for him and not us was unfair. I reported that we were deeply discouraged, that we felt forgotten while we languished in cells. I described the filth, the lack of sanitation, the bad food. I said that these conditions

197

were getting worse. Time is running out for us, I pleaded. I asked why there was a public uproar about Daniloff but we were being ignored. Didn't our country value us also?

Ali returned in an hour, scanned my letter quickly and took off again, promising to come back.

With almost every square inch of my body either a throbbing ache or a stabbing pain, I lay on the floor, on my back, clasped my hands on my chest and prayed to my Lord. I thanked Him for sparing my life and then I surprised myself by mumbling aloud,

"Thank you, Lord. I needed my privacy." It was a strange reaction, but except for my first weeks in captivity I had not had a moment alone for fifteen months. Even in this desperate moment, sorely afflicted, I welcomed the change.

Chapter 13

Communications

As I waited for Ali to return, a guard brought a glass of cool water and some freshly washed grapes. "We are sorry, Mr. David," he said softly. Until that moment I had not realized how parched my throat had become from the stress of the beating. The water and grapes improved my spirits.

A full hour elapsed before Ali reappeared. He sat at the table and told me to take the chair facing him. "They do not trust you and what you have written. They have written the letter for you." He held up several pages, handwritten in Arabic. "You are to write exactly what I say and I have been instructed to check every word."

He began to dictate. "Four hundred seventy-five days and I David Jacobsen, and my friends Anderson and Sutherland, we feel homesick, our bodies are sick and our psychological state is bad." I immediately interrupted him. "That's not a complete sentence and it's not grammatically correct.

He rejected my criticism and again told me just to copy down his exact words. I transcribed his translation, continuing to point out poor syntax and misspellings when he opted to supply the letters for a word. And he dismissed my corrections without exception.

The theme of the missive remained a comparison of the Beirut hostages with the treatment of Daniloff. "Why was Reagan interested minute by minute with spy journalist Daniloff but he is not interested one minute our story and he didnt do anything to solve it. Are we citizens from tenth

Bizarre grammar and syntax marked the September 15, 1986 letter I wrote under the dictation of my kidnappers.
(Courtesy AP/Wide World Photos)

degree? Are not we Americans. What are you waiting for? For us to die one by one."

The dictation from Ali also included greetings to our families with a "special hello to Peggy Say." As stated earlier, Peggy Say was Terry Anderson's sister, and she had traveled to the Middle East seeking freedom for him. Her presence there and in Washington had been noticed. Ali had me do a paragraph in which I mentioned Ben Weir, Marty Jenco, and Jeremy Levin, as well as Peggy Say, and then continued, "We want from them to continue their efforts because you are our only hope and you know our suffering very much . . . Don't get trapped by our government and don't believe their lies and don't believe their promises."

The aim of the letter was to apply pressure to the people back home by questioning how the Daniloff case, in which there was no hesitation about negotiations, differed from ours. On this issue I have no quarrel with my captors. I was all for talks to free us as well as Daniloff.

When I completed the letter under the eye of Ali, I took him to task. "Some friend you are! Why didn't you help me when I was being beaten? I didn't send any coded message. You know better than that."

He shut me off. "That is in the past and there is no need to discuss it further. Let us only be concerned with the future. This time I will protect you." Given his track record and his loyalty, it was less than reassuring.

Satisfied with their literary output, the Hajj and his gang dispatched copies of the letter in my handwriting to the various news agencies housed in Beirut. They also included a photograph of me and their own typewritten statement in Arabic which castigated the president as "cheating the American people" by making concessions in the Daniloff case.

On the following day, newspapers around the United States printed portions of my letter and the State Department mounted its usual damage control operation, to our detriment. As I feared, officials and some commentators focused on the style instead of the content. A New York *Times* dispatch described the letter as ". . . in English supposedly written by him [me]. But awkward phrasings sprinkled through the letter suggested that it was coerced or was written by the captors." A State Department spokesman, Bruce Ammerman, said, "We think there is a good reason to question whether the letter was freely written and represents anything more than the views of Mr. Jacobsen's captors." Real stop-the-presses scoops! I did not have freedom of expression while being held hostage.

My son Eric analyzed the import of the letter perfectly. He agreed it was not similar to others I had written. "There is a possibility it was written by his captors. But that doesn't lessen the importance. The captors are communicating through him." Then Eric criticized the Administration. "For Reagan to respond to Daniloff and neglect to do that for my father and the others just angers me beyond words. They all deserve the treatment Daniloff got. They got Daniloff out in a matter of days. My father's been in there sixteen months and has received no assurance from the Administration that they will work for his release."

Once again, the media made my life tougher. When the letter was shown on television, the broadcasters circled every single mistake in spelling or grammar, adding a notation, "mistakes in dictation." Ali later told me that this emphasis upon errors in composition angered his superiors. They suspected me of sabotage until he managed to convince them that I had followed his orders precisely.

The authorities in the United States may also have been wounded by the swipes taken at their integrity. Among the *bon mots* I dropped was a plea not to believe "the lies and promises of the American government." Those in charge should have been intelligent enough to recognize that in spite of the letter's origins and pejorative tone, a bunch of U.S. citizens were in desperate need of their help.

As a matter of fact, we had not been totally forgotten. In addition to the efforts of Ray Barnet and Terry Waite, one other private effort was mounted. Peggy Say and my son Eric were joined by Ben Weir, Marty Jenco, and Jeremy Levin in a campaign to get the American government to change its avowed policy of non-negotiation with those it considered terrorists. Weir, Jenco, and Levin had all come to Washington a week before the Daniloff letter and, although they failed to generate a great deal of publicity at home, the Beirut newspapers gave their mission front-page coverage. Possibly, that had inspired Islamic Jihad to create my letter about the Daniloff affair.

My children, individually and collectively, must have traveled to Washington several dozen times. Almost immediately, they had picked up disquieting signs from the families of other hostages who had already been through the drill with the officials. These kin were extremely critical of the efforts of the State Department. Eric and Paul at first did not believe what they were hearing.

It was as if they were in the waiting room of a hospital along with the families of other patients. When the doctors, that is the State Department people, came to Eric and Paul to describe their father's condition, the treatment and prognosis, the others would sneer that the physicians were no better than quacks and the hospital was more of a morgue than a place to receive professional help.

It did not take long for my sons to realize that the negative comments were accurate. To a question by my family about some aspect, rumor or even fact, the people at the State Department would respond with the monotonous formality of a police officer reading a suspect his *Miranda* rights: "We are working night and day to secure the release of your father. This is a sensitive situation and we cannot discuss any details of the efforts being made, nor can we comment on unofficial reports, speculation or rumor. Let us reassure you that we appreciate the gravity of the situation, your concerns and we are doing everything possible. You must remember that we are dealing with shadowy people in a shadowy land."

The families and their supporters arranged for a congressional awareness day to acquaint legislators with the situation. Several senators and representatives appeared but some of these guys didn't even seem aware there were hostages in Beirut.

Eric received excellent advice from Jeremy Levin. He briefed him on the Washington scene, who was sincere and might help and who was at best an obstructionist. He forewarned Eric, "You're going to hear this and that and you will be discouraged. Don't lose hope. You just happen to be talking to a guy who has a certain kind of job." Levin produced a tape that explained about the Dawa prisoners in Kuwait. He sent it to Robert Oakley, the Ambassador for Counterterrorism, and hounded Oakley until he admitted receiving the materials. Nevertheless, the Foggy Bottom crew continued to spew its usual smokescreen about the "shadowy group, with shadowy motives in a shadowy part of the world."

It became a very tired refrain and of course it was not true. They did know who kidnapped us and what was being demanded as a ransom. They had been given the word by Jeremy Levin, Ben Weir, and Marty Jenco.

The people at the State Department held their cards so close to their vests that they refused to confirm to my children that Ben Weir had been let go even after he spoke to his wife and it had been reported on television.

My offspring realized that if there was to be a genuine attempt to gain freedom for the hostages, it would have to come from some other agency of the government.

Looking for help elsewhere, the families and the freed hostages pressed the case with the White House and the National Security Council. The group asked for a meeting with Vice President George Bush. The White House agreed to the meeting on the condition that Jeremy Levin and Ben Weir be excluded. The intended snub infuriated the families.

Both Levin and Weir had annoyed DOS by their stubborn refusal to accept the party line. Levin was extremely percep-

Ben Weir (left), Jeremy Levin (center) and Marty Jenco (right) met in Washington, D.C. on one of the missions to generate pressure for release of the hostages. (Courtesy AP/Wide World Photos)

tive, knowledgeable, and articulate. He insisted that the meeting with Bush proceed even if he could not attend. He pointed out that high government officials were unhappy with the possibility of him raising questions in the presence of the hostage families. After a lot of offers and counter-offers, the White House agreed to permit Ben Weir to attend, but not Levin. The childish behavior of the White House staff caused Eric and Paul to lose confidence in the President's men.

The session with Bush produced some minor improvements. The State Department assigned Doug Jones as the contact person in the Citizens Emergency Center and he supplied better communications. Late in 1985, John Adams replaced Jones and he established even finer rapport with the families. The State Department started to make weekly calls

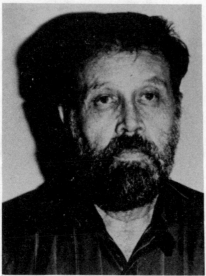

This picture, released in August of 1986, suggests I am holding up reasonably well. (*Courtesy AP/Wide World Photos*)

to the families. When rumors circulated the Center responded with explanations. Everyone in the hostage family community became very fond of the man they dubbed "Little John."

The hostage lobbying group also gained meetings with National Security Adviser Robert McFarlane, his assistant Admiral John Poindexter, and White House Chief of Staff Donald Regan. During a visit to Washington, Eric was at the White House when a man sought him out. "I'm Ollie North," he said. "I work here." Eric ran into North again on several occasions but whatever North's assignments were, he held them close to his tunic.

"Every official was very sympathetic," Eric told me later. "But nobody offered anything substantial. We were told to work through the Syrian, Kuwaiti and Algerian embassies."

But the criticism of the government's position incurred the wrath of some super patriots who considered any deviation from the policy to be disloyal. The New York *Post* in an editorial in October 1985 even accused the American Hostage Committee, a volunteer organization to support and inform families and raise public awareness of the kidnappings, of being a front for the Palestine Liberation Organization.

Eric toured the talk shows drumming up interest in our situation, which had faded from the media. He and Paul composed a song, "When the Word Comes," to heighten public consciousness of the hostages. They recorded the song and performed it on major network programs. Like Eric, Paul and my daughter Diane traveled to Washington and tried to heighten awareness of our plight. My sisters, Carla and Doris, pitched in also. Mary Ellen Mohler, John Mohler's wife, organized the USC faculty wives to write letters and sign petitions on our behalf, even though I am an alumnus of USC's most ferocious rival school.

Eric became increasingly impatient with the process. When he heard Henry Kissinger declare we'd have to get out through our own resources, he telephoned Washington officials and only half-facetiously suggested they trade Kissinger for those in captivity. Eric wanted someone in authority to offer a concrete scenario with a plan of action rather

In this photo, from September of 1986, the effects of my beating are evident. (Courtesy AP/Wide World Photos)

than tea and sympathy. He despaired of the paucity of information from official sources. He learned more from rumors in the press, from Arab organizations and church people traveling in the Middle East. One persistent piece of gossip hinted at secret dealings with the Iranians, but Eric could never find any confirmation.

Meanwhile, instead of being returned to the company of Anderson and Sutherland, I remained in the cell where I had been whipped. Quite likely, the idea was to hide my battered body from the others. A swelling on my leg, possibly a hairline fracture, remained for an entire month. In those first few days in my new room I could barely move. Blood showed in my urine and I wondered how much damage they had done to my kidneys or bladder. More than six weeks later, a medical exam detected traces of blood in my urine.

As I slowly healed, I settled into the familiar pattern of survival, including my old stress relief exercises and concentration upon my faith. I performed my own mass twice a day. "Welcome to the Church of the Locked Door, Annex Division," I murmured. "When two or three gather in His name, He is among us. Lord, even though I am physically alone, spiritually I am joined with my family, friends and the others down the hall." I extended greetings. "Peace be with you, Eric. Peace be with you, Paul. Peace be with you, Diane. Peace be with you, Kerrie." I offered the salutation to every family member and friend, specifically naming them. I told myself that while I was physically alone, spiritually I was with my family, friends, and the others down the hall.

I served as both the celebrant of the mass and its congregation. I consecrated with a prayer a scrap of pita bread I'd saved from mealtime. Tap water substituted for wine. Words flowed easily as I found myself able to mouth huge sections of the scriptures. The stress and the isolation seemed to enhance my memory.

My readings focused on St. Paul. As Saul he had been an evil fellow. Upon his conversion he suffered horribly but he persevered, overcame physical problems and organized himself for a life's work. He was an opinionated person who got things done. I certainly was no saint but I could detect similarities in our personalities.

While I was in this cell, I saw my opportunity to blast my way to freedom. One night, I noticed someone had hung a Soviet solder's rifle, an AK-47, complete with ammunition clip, on a wall hook just outside my quarters. If I could grab it from its perch and pull it back into my cell, I could spend the night familiarizing myself with its workings—how to cock it, the location of the safety. In the morning when the guard opened the door to escort me to the toilet, I could see myself saying, "Greetings!" and then opening fire. I could take out Mokmoud and Fadl, who were on duty, and then break to the outside. I had no qualms now about killing. The "boys having some fun" had squelched any inclination to turn the other cheek.

As darkness and quiet fell on the compound, I decided to go for it. Standing on tiptoe, I could get my fingers through the bars of the transom and touch the weapon. Straining, I managed to get one hand on it, then forcing my face into the door I extended my other fingers and lifted the rifle free. I pulled it back to me. Then I began to sweat. I could not slip it between the bars of the transom. I tried maneuvering it every possible angle. My hands and fingers began to ache but I continued to struggle with the rifle. I moved with extreme caution. If I dropped the weapon or banged it against the door, someone would hear. There would be no questions. They'd come up shooting.

No matter what I did, the piece just was too big for the opening. Now the problem was how to get it back in place. If I abandoned it on the floor, I was a good candidate for a summary execution when it was discovered the next morning. All together, I spent nearly an hour clinging to that AK-47 with horrible cramps seizing me in the back and arm muscles. Finally, I managed to engage the wall hook. I was shaking when I finished, knowing how close I had come either to a violent escape or a fatal volley of shots from the guards.

In the solitude of my cell, I became fascinated with a fellow resident, a mouse who surfaced every evening at bedtime. I plugged his hole in the wall with paper but by morning the obstacle would have disappeared. The puny rodent refused to accept my limitations on its freedom.

Other than that small creature, I enjoyed a small but growing audience of visitors. All of the publicity had transformed me into something of a local celebrity, or more appropriately, a famous attraction at the zoo. They came to stare for a few minutes and then left without a word. None of them threatened me with a weapon.

One visitor improved my life. An elderly Hizballah cleric spoke to me in English. "How are you. I hope you are now all right." I asked him if I could have a broom to sweep the place and some hot water to wash the floor. He must have been a man of some authority for instead of simply acceding to my request, the keepers transferred me to a new, cleaner cell. As I was being led there, I felt a familiar touch and a hand bearing a glass of water. Instantly, I knew Sayid had returned.

I put my arm around his shoulder. "How are you, Sayid, my son."

"Mr. David, I am hurting. I have a bellyful of metal, but I am recovering. While I was working on my car, an incoming artillery shell hit nearby and wounded me badly." He asked, "And how are you?" I told him I was surviving and we agreed to talk later. I learned that he had been treated for his injuries at my hospital.

Once again, my captors chose me to star in one of their videos. Before I left the cell, the ever helpful Ali warned me, "Just one mistake, one added word, one mispronunciation and something awful will happen. You will be forced to watch while Tom Sutherland is killed. Then you will live with that memory forever." I understand that some viewers commented that I appeared to be under extreme stress. For once, the speculation was accurate.

When I opened my eyes to stare into the camcorder lens, the pin-headed, pear-shaped technician of my previous performances was not behind the machine. Instead, I saw Imad Mughniya himself, dressed in a light green jumpsuit, penny loafers on his feet. For some inexplicable reason, he believed he hid his face from me by draping a newspaper in the shape of a V over his head. I had a long look at his slender build, clean-shaven features, well-groomed hair, and dark, sad, inquisitive eyes. He was a handsome fellow, perhaps thirty-five years old then.

The tape, made October 2, 1986, was triggered by the swap of Daniloff for Zhakarov. I made the same points as before about the differences in the way our situation was treated and how desperate our status was. This show also received bad notices in Washington. President Reagan, asked by reporters about the comparison of the Daniloff affair with the hostages in Lebanon, answered, "There is no comparison between the two situations. In one we were dealing with a government that under its laws arrested one of our citizens—we think unjustly. We were able to get him back. There has never been a day that we have not been trying every channel to get our hostages back from Lebanon. But they were not seized by a government. We don't know who is holding them. There's never been any contact between their kidnappers and us, other than an indirect one." I think the President was either misinformed or ill-advised. The information from Ben Weir and Marty Jenco certainly established who the guilty party was and what the demands were. The messages carried by the freed hostages were directly addressed to the American government.

My son Eric was highly offended by the remarks from the White House. He all but called Reagan a liar on a national broadcast. He was upset because in defending the actions taken on behalf of Daniloff, the White House pointed out

Terrorists continued to seize hostages, although the policy of no negotiations supposedly was designed to discourage further kidnappings. Edward Austin Tracy, an American writer, was taken in October, 1986. (Courtesy AP/Wide World Photos)

that the journalist was held in a cell with an informer and was only permitted to see his wife once a day. Compared to the information from Weir and Jenco on how hostages in Beirut fared, Daniloff's brief sojourn sounded more like the equivalent of a two-week camping trip.

In my new six foot by six foot quarters, I could stand erect, my head grazing the ceiling in a few spots. I paced the room, back and forth, counting the steps, burning up the weight of time by concentrating upon the numbers. I continued my twice-daily religious services.

I had healed enough to exercise. Sometimes I jogged in place until the sweat rolled down my body in streams and I felt exhausted. My muscles often rebelled against vigorous calisthenics but I forced my will upon them. Brooding about the brutality and injustice heaped upon me, anger swelled to rage. My hands balled into fists, my heart picked up speed, the muscles of my face tightened. To choke off a futile outburst against the guards, I would sentence myself to push-ups, anywhere from twenty-five to one hundred at a shot.

Some days I calculated that I performed from six hundred to a thousand push-ups. The effort was worth it. Not only did I avoid provoking my captors but I also shook off the miasma of melancholy permeating my cell.

During the period Terry Anderson and I shared quarters we had worked out a primitive code in the event we were ever separated by a wall. One tap signified the latter *a* and two knocks meant *b* until one reached twenty-six for *z*. The code wasn't suitable for lengthy discussions but when we tried it we found that given a few vowels surrounded by consonants, one could often guess the word intended.

I rapped on the wall between me and the hostage in cell 8, "D. Jacobsen, AUB." I repeated the message once. I was thrilled to decipher the responsive taps, "Frank Reed." Reed intuitively grasped what I was doing. He had been the director of the International School. I banged out my name on the opposite wall, believing I might contact my good friend Joe Cicippio, comptroller at the AUB. But there was no answer.

During my trips to the bathroom, I tried to converse with the guard escorting me. And as we passed the room where Anderson and Sutherland lived, I talked as loudly as possible so that they might hear me, realize that I was alive and well. I never saw them, but I knew they were still there from the sight of their towels hanging on the transom to dry in the damp air.

My crude link to a neighbor and the slight attempts to stay in touch with Terry and Tom aside, I focused on maintaining the immutable, inviolable connection with those outside my tiny world. I was able to do so by concentrating on my sense of time. My sanity depended upon always knowing the day of the week and the date. These identified me with my family, Kerrie, friends back home, and the companions down the hall. If I lost track of time, I would fall off the bedrock upon which I could construct my future. Hope would end and I'd collapse into the abyss of depression.

I no longer had access to pencil and paper but, fortunately, the floor provided an easy reference point for the days of the week. There were exactly seven ceramic tiles from the door to the wall. I used an empty medicine vial as a marker. Every night I moved it to the next tile and when it reached the wall, it was back to square one.

For a calendar, I saved the pits from the olives served with my meals. As a day of the month passed, I added a pit to a pile in the corner. At any moment I could count them, note the position of my medicine container and figure what day it was in which month.

The olive pits also served as drawing instruments. I scratched some art on the ceiling but I was fascinated by a picture made by a previous occupant. It showed a man and a small boy. As I lay on my mattress staring up at the portrait, I passed hours speculating on their stories. Was the father ever reunited with his son? Had they both survived the terrible war or were they just two more anonymous victims?

As he promised, Sayid visited me. He chatted about his children and his wishes for the future. He desperately wanted to amass enough money for a dowry that would bring a new wife willing to care for his brood. He was reluctant to speak about his hospitalization and he continued to suffer pain from his shrapnel wounds.

Sayid brought a most welcome gift, a new Bible for my exclusive use. Previously, I shared a copy with others. I devoted myself to the passages from Ecclesiastes, absorbing emotionally his eloquence on a season and a time for everything. I interpreted the words as a message urging patience upon me, something I all too frequently abandoned.

One morning I awoke with a powerful memory of a dream, one in which my freedom was at last granted. I'm not a believer in the prescience some say comes from dreams or mysticism. But the images from my sleep refused to dissipate. I saw myself as going home early in November. The feeling was so strong that I worried I was losing my sense of reality. At the same time, I pored over my heap of olive pits, calculating the days until November.

The only illumination for my cell came through the transom from the floodlight in the corridor ceiling. One day as I read the Bible, a guard inexplicably unscrewed the bulb and left me in darkness. It was a moment of great frustration, but I sought comfort in Ecclesiastes. I put down the Bible and stretched out for a lengthy nap. "All things have a time and a place," I reminded myself. And indeed, my nap was interrupted by the return of the bulb and light flooding into my room. I began to read again.

The removal of the bulb was repeated on the following day. I forgot my injunction to patience and buzzed for the guard. He spoke no English but I gestured to indicate the problem, that I could not read without light. He went off and returned with another bulb. It was a mercury type, however, requiring minimum voltage to stay lit. It flickered, died, revived, flickered and quit. Reading under these circumstances was impossible. I pressed the buzzer again. There was no response.

I gave up and turned to sleep, fearing that for the remainder of my days I would live in faint, intermittent rays of light. That night, the floodlight was installed back in place. As its beams struck me, I counseled myself, "Patience, patience." Although I had been deeply disappointed by broken promises and false signs of release a number of times, I took the incidents with the bulbs as favorable omens to go along with my dream. A sunny optimism enveloped me.

Late in October 1986, Sayid and Mokmoud entered my cell. Sayid said, "You can really be proud of your son Eric. He is working so hard for your release and he loves you so much. Come with us. We have a surprise for you."

They led me down the hall and we halted in front of the door to the room where I had been tortured. I almost balked. "I didn't like the last surprise I received in this room."

They both chuckled. "Trust me, Mr. David," said Sayid. "Yeah, sure."

Inside, I was instructed to remain standing while they assembled a folding cot. When it was set up, they told me to sit on the head section. I no sooner lowered my butt when the thing collapsed, spilling me on the floor. We all laughed.

Peggy Say, Terry Anderson's sister, has waged a vigorous campaign to apply public opinion and U.S. government pressure on behalf of her brother. She joined with the freed French journalist Jean-Paul Kauffmann in a birthday greeting to Terry in October, 1988. (Courtesy AP/Wide World Photos)

When the cot was upright again, I gingerly sat in the middle. To my delight, Tom Sutherland and Terry Anderson appeared.

We were ordered not to speak or lift our blindfolds but to look straight ahead. Terry reached over from his position on the cot and tapped a message on my knee. "Good to see you."

They brought in a TV set with a VCR and inserted a tape. We were told to raise our blindfolds but to stare straight ahead. Sayid announced, "You will be proud of Peggy Say and Eric." We watched what was a panel discussion with the participants arranged in a U-shape. On the left was a boy and a woman. Later, I learned they were the family of Alec Collett, the British journalist murdered at the behest of Libya after the American bombing attack. I didn't recognize the group leader but Terry told me he was Jeremy Levin. Next to Levin sat our old friend, Ben Weir. He looked hale and hearty. It was great to see how well he had recovered from his ordeal.

The first voice we heard was a woman's. Terry proudly identified her. "That's Peggy, my sister." He had always boasted about her. She had returned to college as a mature adult and achieved substantial success in her field of social welfare. She had acted as a kind of substitute mother for him when he was very young. Like Terry, she was very assertive. She was an effective advocate for our cause.

My pale face must have glowed as I heard Eric offering his views. The camera never showed his face, but only his hands. I caught a glimpse of a prayer bracelet with my name on it around his wrist. Why his face was not shown I have never understood. Terry and I were pleased by the videotape, but Tom was disappointed because his children did not appear. The program lasted for about fifteen minutes and we asked to watch it again. To our surprise, the guards agreed. The tape was replayed; we hung on every word, just as when we watched the first time. Then we rose, shook hands and said goodbye. Since that moment, I have not seen these two men with whom I had shared so much pain, from whom I drew so much support and grew to love while I was in Lebanon.

Chapter 14

Freedom

On Saturday night, November 1, 1986, I went to bed supremely confident that my seventeen-month nightmare was about to end. Just about every hostage had been released late on a Saturday. The reason lies in the religious observances. Friday is the Moslem sabbath. After the services, the elders and officials meet to decide important matters. By the time they complete their deliberations, daylight has arrived. To protect themselves, the hostage-takers wait for the dark of night or early morning hours to free a captive.

Apart from the omens I had collected, hard evidence of approaching deliverance piled up. For a week, I had enjoyed a haircut and beard trim every other day. The guards indicated they expected me to leave shortly. And on this evening when my turn for a shower arrived, I was told to take as much time as I wanted, to leave my underwear in the bathroom and come out naked. That was most unusual, even shocking. My captors always exhibited extreme modesty; they were affronted if one of us appeared without the requisite boxer shorts over the jockey style underwear to cover the outline of genitals. Now, after I followed orders, someone handed me new white undergarments. I received a second towel to thoroughly dry my hair. A guard combed my hair and beard. The conversation and the touch of the person grooming me were extraordinarily kind and gentle.

I lapsed into sleep but not for long. A loud commotion outside the room roused me and the bolts to the doors clicked open. I immediately covered my eyes and sat up. I recognized the voice of Imad Mughniya.

As he squatted down on my mattress he said, "You are going home in a few hours. But first, we must move your friends." We chatted about inconsequential matters while I saw, beneath the blindfold, the lower legs and feet of other hostages parading past my cell. Everyone appeared to be moving out; subsequently I learned it was only one more masquerade. The marching feet were strictly to fool me, and the other captives remained at this location another three months.

My joy curdled suddenly as Mughniya unexpectedly raised an old specter. "Your name, Jacobsen. That's a Jewish name, isn't it?"

As calmly as possible I reiterated that mine was a Danish name, spelled with an *e*. I added that if it had an *o* it would be Swedish. I caught a whiff of cigarette smoke as he exhaled. Silent moments passed and then he said, "We will talk about it later, but it really doesn't matter."

We had been talking in English and he seemed fluent. But then he called for Sayid to translate. Speaking in Arabic, he now gave me a message for President Reagan and instructions on how I should personally travel to Kuwait and seek the release of the Dawa prisoners.

Slowly, he dictated the procedures of my release. When ordered to leave the van, I was to take off my blindfold and keep my eyes closed tight. After waiting for a minute I could look straight ahead and then walk to the wall. I would then pretend to urinate and after a few minutes face left and walk to the U.S. Embassy.

"Do you mean the place in East Beirut?" So far as I knew that was the only U.S. Embassy in operation. The old one in West Beirut had been abandoned after the car bomb attack of April 18, 1983.

"No, no, in West Beirut," they insisted. "There are still security forces on duty there." The place adjoined the American University. The housing shortage, thanks to the intermittent shelling, firefights and car bombs, meant that squatters hunkered down in any unoccupied structure, including damaged buildings or those under construction. Grateful for a roof overhead, the squatters would occupy these places even though they were without running water or sewers. The refugees and homeless usually tapped into the electric lines that lead to nearby houses. Since no one in Beirut paid power bills anymore, the neighbors never complained. To prevent interlopers, building owners hired security guards.

"Above all," sternly commanded the Mughniya, "you must not go into the Riviera Hotel, because the Syrians are there. We do not want the Syrians to take credit for your release. If you make this mistake and they do claim to have saved you, we will harm your friends. Do you understand?"

I nodded vigorously. I was aware of the deep-seated antipathy toward the Syrians. The Shiites considered them too worldly, a thieving bunch, and made fun of them by jabbering away in the high-pitched voices they insisted typified the Syrian way of talking.

I absorbed all of this material as Mughniya chain-smoked, fouling my cell. Abruptly, he ended his monologue and through Sayid now said, "Forget my instructions about Kuwait. Go home, see your family, have a good vacation and then come back to work as the director of the American University of Beirut Hospital. We need you and you will be safe and protected from all further harm." On that note he stood up and left without further comment.

Once he departed, the crew who had watched over me for so long came to celebrate. Mokmoud, Fadl, and Abu Ali joined Sayid in hugging me and bestowing traditional Arab kisses on my cheeks. They bubbled with pleasure at my imminent release. They begged my forgiveness for what they had done. They assured me the kidnapping and my long captivity was not aimed at me personally. It was only a job and they always sought to be kind and protective.

Aware I was divorced and considering a new life with

Kerrie, they advised, "Go home, get married and come back to spend your honeymoon in West Beirut. We will protect you." I burst out laughing. Even they had to smile at the naivete of the suggestion.

Still maintaining the fiction of shifting the other hostages, they told me I would have to wait several hours before the actual release. I was given a choice of napping or sitting around talking. I was too excited to sleep so those who were changing from guards to "friends" remained with me. We exchanged the kind of farewells appropriate to such an occasion, although to an outsider the sentiments, considering the previous seventeen months, might have sounded weird.

To Sayid I said, "I trust that someday things will be peaceful in Lebanon and that your children will enjoy a safe future. You have endured too much personal sadness and I share your grief with you. Be careful." We both spoke optimistically of the future. My sentiments to Sayid were sincere. My hostility and anger were directed at his superiors and those who failed to make their best efforts to free the hostages. I also chatted with Mokmoud. We discussed the impending birth of his first child. "Mokmoud," I joked. "If it is a boy, he should be named Duwad"—David in Arabic.

Five hours passed in this fashion. Once again, they brought me the new trousers and shoes issued on the other occasions when I was supposed to be freed. Instead of the sport shirt supplied previously, however, this one bore a Sears label. I figured it must be the one Tom Sutherland demanded when we were all transferred from the penthouse to the dungeon cells.

At 6:00 A.M., with my blindfold securely in place, they escorted me up the spiral staircase and out into the faint rays of the early morning sun. Imad Mughniya greeted me. "Do you remember your instructions?"

"Yes," I answered. It surely was not the moment to ask for a clarification or recapitulation.

He offered his benediction. "Goodbye, good luck. Have a safe trip."

Sayid gripped my arm. "Let's go. It's time for you to go home." As he guided me to a van, I stepped over piles of steel building rods and sand—the typical junk that litters the Beirut streets. This time I was delighted to be walking through it. The interior of the van quickly brought me back to the ambience of the city. The stench of death saturated the carpet; God knows what slaughtered animals or murdered humans had been hauled by the vehicle. The odor reminded me of the hospital morgue following a battle in the streets or a car bombing. Once smelled, it is never forgotten.

I lay there while the driver zigzagged over paved and dirt roads. I don't think the aim was to confuse me but instead to avoid militia checkpoints sprinkled through West Beirut. Sayid accompanied me for part of the ride. He again defended the entire business. "Do not think badly of us. We are all soldiers following orders." He repeated the wish that I would return to Beirut and the hospital. "We need you to help us," he said. "Give my regards to Father," meaning Marty Jenco. "He is a good man."

I responded as neutrally as possible. "I hope someday we will meet under better circumstances. I hope you and your children survive and can grow up free of injustice."

Then, he instructed, "In a few moments we will change guards. The new men will be with you for a short distance. When it is time to get out of the van, remember to keep your eyes shut when you take off your blindfold. Do not open them until you face the wall. Be careful. May Allah protect you. Goodbye."

He hardly finished speaking before the van halted. The exchange of guards required but a few seconds and then the van sped down the road. An unfamiliar voice said, "Take off your blindfold, keep your eyes closed and sit up." I complied. The vehicle stopped; the side door slid open. Someone pushed me out and I took my first steps as a free man in 532 days.

I saw the wall, stepped over to it, stood there for two minutes and now headed left. To the east, the mountains stood out against a rainwashed and clear sky. In the other direction, sequins of sunbeams dappled the deep blue Mediterranean. The brightness of nature seemed to bless the day, except the same sun had shone on the darkest hours of my life.

I heard dull booms out at sea as the Beirut fishermen ignited explosives to stun their catch. I was on the inland side of the Avenue de Paris and my path skirted rolls of barbed wire, garbage, puddles of rainwater, and neat piles of raked leaves.

Across the divided highway, beyond the ragged palms of the center island, parked cars lined the curb. The aroma of Arabic coffee brewed on small trucks selling refreshments wafted to my nose. Joggers, some accompanied by dogs on leashes, passed me in both directions. They moved at a pace barely above a walk. The Lebanese are not much for athletics but their warm-up suits were stylish and beautifully tailored.

This site, on the coastal highway, is where I was released.

The Riviera Hotel, which served as headquarters for Terry Waite when he negotiated the hostages, was supposedly controlled by the Syrians, although I later learned it fell under the domain of the Druse militia.

Suddenly it struck me that I might be recognized. I hoped not. There were those who might perceive an advantage in my death. The Druse, Sunnis, Lebanese Christians, Israelis, and Syrians could all exploit my demise as a means of discrediting Hizballah and the Shiites. This last day was the second most dangerous of the hostage ordeal; the first, of course, was the day of the kidnapping.

Now I realized I was in front of the Riviera Hotel. I saw a pair of soldiers, armed, dressed in fatigues. I remembered my instructions. Those must be the Syrians, to be avoided at all costs. I directed my gaze away from them. I told myself, "Do not look at them again. Do not change the pace of your walk. You do not want to attract their attention." I plodded on, leaving them behind.

I passed rows of drab stone and concrete block apartments. Steadily, I approached the site of the bombed-out U.S. Embassy. "Oh, Lord," I silently beseeched. "I'm so close. Don't let a stray bullet get me now. Not after all I've been through. I am fit enough to resist but I cannot outrun a bullet. Please, God, don't let somebody else pick me up before I get to the Embassy."

Panic and terror struck. I felt a sharp tap on my shoulder. I stopped dead. A voice in broken English commanded, "Do not turn around. Read note. Wait one minute." He slipped a scrap in my hand. I estimated sixty seconds and then glanced at the paper. It said, "You walk too far. Turn back one hundred meters."

Relief flooded over me. I was still free and my kidnappers, ironically, had remained on the scene to *protect* me. I understood the new instructions. I had failed to recognize the U.S. Embassy they designated because it was a new building put up to replace the old one. The original embassy had been abandoned after the 1983 bombing. It had been replaced by this building but when officials decided it was too vulnerable to attacks, the Embassy moved to a third home in East Beirut. The second site was well set back from the road. Furthermore, there was no sign identifying it to passersby. The same two soldiers stood nearby. I could not decide whether they were Syrians but I could not take the pressure any longer. I decided to turn myself in no matter who they were.

I accosted them, stuck out my hand and announced, "Hi, I'm David Jacobsen, the American hostage from the American University of Beirut."

As a declaration of identity it fell flat. Neither spoke English. But one of them summoned a superior, the sergeant of the guard. His sweet words were, "We are the security force for the Embassy. Quick, get inside. There is a lot of metal in the air today." Relief overwhelmed me. They were not Syrians but Lebanese employed by the United States.

In the building a tall, slender young officer in a black leather jacket took charge. Someone served me a cup of hot coffee while he telephoned the U.S. Embassy in East Beirut, which was still operating. The word was to sit tight for a few minutes and they would call back on how to proceed.

I felt as if I were still trapped in a world I could not control. I tried to figure out what I should do with myself while I waited for the Embassy to contact us. I asked to use the telephone and tried to reach my former deputy at the AUB, Ahmed Nasrallah. The call went through the AUB switchboard and the operator paged him but he failed to respond. I preferred not to use my name because the news would spread to a thousand people, but there was no avoiding it. I gave my name and the number where Ahmed could reach me. When he called back, he, of course, was full of questions. I told him I could not speak but would he please see if he could find my passport, briefcase, picture albums, and several other sentimental items I had left in my apartment seventeen months before.

After I hung up I felt so restless I thought of stepping outside for some more fresh, free air. The security officer demurred. "There's too much metal in the air," he reminded me.

Soon the Embassy responded. It organized a convoy of five vehicles. Out of the twenty-five Lebanese nationals employed by the United States every single one on duty had volunteered to make the dangerous round-trip journey across the green line. The participants came from every segment of the country's major groups—Christians, Druse, Sunni, and Shiite Moslems.

The vehicles arrived at about 10:00 A.M. and they loaded me into the third car in the line. Two Marines were in the front seat and the military attaché sat beside me in the back. The first car in the procession was naturally designated the leader, the last the chase car. The second and fourth were packed with heavily armed security people. The parade wound and weaved through the streets, with the other cars sometimes changing position but my vehicle always remaining in the middle. To clear the right of way at intersections, someone would fire an M-16 into the air as we approached the crossing. It was the same system used by ambulances on their emergency runs. There is nothing like gunfire to break up a traffic jam.

The drive to East Beirut lasted thirty minutes and delivered me to the residence of the U.S. Ambassador. He greeted me at the door, "Hi, I'm John Kelly. How are you? Would you like coffee or tea?" Now I really felt free. I was with friends, in the bosom of the American government.

A colonel on the staff arrived and a preliminary debriefing followed. Everything now happened so fast it tended to blur. I chatted with Ambassador Kelly, who had only been in the country for three months but quickly demonstrated to me a strong understanding of the factions and different mentalities that drove the various forces.

I wanted to telephone Eric to personally give him the news. But the call would not go through. Finally, we tried through the State Department in Washington, which relayed a message to Eric. Only then did I discover that in my excitement I transposed the numbers for his telephone, making it impossible to reach him. At that moment he was out and only later heard the news on his answering machine tape.

From the Ambassador's residence a car carried me to the Embassy itself, situated on a protected hillside with its own airstrip. To my great delight I met in person the gentle giant who had sought to free us, Terry Waite. Our conversation, consisting of my thanks and his deprecation of his efforts, indicated the emotional context of the moment. He and the Ambassador asked if I minded waiting a day or so in the event that another hostage might be released. I answered, "I will stay, a day, a week, a month if it will enable someone else to be set free."

The day stretched out and my daze, engendered in part by lack of sleep, continued. I still cannot remember what I ate but I will swear it was the best food I had in seventeen months. At some point in the afternoon I indulged myself in a prolonged hot shower. It was difficult to tear myself away from a luxury that I had once regarded as mine by birthright.

The U.S. Embassy in East Beirut is covered with netting that protects against rockets, mortar shells, bombs and rocks. (Courtesy AP/Wide World Photos)

Following dinner and some post-meal drinks, I retired at about 10:00 P.M. Clean sheets and a soft sleep-inducing mattress awaited me. But when I lay down I was totally uncomfortable. I had grown accustomed to a thin pad on a floor. As much as I tossed and shifted my body I could not relax. I would have resorted to the floor but how would Ambassador Kelly react if he looked in and discovered me in that position. He would think I fell out of bed!

My wake-up call was for 5:00 A.M. and I probably managed to nod off for only an hour or two at the most. None of the items Ahmed Nasrallah finally managed to locate caught up with me until weeks after I left Lebanon. Therefore, I still wore Tom's shirt along with the chocolate brown trousers and Italian shoes supplied by my captors. Because I would be leaving for chillier climes, Kelly gave me one of his sweaters. We traveled out to a maximum security area by the air strip. Fences, barbed wire, and men packing automatic weapons surrounded the area. We rendezvoused in a single-story building. Some secretaries and other Embassy employees were scattered about. Ambassador Kelly and Terry Waite were on hand and everyone sampled a buffet breakfast while awaiting the arrival of helicopters.

An enthusiastic man in his late thirties or early forties, wearing a safari style jump suit, approached me and identified himself as being with the National Security Adviser's office. "My boss is coming in. He'll want to meet you and talk to you. His name is William P. Goode. He's a dynamo, a real workaholic."

I built up an image of a physical giant who would instantly dominate the scene. And when the choppers landed, I was not prepared for the rather slightly built fellow in matching beige pants and safari jacket who accosted me, "Hi, I'm Ollie North, from the White House." I realized this was the "William P. Goode" I had heard about.

Our conversation was brief. Lots of "Nice to have you home," "Glad to be here" stuff. Ollie explained to me that their expectations of another man's release had been dashed. He thanked me for agreeing to wait but now it was time to leave. We loaded into the helo. I sat between Waite and North while a Marine guard crouched in the jump seat.

The roar of the engines during the forty-minutes flight to Cyprus destroyed any further attempts at conversation. I passed a note to North inquiring, "Is it true that the inflight movie will be *Bedtime for Bonzo*?" He scribbled back, "I won't tell the Boss about that." He shared the notes with Waite, who chuckled. I thought about those left behind, how desperately I wanted Terry and Tom with me. My head had started to clear as the numbness caused by the sudden flash of freedom ebbed. I had reported to Ollie North how the kidnappers tried to fool me into believing they had moved the others upon my release. I volunteered to sit with any intelligence staff people and try to pick out our location precisely.

At the Larnaca Airport on Cyprus, an official delegation consisting of a U.S. Air Force General and the U.S. Ambassador to Cyprus welcomed me. Terry Waite had arranged for a press conference. It would be the first of many, and I approached the microphone with great trepidation. I wondered what I should say. Back in our cell, Terry Anderson and I had talked about the problems that could occur during what Terry referred to as a "media gang-bang." They would

At the Larnaca airport on Cyprus, wearing Ambassador Kelly's sweater, I enjoyed a laugh with Terry Waite. (Courtesy AP/Wide World Photos)

all be hungry for something to please their editor:
pers, or pull viewers to the TV set.

In my few minutes at the microphone, I cor
erroneous impression drawn from videos and le
duced in captivity. "I'm darned proud to be an Ame
proud of the American government and the Amer
ernmental employees, and I would also hope that a
cans would be proud of our government also." A
had been critical of the apparent absence of effor
my freedom, I now recognized that, thanks to Olli
was free.

I paid homage to Terry Waite. "It is a great pleas
this guy here. He gave us hope, he gave us hop
would be free men again. And we love this guy."
the Twenty-seventh Psalm and how it had helpe
me. I recited the last verse. "I believe that I sh;
goodness of the Lord in the land of the living. T
Lord. Have faith. Do not despair. Trust in the Lo
there is goodness." I said I would never have sur
not retained my faith.

I reported that Terry Anderson and Tom Suthe
both well. I noted, however, that efforts to free th
be increased for their situation was most unplea
Waite had organized the session and served as mo
mercifully kept the proceedings short. Newspape
the press conference described me as "hagga:
shaven" and indeed, anyone who knew me was t
by my hollow-cheeked face and the thousand-y
the battle-fatigued soldier. My ordeal as a ho
physical imprint that lasted for months. But I in
felt strong and remarked, "Anybody want to chal
a six-mile jaunt around this airport?"

Now we moved over to a sleek, dark red L
zigzag blue and tan stripes on its nose. As we we
aboard, the Marine escort from the helicopter h
cap. It belonged to Ollie North and on the bill he
the words of the Twenty-seventh Psalm. Out of

reporters, he had been listening to me. The flight crew provided another souvenir, a velcro patch with the American flag.

On the trip from Larnaca to a U.S. base in Wiesbaden, Germany, I wallowed in comfort. The most beautiful stewardess I've ever seen toted platters of hors d'oeuvres, grapes, kiwi fruit, sandwiches, and drinks. Again I thought of the accustomed diet of rice, pita, cheese, and olives being served to Terry and Tom. Because of my appearance, the stewardess looked as if she might burst into tears.

The jet soared above the clouds, even higher than several 747s, creating spectacular views of the scenery. I owed the luxury not to my government, which still seemed ambivalent about dealing with me, but to Gen. Richard Secord. He had leased the Lear from a Swiss company.

In Wiesbaden came my first teary-eyed, yet exuberant reunion as Eric, Paul, and Diane met me there. I learned that not only had Paul married but my daughter was now Mrs. Duggan and I could soon expect grandchildren. Kerrie also greeted me. She had been reluctant to intrude upon the family. But Terry Waite, in his typically kind and loving fashion, had persuaded her that she would be most welcome.

Before Waite left the military hospital at Wiesbaden, he, Kerrie, and I shared the biggest banana split I had ever seen. Kerrie remarked, "Only Americans could eat such a mixture of ice cream, fruit, chocolate syrup, whipped cream, and nuts." But all three of us dug into the huge bowl of goodies. The Briton, who had never sampled a dessert like this before, remarked, "By Jove, this really is delicious. You colonists have one good idea." And then we said goodbye to him.

At Wiesbaden in the base hospital doctors examined me and pronounced my physical condition quite good. The occasional blood in my stool, which I feared augured cancer, came from an uncomplicated hemorrhoid. And even though the prescription by Dr. Hallak for medication to treat my hypertension ran out after only a few weeks, I no longer suffered from high blood pressure. A salt-free, low-protein,

On the balcony of the U.S. Air Force Hospital at Wiesbaden, Germany, my sons stood with me, Paul behind me and Eric on my left.

high-carbohydrate diet and all of those stress reduction exercises had cured my condition.

Prior to my kidnapping I jogged six miles a day at the AUB campus. The routine included four miles on the track, where Tom Sutherland clocked me while enjoying his cocktail, one mile on the road to the upper campus and then a loop past the classrooms to bring me back on to the track for some final laps. I carried 176 pounds but I was really fit. I also lifted weights with Mehdi, Tom Sutherland's police guard, who happened not to show up the day they grabbed Tom. Sometimes I ran with Mehdi, who was at least twenty-five years younger. He would gradually pick up the pace and at the four-mile mark, my body would scream, "slow down!" Then Mehdi would leave me in the dust.

I only dropped three pounds in captivity but my muscles atrophied and a fat belly replaced them. The push-ups and sit-ups enabled me to retain upper body strength. Once I returned home to California, I joined a health club and embarked on a vigorous program of weight lifting and exercise machines. I also started running on the beach five, even ten miles. But I've never regained the speed I once enjoyed for at least four miles.

Once the doctors in Wiesbaden decided I was healthy, I had more immediate goals than a return to a fitness regimen. I was determined to do whatever I could to help free my associates. My release date was November 3, 1986, and I spent two days at U.S. military hospital in Wiesbaden. During this time I also went through extensive debriefings. When the medical and governmental investigators finished with me, I flew home on November 6.

Chapter 15

Aftermath

From those who debriefed me in Washington, from various accounts in the media, and finally as a result of the Iran-Contra Congressional hearings I learned the basic facts of how Ben Weir, Marty Jenco, and I were freed.

Except for the nine-month period at the end of 1979 during which the Iranians held the staff of our embassy hostage, the Israelis had surreptitiously engaged in arms sales to Iran. After the Iraqi invasion of Iran, the beleaguered country desperately needed certain weapons to halt the assault. Various agents, including the notorious Iranian wheeler-dealer Manucher Ghorbanifar, Saudi entrepreneur Adnan Khashoggi, and some Israelis, suggested to the CIA and the National Security Adviser's office that the United States could regain influence in Iran and possibly obtain release of hostages in Lebanon by doing business with Iran. Furthermore, people like Ghorbanifar alleged that the Iranian regime was losing its popularity and that by a judicious application of U.S. largesse, a more congenial bunch might be able to take over. This aspect proved to be a figment of Ghorbanifar's imagination.

Discussions within the U.S. government about taking this approach began in the summer of 1985, a few months after I was first taken captive. According to Michael Ledeen, a consultant to the National Security Council and a longtime agent for various U.S. international operations, a top priority was the release of William Buckley, the CIA man. The American authorities at the time did not realize he was already dead.

The first deal arranged by Ollie North's boss, National Security Adviser Robert McFarlane, was a sale of five hundred TOW missiles that would make their way to Iran via Israel. To guarantee the release of a hostage, the shipment was to be broken into two lots. Upon the arrival in late August 1985 of the first one hundred TOWs in Tabriz, the Iranian Revolutionary Guards grabbed the merchandise and instead of arranging for a hostage swap put Ghorbanifar, who accompanied the shipment, through an intense interrogation.

The delivery of the missiles, however, convinced the Iranians that, through Ghorbanifar, the United States would supply the desired weapons. North became deeply involved in the subsequent transfer of the remaining four hundred and eight missiles. According to Ledeen, a meeting of Ayatollah Khomeini's son Ahmad, certain factions within Iran, and Lebanese Hizballah leaders ended with Ahmad ordering the release of one hostage in return for the TOWs. The American government was told by its Israeli contact, David Kinche, to pick a hostage. McFarlane chose William Buckley; we hostages nominated Terry Anderson, and Hizballah sent home Ben Weir. According to Ledeen, Weir's attitude so angered Ollie North and others that Ledeen jokingly asked Ghorbanifar if it were possible to return Weir in exchange for "a patriotic American."

Ben Weir, of course, could confirm the death of William Buckley, which eliminated negotiations to gain the release of a valuable CIA agent. However, there was still a small push of public opinion for the remaining hostages. Congressman Bob Dornan from my state constantly agitated for the government to make an effort to free us. The Rev. Canon Samir Habiby, and the Rev. Canon Harold Hultgren and Bishop Allen of the American Episcopal Church actively lobbied the White House and the Archbishop of Canterbury during the entire time I was a hostage. The Kiwanis Club of Alhambra, California, campaigned vigorously on my behalf. Patients at the Hylond Convalescent Hospital in Westminster, California, although prisoners to the infirmities of age and illness, wrote letters seeking to influence policy. An employee there, Nancy Fontaine, organized a network for support of hostage families. Such actions, along with those of Jeremy Levin, Ben Weir, and their relatives, as well as the kin of remaining hostages, I believe goaded the policy makers in the White House to continue negotiations.

Oliver North now became the point man for an expanded operation. He enlisted Gen. Richard Secord, a retired U.S. Air Force officer, to assist in the complicated transfer of Hawk surface-launched anti-aircraft missiles out of the Israeli inventory at a price to the Iranians of $24 million. Working with Secord and North was the former's Iranian-born partner, Albert Hakim.

This outing, however, proved a near disaster. The first effort was aborted when the aircraft carrying the eighteen Hawks was just about halfway to its destination. Then the Iranians were enraged when the missiles finally arrived on November 28, 1985. Not only did the Hawks still have their Israeli markings, but when one was tested it proved defective. Furthermore, the Iranians had believed they were to receive a new improved version of the missile. The remaining seventeen Hawks were returned and to assuage the outraged customers, most of the $24 million was immediately refunded.

In December 1985, Adm. John Poindexter replaced McFarlane as National Security Adviser and, according to Ronald Reagan's memoirs (*An American Life*), argued that the arms-for-hostages arrangements should continue. Both Secretary of Defense Caspar Weinberger and Secretary of State George Shultz "argued forcefully" against the policy.

The first one hundred TOW missiles from a planned shipment of five hundred and eight had arrived in Iran in late August 1985. The remaining four hundred and eight went September 14. Ben Weir was released on September 15, so it would seem that this shipment was the ransom for him.

As 1985 drew to a close, Ollie North and others urged that

237

Robert "Bud" McFarlane (left), the National Security Adviser for President Ronald Reagan, and who began the arms-for-hostages deals, resigned in December of 1985, to be succeeded by Vice-Admiral John Poindexter (right). Poindexter continued the trading with the Iranians that resulted in my freedom. (Courtesy AP/Wide World Photos)

several thousand TOWs be sold to Iran in order to show good faith. (TOW is an acronym for "tube-launched, optically tracked, wire-guided." The TOW is a portable anti-tank weapon.) President Reagan approved the deal. North and his associates began the intricate maneuvers designed to liberate hostages and provide added financing for the Contras, diverting the profits from missile sales to funds for the Nicaraguans. The sale of one thousand TOW missiles in February 1986 produced revenues for the Contras but freed no hostages.

On May 25, 1986, an American delegation led by McFarlane (as a consultant), Ollie North, and several others, plus an Israeli representative, arrived in Tehran aboard a plane that also hauled replacement parts for weapons. The U.S. aim was to determine what was required for a genuine renewal of United States-Iran relations as well as the prospects for hostage releases.

The Iranians showed considerable hostility and little inclination to moderate their attitude toward the United States Furthermore, they insisted the Israelis must withdraw from their Golan Heights positions overlooking the Syrian and Lebanese borders, and that Kuwait must free the Dawa prisoners. McFarlane flatly rejected the demands. Quite possibly, Hizballah in Lebanon, which had turned over Ben Weir at the behest of Iran, now asked that it be compensated. The fine, cruel hand of Mughniya undoubtedly lay behind such a proposal.

McFarlane's hosts maintained that if details could be worked out and a plane loaded with Hawk spare parts could be dispatched, four hostages would be freed. McFarlane concluded that their offer was bogus. He had orders not to deliver any more weaponry without the actual liberation of captives. His patience exhausted, he ordered the American party home.

Apparently, the Iranians were as desperate for military hardware as we were for our freedom. As a result of conversations with various parties, including North, Marty Jenco received his freedom on July 26, 1986. By August 4, in recognition of the action, U.S.-made weapons arrived in Iran.

The Iranians grumbled about price gouging and maintained that some of the items did not work or were unsuitable. They wanted help in deposing Saddam Hussein of Iraq and they still wanted the Dawa prisoners freed. But most importantly, the arms-for-hostages deals were back on track. Another one thousand TOWs arrived in Iran at the end of October 1986. And as a result, I took my freedom walk on November 2.

According to Richard Secord—and I consider his sources reliable—the KGB knew about our arms sales to Iran in exchange for hostages and they also knew about the funds being diverted to the Contras. Because they supported the Sandinista government in Nicaragua, they wanted to do whatever possible to halt aid to the Contras. So the KGB tipped off the Syrians, who sent two intelligence agents to one of the Beirut daily newspapers. The daily refused to print the story so the Syrian agents went to the publisher of another newspaper, *Al Shiraa*. At first, he also refused but the Syrians returned the following day and announced "You don't print that story, we make you dead." He printed the story, including details about McFarlane's visit to Tehran, and that is what broke the Irangate scandal and ended the arms-for-hostages process. Indeed, it would be more than three years before any other American was unfettered.

Following my brief stay in Frankfurt I flew home for a series of celebrations and consultations with Washington officials. Naturally, the height of all of the ceremonial affairs was the White House reception. In addition to President Reagan and his wife Nancy those present included Admiral Poindexter, Vice President Bush, Reagan's chief of staff Donald Regan, and a number of representatives of the State Department.

Retired Air Force General Richard Secord, who played an instrumental role in the deals with the Iranians, joined me in a discussion about the plight of the hostages.

On the flight from Germany to the States, Kerrie, and John Adams of the State Department, flanked me.

Everyone came across as warm and friendly. They asked how I managed to survive. I told of the strength derived from religious faith, from my companions and in a backhanded way from the cold rebuff by Henry Kissinger. In hindsight, I explained, his remarks fired me up, made me determined to make it. I congratulated the President for never having employed Kissinger in any official capacity.

I remarked to Vice President Bush that the second lowest point in my captivity came with his public declaration of no negotiations. I recall Bush's distinct lack of reaction to my remark; one of the aides abruptly changed the subject and the conversation moved on. I described those who had been imprisoned with me, who our captors were, talked about the irresponsibility of the media and how it led directly to my beating. I explained to Mr. Reagan that, although the Hizballah people sought the release of the Dawa men in Kuwait, they were aware it was unlikely. But at this point, they needed to talk with American representatives and work out a face-saving resolution. It was imperative for our kid-

On November 6, 1986 I chatted with President Reagan in the Oval Office of the White House.

To David Jacobsen – With every good wish & Warm Regard.
Nancy & Ronald Reagan

The President autographed this picture of me with him and the First Lady.

The entire Jacobsen clan posed with the Reagans: from left to right, my son Paul, his wife Lori, my daughter Diane, her husband Jake, the President, me, Mrs. Reagan, my daughter-in-law Cathy, her husband and my son Eric, and Kerrie.

nappers to show their supporters some tangible result of their actions. I was somewhat surprised by the lack of knowledge demonstrated by these individuals who occupied the top posts in the government.

I kept expecting the President to cut short my visit but he seemed in no hurry. We adjourned to the Rose Garden for the standard photo opportunity. During the din of shutters clicking and whirring, some of the media shouted questions. One of them raised a sensitive issue concerning negotiations. Before the President could answer, I gently nudged him aside, usurping his prerogative. In a loud, firm voice, I said, "Irresponsible speculation like your question nearly resulted in my death. You have endangered the lives of hostages remaining in Lebanon. I don't want that to happen and I don't think you want that on your conscience. So in the name of God back off."

Every released hostage hesitates to speak out, fearing that his remarks may be misunderstood or that a journalist will put a spin on the meaning of the statement that will arouse the fury of the kidnappers. I was ignorant of the details of the arms deals with the Iranians when the White House Rose Garden incident occurred. And I foresaw great problems for those still held if reporters speculated about whatever details they could ferret out. Subsequent events proved how right I was.

Afterward, the Reagans insisted on chatting further. The First Lady picked up my theme about the problems caused by the publication or broadcast of rumors. She asked if I had any ideas on how to control the media. I had none. In a free country one must depend upon the discretion and judgment of the journalists. All we could do was to warn them in advance of the potential consequences of punditry and over-zealous pursuit of a scoop.

When the reception ended, Ollie North insisted I meet his staff, including the soon-to-be-famous Fawn Hall. The people who worked for North obviously revered him. They were extremely gracious to me. And by now I had learned from various sources that it was North who had been engaged in behind-the-scenes bargaining with Iranian power brokers on behalf of the hostages. Within a few days the entire affair revved up with the added spice of deals that helped finance the Contras battling the Sandinista government in Nicaragua.

The AUB paid for my stay in Washington at the Jefferson Hotel. Dr. Robert Schuller, whom I consider a great Christian leader, befriended me on my return to the States. When I went to the White House, I still had no credit cards and no access to money to pay my expenses. Through him, my family and I flew home from Washington aboard a corporate jet. As usual, the State Department showed no interest in my immediate welfare. While I was in Washington I had an opportunity to meet with relatives of William Buckley. I was able to comfort them with a true account of his last days and to assure them that from what I and the others knew, he had never betrayed his country no matter what torment he endured.

I spent days working with various counter-espionage and intelligence people. In Wiesbaden the crew that interrogated me consisted of eight officials representing, respectively, the FBI, CIA, the State Department and the Defense Department. Between the debriefings in Germany and those upon my return home, I passed a total of about seven full days, eight hours apiece, providing detailed information to government officials. I would have put in even more time if it would have helped because I was eager to contribute anything that might aid in a rescue effort. I knew I had to offer as much data as possible, quickly, because critical days would pass while a mission was planned.

We had not been moved for twenty-nine days after Ben Weir was released, and nine days elapsed after Marty Jenco departed before we were taken elsewhere. In fact, after I was freed, my former associates stayed put for ninety-one days! I am convinced that the logistics of a Beirut rescue mission were not insurmountable. The strike force could hit the beach and arrive at locations where the hostages were held within ten minutes, either by helicopter or surface vehicle. And I am sure there were plenty of potential confederates already on the ground in Beirut who could be enlisted in support. All we had to do was determine where to strike and the going price for on-scene help.

I peered at aerial photographs of the Beirut airport area, trying to pick out the location of our prison. I was unsuccessful. I drew floorplans and maps of estimated locations. I described what I heard while incarcerated, how Terry Anderson had figured out the neighborhood in which we were held and placed our dungeon on the coastal road. Possibly, with this information, espionage agents in Beirut could pinpoint the site. But our intelligence from Lebanon was terrible. The government had no one on the scene capable of a reliable survey. There were numerous hustlers in Beirut who peddled worthless tips or ran scams to squeeze out some dollars. Indeed, Ollie North and his associates believed we were scattered all over the city until Marty Jenco reported that we were together in a single building.

My efforts on this track were academic. The fallout after a failed rescue of the hostages in Iran during President Carter's administration, and the many dead and wounded from the bombings of the U.S. Embassy and the marine barracks in Beirut, had made officials gun-shy.

At any rate, the debriefing team was an impressive bunch. Their professionalism and attention to detail led me to entertain hope for the release of my fellow captives. After the debriefings I continued to consult with members of the team by telephone whenever some new piece of information occurred to me or came my way. We stay in touch and I consider some of them good friends to this day. In my opinion, if the hostage-rescue efforts were once and for all delegated to a team of pros from the FBI and CIA they would have a much greater chance of success.

The clothes I wore home, including Tom Sutherland's favorite shirt, became part of the physical evidence that might someday be used in trials of the terrorists. Based on Ali's gaffe of "my Wolverines," I studied the yearbooks from the University of Michigan to see if I could identify Ali. Also, there were tidbits of information on Sayid. We knew his wife had been treated at the AUB hospital in June 1985. He, too, had been brought in with shrapnel wounds early in September 1986.

To find out Sayid's real identity I enlisted the help of an FBI agent. I wrote a letter to someone whom I knew worked at the U.S. Embassy in Beirut and the agent arranged for it to be carried in the diplomatic pouch. Inside the envelope addressed to the Embassy person, I inserted a sealed letter to be forwarded to an employee of the AUB hospital whom I knew I could trust. I told the individual at the hospital the approximate date Sayid's wife arrived at the emergency room and the fact that she had succumbed while pregnant. I also included information about Sayid and his treatment. My contact was to match the name of a critically injured pregnant woman who died in June or July with the name of a man suffering abdominal wounds in September 1986. There would have been no reason for Sayid or his wife to have concealed their real names when they were treated. The outcome was that we obtained accurate information on Sayid. As a kind of unexpected bonus, we also obtained a complete medical record on Mughniya, which would be invaluable to confirm his identification if he is ever apprehended.

The State Department's Ambassador for Counter-terrorism, Paul Bremer, who had rebuffed every effort I made to contribute information or suggestions, learned what I had done behind his back. He reacted like a bureaucrat cut out of the loop. He argued I had endangered the lives of innocent hospital employees and wrongfully inveigled access to the diplomatic pouch. He demanded that the FBI severely reprimand the agent who facilitated my scheme.

Bremer's behavior convinced me beyond any doubt that the State Department would not be able to work effectively to resolve the hostage situation. Punishment of an FBI agent for a creative step toward gathering evidence struck me as inexcusable. I can accept the stance of professionals who do not want amateurs to become officially involved. But the refusal to accept any help or suggestions from outsiders is, to me, just a case of the fourth graders barring third graders from their sandpile.

Through photographs of individuals associated with Islamic Jihad I actually identified Imad Mughniya. And I learned the reason for his lethal dedication to the cause. Born in a small Shiite village near the Lebanese port city of Tyre, he was the son of Sheik Muhammad Jawad Mughniya, a mullah of considerable repute. The elder Mughniya had published an acclaimed book, *The Enturbanned Spy*, which denounced Iranian mullah Imam Moussa Al Sadr. The latter

Imad Mughniya masterminded my kidnapping, made hostages of Terry Anderson, Tom Sutherland, and Terry Waite among others, and directed many acts of terrorism including the hijacking of TWA Flight 847. While I was his captive, Mughniya was clean-shaven. This photograph, obtained by the Paris-based publication MEDNEWS, was copied from Mughniya's 1983 passport. (Courtesy MEDNEWS)

had preached the virtues of Moslem fundamentalism and promoted the idea of an Islamic state ruled by a supreme Ayatollah. *The Enturbanned Spy* counseled against a government subject to the whims of a mere mortal vulnerable to human weaknesses.

Moussa Al Sadr actually founded the Shiite Amal movement. But he disappeared under mysterious circumstances after a visit to Colonel Khadafi's Libya. The Ayatollah Khomeini assumed leadership of Shiite fundamentalism and Imad Mughniya, the son of the mullah who had bucked the movement, rebelled against the beliefs of his father and joined it. The success of the Islamic revolution in Iran meant that, like other Lebanese Shiites, the younger Mughniya no longer needed to settle for a subordinate status to the Sunni Moslems and Maronite Christians. Imad Mughniya received the post of security chief for the leading Moslem fundamentalist, Sheik Fadlallah.

Forced to move to the Beirut suburbs after the Israeli invasion in 1982, Mughniya met a physically handicapped young man with a streak of engineering genius. Mustapha Badr-el-Din joined the Mughniya clan when Mughniya married his sister.

Badr-el-Din demonstrated his revolutionary zeal through his skill at manufacturing explosive devices. He is believed to have constructed the device that demolished the U.S. Marine barracks in Beirut. He was among the Dawa group that infiltrated Kuwait and sought to blow up key installations in 1983. Along with the other conspirators, Badr-el-Din was captured and lodged in a Kuwaiti prison.

His freedom became the terrorist cause of Mughniya, who began with the abortive kidnapping of Frank Regier and followed up with Jeremy Levin and William Buckley. Mughniya and his men embarked on a reign of terror; by 1987 they had racked up forty-seven violent acts against persons and property with twenty dead (including four Americans) from executions or bombings. The kidnappings, assaults, and hijackings were announced by organizations with different names. Some were proclaimed in the name of Islamic Jihad, others included the Revolutionary Justice Organization, Islamic Holy War for the Liberation of Palestine, the Organization for the Oppressed on Earth—as many as eight overall. But in truth there was only one group responsible. The aliases were intended either to suggest widespread opposition to the West or to disguise the identities of the guilty parties.

Ironically, the Dawa prisoners and the Western hostages shared one common characteristic. Both groups were an asset only as long as they remained alive. It is obvious that a dead hostage holds no value. In the case of the Shiite bombers, the government of Kuwait treated them as hostages and made it clear that any further attempts to assassinate the Emir or perpetrate further terrorism would bring death to those already in prison.

It was Mughniya's misapprehension that his brother-in-law and the others would all be instantly liberated through a simple telephone call from President Reagan to the Emir of Kuwait. Obviously, things don't happen that way and I had the scars to prove it.

Contrary to the handouts from the Department of State insisting that no one knew who the terrorists were, the American government seems to have been well aware of Mughniya's role. Oliver North had fingered Mughniya to my son Eric, for instance. A dispatch carried in the Orange County *Register*, on September 19, 1986, more than six weeks before I was released, reported that Mughniya had visited France in 1985. Alerted by intelligence agents, the United States requested that French security forces arrest him. Although the French tailed the quarry, they failed to grab him, supposedly for lack of evidence that he had participated in the hijacking of TWA 847. My sources in intelligence believe he was involved.

I absorbed all of the information and I accepted the theory that the key to the hostage cells could only be acquired through resolution of the Dawa problem. Meanwhile, my celebrity status palled quite soon. I already knew that the media could show a friendly face and then bite. Eric assumed the job as frontman for interviewers. Although I did not publicly identify the commentator who cost me a savage beating, I refused to appear on any program with him. However, I did talk with other correspondents on the network's evening news show. I learned that Bryant Gumbel, the anchor for the Today Show, after having Eric and Paul on the show, tossed off some contemptuous remarks about them to a magazine reporter. I also crossed him off the acceptable list. Some months after my release, he suddenly surfaced for a brief interview by remote in which I was in California and he in New York. The talk was short and bland.

In view of their public images, neither Dan Rather nor Joan Rivers were as tough as I would have imagined. Their interviews showed warmth and compassion for the hostages. Sitting in a club in Washington, D.C. one night, caught up in piano renditions of Cole Porter tunes, I was approached by a man who introduced himself as Larry King. We fell into talk about music and popular culture. In the course of conversation, he asked if someday I'd appear on his program. Subsequently he invited me on his CNN show and I was delighted by the opportunity to make the case for the Beirut hostages.

I've been critical of some people in the media but I also met many who, within the limitations of a highly competitive business and a premium on time and space, reported in a responsible way. Connie Chung, Lori Singer, Harry Smith, and Paula Zahn of CBS TV, Barney Morris of Los Angeles ABC TV, and Vikki Vargas of NBC TV are among those who come most immediately to my mind.

The worst demonstration of print press irresponsibility occurred in Great Britain. A little more than two weeks after my deliverance I flew to England to meet with Terry Waite at Lambeth Palace, the headquarters for the Anglican Church which sponsored him. Marty Jenco and Ben Weir joined me in expressing our thanks to Waite and others who had risked their prestige and safety for our freedom.

At Lambeth Palace in London, I was reunited with my former cellmates, Marty Jenco and Ben Weir, for the first time since captivity. Also on hand were some of those who worked so hard for our release. From left to right, the Rev. Dr. Charles Cesaretti, then Deputy for Anglican Communion Affairs of the Episcopal Church; Marty Jenco; Ben Weir, the Rev. Canon Samir J. Habiby, then Executive Director of the Presiding Bishops' Fund for World Relief; Terry Waite; myself; Dr. George McGonigle, then Senior Executive Officer of the Episcopal Church. (Courtesy Rev. Samir J. Habiby)

Terry Waite first became involved because his efforts to free hostages in Iran and Libya were duly chronicled in the press. Three separate United States church representatives approached Waite through his sponsor, the Church of England. Ben Weir had worked for the Presbyterian Church's Near East School of Theology in Beirut for three decades. Baptists in America took up the cause of Terry Anderson through the intercession of his sister Peggy Say. And Episcopalians were active on my behalf.

Waite had developed his own contacts in the Middle East and Africa. Working with Terry Waite was a Palestinian-born American, the Reverend Canon Samir Habiby, Past Executive Director of the Episcopal Church's Presiding Bishops Fund for World Relief. Habiby also had excellent contacts in the Middle East. Indeed, while the Church of England paid Waite's salary, all of the expenses for his many trips, his hotel rooms and other costs were met by the Presiding Bishops Fund.

Habiby and Waite and representatives of the various church groups met in London under the auspices of the Archbishop of Canterbury. As a result of the conference, Waite came to the United States to talk with White House officials, including then Vice President George Bush, and top people at the United Nations. The meetings were well publicized because it was important for the kidnappers to know that Waite had the ears and the confidence of leaders in Washington and the international community. Waite was determined to present hostage-taking as an international problem.

There was a session in Geneva with the International Red Cross, attended by Waite, Habiby, a Saudi official and someone designated only as a "guest." The circumlocution disguised the identity of the Kuwaiti Ambassador to Switzerland, who would not officially engage in negotiations concerning the Dawa prisoners. Waite and Habiby also traveled to Rome for a consultation with Vatican authorities concerned specifically with the welfare of Marty Jenco and Terry Anderson.

At the same time, contacts had been established with the Druse leaders in Lebanon for Waite's missions. He had kept his aplomb even though he was forced to wear blindfolds when meeting with representatives of the hostage-takers, and he was surrounded by gunmen.

After I was released on November 2, 1986, and in spite of the growing controversy about the circumstances surrounding the release of the Weir, Jenco and me, Waite decided to return to Beirut and plead the case for Terry Anderson and Tom Sutherland. His itinerary also included a scheduled trip to Kuwait to demonstrate to the kidnappers his willingness to address the question of the Dawa prisoners.

Even as he prepared to leave for Beirut, some newspapers

in London had begun to circulate stories that suggested Waite participated in secret intrigues designed to benefit political ends rather than the humanitarian causes he espoused. During my trip from Beirut to Wiesbaden, and while in Washington, Ollie North had never discussed with me the behind-the-scenes events. Both he and Terry Waite maintained a distance between them throughout the time we were together. The British press, never loathe to think the worst of Americans, even when a victim may be a countryman, had attacked the arms-for-hostages arrangement like starving piranhas coming upon a plump carcass.

To shut up those analysts who implied he had served as a cover for a cloak-and-dagger operation, Waite issued a statement that described his work for the Anglican Church as involving many more matters than the hostages. He spoke of his efforts on behalf of the Church's own Bishop Desmond Tutu and the campaign for justice for "the black and coloured populations" of South Africa. He noted the attempts to alleviate suffering in the Sudan and neighboring countries. He said, "The 1939–45 World War is a most horrible reminder to us of what happens when the value of the individual is forgotten. The whole Jewish people have been scarred by that experience for generations to come. In my own work I try to look with the same compassion on the sufferings of the Arab people, many of who have been driven into hopelessness and despair."

Waite declared he regarded "it as absolutely wrong for innocent people to be used as pawns in a larger political game. Hostage-taking and acts of violence against the innocent are wrong and bring nothing but disgrace to the faith of those who practice such acts, be they Christian, Moslem or Jew."

He addressed himself to the hints of sinister motives for his actions. He squarely opposed secret arrangements and unequivocally stated he would have nothing to do with any deal that seemed to breach the code to which he subscribed. And he remarked that the American authorities, with whom he had dealt, had respected and honored his stance. He warned "the rumor and speculations of the past week have done immense harm," endangering the security of the remaining hostages.

The manifesto sought to establish his role as driven purely by humanitarian desires to serve as a middle-man for the release of the hostages, and to spread an awareness of the grievances of the kidnappers so that their problems might be solved. While the evidence shows that it was the military hardware that bought our freedom, I am convinced that Waite's efforts created a climate which contributed to our well-being. All of us hoped Waite's eloquent presentation would quiet the whispers and end anonymous stories that jeopardized his mission.

Incidentally, while at Lambeth Palace, I enjoyed a pleasant meeting with another former cellmate, Wadgid Duomoni. Smiling, he embraced me and placed a gift in my hands. I said, "Wadgid, I'm thrilled you remembered our conversation. But how on earth did you manage to squeeze a Mercedes into a tie box."

But time continued to drag on for those still locked up in Beirut. I was heartened by Terry Waite's resolve to pursue the matter in spite of the dangers to him. Indeed, reports connecting him to U.S. operations continued to appear.

On January 14, 1987, Waite arrived in Beirut. He took up residence in the Riviera Hotel, which is in the sector controlled by Walid Jumblatt's militia. As in the past, he contacted Dr. Adnan Mroueh, who was the physician to the family of Sheik Fadlallah, spiritual leader of Hizballah. He explained to Mroueh that before he could begin to bargain, he would need to meet personally with some of the hostages. On the other hand, Waite also said that his talks with U.S. and British authorities had indicated a willingness to work toward a solution acceptable to the kidnappers.

It has been reported in some newspapers that Ahmed Nasrallah and Gladys Mouro, the erstwhile object of Joe Cicippio's affections at the AUB hospital, had been among those who saw Waite with Dr. Mroueh. That is not true, although the pair did talk with the physician.

Midway during Waite's stay in Beirut, the *Times* of London printed a damaging story, only a month after Waite's vigorous denial of his links to U.S. government policies and programs. While the piece agreed that Ollie North never informed Waite of his separate effort to trade hostages for arms and divert the profits to the Contra rebels, it nevertheless besmirched Waite. The account attributed to "a highly reliable source" information that "Colonel North arranged for Mr. Waite to be dropped in Lebanon by a U.S. helicopter in the dead of night. The security details which enabled him to enter highly dangerous areas, negotiate with captors, and leave again were all provided by Colonel North."

The writer was dead wrong. During Waite's visits to Lebanon, well-armed Druse forces under command of their leader, Walid Jumblatt, guarded him. The bodyguards escorted Waite everywhere, never leaving his side unless his safety was secured. The Druse militiamen made sure no one followed Waite when he left his hotel for a meeting. They informed the press and other parties that they would shoot out the tires of any vehicle that sought to follow the Druse convoy when it carried Waite. When Waite attended meetings with the physician intermediary, the Druse gunmen remained until the doctor appeared. The presence of the physician, also a Shiite official, guaranteed Waite's person.

Other members of the media reinforced the erroneous account of the *Times. Time* magazine reported frequent contacts between Waite and Ollie North. Once again the press failed to realize how closely Hizballah read the news and how much credence they accorded Western journalists. To be sure, Waite spoke to North as well as many other individuals engaged in the intrigues of the Middle East. Only by talking with people could he accumulate the scraps of information that would provide keys to successful negotiations.

In any event, the publicity and intelligence indicated Waite was at extreme risk. Druse militia boss Wadi Jumblatt

Walid Jumblatt, leader of the Lebanese Druse, tried to provide protection for Terry Waite. (Courtesy AP/Wide World Photos)

had warned Waite that he was now in extreme danger. There were calls from British officials advising him to leave immediately. Canon Habiby telephoned Waite from London urging utmost caution, and not to leave his hotel under any circumstances. Instead, he should return home and work on the U.S. and Kuwaiti aspects. Habiby, in fact, was the last outsider to speak with Waite before he disappeared.

There are two versions of how Waite became one more victim of the terrorists. One account blames it all on an unfortunate sequence of events that undid the strategy designed to safeguard the Anglican emissary. Allegedly, when Waite arrived for a scheduled session with Dr. Mroueh, a genuine medical emergency detained the intermediary. Waite had been instructed never to stay alone anywhere, but he was so anxious to see the negotiator that he remained in the doctor's office. Members of Imad Mughniya's forces appeared and, during the routine search of Waite, discovered a hand-held calculator with a memory device for names and phone numbers. In their ignorance, they presumed this was a homing device. Certainly, they were already suspicious of Waite's motives, thanks to the drumfire of media stories suggesting he was really an American agent.

Rank treachery marks the second explanation. The chief

Accompanied by armed Druse militiamen, Terry Waite strolled along the Beirut waterfront in January 1987, shortly before he was abducted. (Courtesy AP/Wide World Photos)

of the Druse bodyguards, Abu Haytham, supposedly sold out Waite for $500,000. About 7:30 P.M. on the sixth day of his visit to Beirut, Waite, against all advice, went to the building that housed Dr. Mroueh's office and home. Waite insisted that the Hizballah people were becoming spooked by the close watch kept on him, and he refused to allow any guards to accompany him inside. From inside the hallway of the building Waite waved off the militiamen. The site is about one hundred yards from the place where I was kidnapped.

One car with guards remained on the scene for surveillance. They watched as Dr. Mroueh suddenly left the building about twenty minutes after Waite entered. One lookout followed him to the AUB hospital. Around midnight, a water truck in a parking lot across the street lumbered off.

Waite had agreed to touch base with the bodyguards after

three hours. When he failed to contact them, Jumblatt ordered a search of the area but nothing turned up. On the following morning, Jumblatt's deputies confronted Dr. Mroueh. He insisted he had warned Waite of his danger and told him if he should go anywhere, to leave behind a note with his destination. Mroueh showed his interrogators a note he had found: "I'm going to a meeting with one of the hostage-takers and if I myself am taken hostage and they ask for a ransom, don't pay anything." According to a story in the French newsmagazine, *L'Express*, an investigation indicated that Waite had been spirited away in the water truck seen leaving the area. However, my sources insist that Waite left in a car in the belief he was being taken to meet the hostages.

Jumblatt was furious with Mroueh, holding him responsible for the debacle. The Druse leader was so outraged by the breakdown in security that he offered himself as a substitute hostage for Waite.

Waite rode in a car with his bodyguards, in the last photograph taken of him before he was kidnapped. (Courtesy AP/Wide World Photos)

Subsequently, Abu Haytham, the man who was reported to have betrayed Waite, was arrested by the Syrians. In their hands, he allegedly confessed to having participated in the assassination of one hundred eighty five people, including a Sunni sheik and a Druse sheik. According to the Syrians, these murders were paid for as part of a plot concocted by Israeli agents seeking to start a religious war between Sunni and Druse factions. Abu Haytham was also said to have attempted to kill Jumblatt by means of a pen packed with plastique. That scheme failed when a Jumblatt bodyguard happened to play with the pen. The unfortunate man set off the charge and was badly injured.

Whatever the truth of these accounts, it was indisputable that Terry Waite, that generous and great embodiment of all of the best Christian virtues, had become one more hostage. The kidnappers, with their protestations of their devotion to religion, betrayed the best of the Moslem faith by an act against a man of "The Book." And they incurred the lasting hatred of the Druse, who felt humiliated and abused by the treatment of a man in their care.

Hindsight suggests to me that it may have been a serious error for Waite to become involved at all with North. No matter how discreet they were, their meetings were always at risk of discovery. Leaks, spies and chance observations could have betrayed them.

In addition, when Ollie and his associate Albert Hakim met with their Iranian contacts, it is possible they either mentioned Waite or dropped a piece of information that their opposite numbers would recognize as knowable only by Waite. Given the paranoia of the people in Tehran, their conclusion that Waite was not an innocent but an active source of intelligence for the United States could easily follow. To them, the alliance of North and Waite and their ostensible missions might be part of preparations for a military-style assault.

Furthermore, North's responsibilities and his background differ markedly from that of Waite. As a Marine officer trained to accept casualties in pursuit of the objective, and as an agent of the National Security Adviser's office, North had to view the freedom of the hostages from a different perspective than the gentle humanitarian. North and company may well have entertained adventurous notions; they were experienced in the use of force. Such an operation would have been totally alien to a Terry Waite. To him or for that matter to Ben Weir, casualties are never acceptable.

No one felt keener anguish than I about Waite's disappearance, even though I had met him a little more than two months before the thugs captured him. Just the awareness of this gentle giant's efforts inspired us all to survive.

Meanwhile, my experience with the State Department followed a similar path to the one trod by my sons. Immediately after my release I was vocally supportive of DOS. I couldn't praise them enough. And having been made aware of how much John Adams had done for the families, I praised him to President Reagan during our meeting. The President wanted to know who this fellow was. I said John was right outside in the corridor with the rest of the DOS staff who had accompanied me to the White House. The President promptly ordered he be invited in and I don't think Little John ever recovered from the shock of suddenly being introduced to the President.

As I learned the facts about the actions—or lack of same—by DOS, exclusive of John's fine work, and saw their seeming lack of interest with my own eyes, my attitude changed. Like those who had gone before me I realized the best chance for rescue of the people in Beirut lay with people outside of DOS. I deeply regret it took me so long to understand the need to approach other government agencies or even to try to work out something by private means. I feel sure that Peggy Say, who went on her own to Beirut in an effort to free Terry Anderson, knows that she has done her utmost.

When I heard criticisms of the people who flew to Iraq to obtain freedom for Americans taken hostage there and in

Kuwait my reaction was, "Good for you. Go for it. You have nothing to lose." And indeed, their people came out and there was no loss of face or power for the United States.

My frustration with DOS is actually limited to a handful of individuals. Unfortunately, most of them are the decision-makers. Others from the lower echelons made it plain to me they did not agree with the policy. But there was nothing they could do about it.

While we were captives we often mulled over the possibilities that would open up to us after we gained our freedom. I assumed I would return to my trade as a hospital administrator, but I discovered there was a certain reluctance to hire me. Sometimes potential employers seemed to fear that my celebrity status, minor though it was, might interfere with work. Search firms suggested I would never be happy in a routine job. Rejections were also couched in terms of "You've been away from things so long and the entire business has changed." That wasn't true. The procedures, paperwork, and innovations were all easily learnable and I knew the latest policies and procedures after only a few weeks of study.

Except for moments when I wanted to exploit my notoriety to make people aware of the plight of Anderson, Sutherland, Cicippio and the others, I had come to abhor the recognition I received. Initially, it was pleasant to have people approach me and say how glad they were I was home. Later, while I appreciated their warmth, I saw no reason for any further celebration. I wanted to get on with my life. During the time I was a hostage, Kerri had gone on with her life. She enrolled in a graduate program at a University more than a thousand miles away from Huntington Beach, my home. The circumstances put our relationship on hold.

I was invited to throw out the first ball to start the California Angels' 1987 season. After a convertible drove me to home plate and I climbed out to bask in the cheers and applause, my rabbit ears heard a young guy shout an obscenity relating to Iran-Contra. I was enraged, aflame with the same anger that had so appalled Ben Weir when gunmen fired on our cell. I wanted to beat the heckler to a pulp. But, I restrained myself. When I had an opportunity, I caught his eye, flicked my thumb from my mouth in the fine old Italian gesture of contempt. Seventeen months of confinement did not soften me into a pacifist.

Actually, I really did not want to return to the day-to-day regimen of running a hospital. No matter how much satisfaction one could derive from making such an institution thrive, I wanted to have a more direct involvement in aiding other human beings.

Destiny, however, intervened. The Catholic Health Corporation hired me as chief operating officer of Mercy Medical Center in Durango, Colorado. Two weeks after assumption of my duties, the president and chief executive officer of the hospital died unexpectedly. I immediately assumed the responsibilities of both of the deceased and occupied myself in this fashion for eighteen months. It was a wonderful time and place to heal. My privacy was respected; the media could not find me. I owe much to the Sisters of Mercy for their trust in me.

Eventually, I felt a longing to be closer to my family. And while Durango is beautiful, it is also isolated. Visits were expensive—in terms of time and money. I returned to California in the spring of 1990 to be closer to my family and friends.

My real vocation became the liberation of the hostages. I wrote letters to editors, traveled the talk show circuit, spoke at any institution or gathering that would have me. My purpose was to remind people that a handful of Americans and other Westerners still endured the yoke in a Beirut hideout. I pleaded for public pressure on the government to make an effort to secure their release. I arranged for Valentine's Day greetings cards to the hostages to be published in a Beirut newspaper, *As Safir*. I knew the guards would tell them, making the captives aware they were not forgotten.

I traveled to Washington D.C. periodically to lobby politicians and on occasions spoke at meetings of NOVA, the National Organization for Victims Assistance. It was formed to provide support for victims of crimes and disasters and their families. The founder, Marlene Young, had started the first victims assistance program in the country.

But my frustration continued. The attention span of the media and its audience was brief. Other news items, anything from a scandal involving a TV star to genuine world and national affairs, crowded out mention of the hostages. And when I was asked for comments on a dispatch from Beirut or some relevant story, it was as if we had never discussed the matter before. The questions, answers, and responses remained the same.

If anything, the situation was worse than ever. The Congressional hearings and the subsequent trials of those involved in Iran-Contra obviously scared those in power. They opted for the safe route of doing nothing while piously proclaiming their sorrow over the fate of the hostages.

We lost allies in the government. Ambassador Kelly, who had demonstrated to me an intuitive understanding of the forces in conflict, was summoned by Ronald Reagan for a consultation at the White House. He obeyed orders instead of following the prissy protocol demanding he report to the State Department and not engage in private talks with the President. The DOS resented hearing after the fact that one of their people had met with a President. Consequently, this able man was disciplined with a posting to a less sensitive area than Lebanon.

In the State Department, John Adams had served as the contact person for Eric and others seeking information on the hostages. Adams received a promotion and no longer dealt with hostage problems. His successor proved to be a totally obnoxious bureaucrat and far less forthcoming.

L. Paul Bremer III, Ambassador for Counter-terrorism, turned out to be a man with one answer. To every suggestion we put forward, he answered no. For example, we proposed that the International Red Cross, members of the Red Crescent Society, or people from Amnesty International visit the Dawa prisoners or have TV cameras film them. From conversations with our captors, I knew there was great concern about how they were being treated. A simple gesture, the imparting of reassuring information, might have led to dialogue. Surely the Kuwaiti authorities would have been receptive. We had reflagged their tankers to protect them against an Iranian attack during that country's war with Iraq. But the answer was no, because of the policy of no negotiations with terrorists.

The State Department Bureau of Diplomatic Security distributed thousands of leaflets headlined "Wanted for Terrorist Crimes." The broadsheets listed rewards to anyone who aided in the arrest or conviction of terrorists. They offered $500,000 for information on the Pan Am Flight 103 disaster in Lockerbie, Scotland; $250,000 for help in capturing those responsible for the TWA hijackings; the same sums for the gang that boarded the *Achille Lauro* and engineered a Kuwait Airlines attack. There was $100,000 for assistance in solving the murder of the Marines in El Salvador. But not one cent was tendered for similar data regarding the Beirut hostages. The Lebanese are poor, many on the ragged edge of subsistence. Hundreds of people must know the who and the where. But the United States has done nothing to encourage them to come forward.

I achieved one small success. After George Bush's election in 1988 we exchanged letters. I blurted out my frustration over the negative reaction to all proposals. He assured me I need not worry about the chief obstructionist. I drew some satisfaction when Bremer subsequently "retired" as head of counterterrorism. (Civil servants with Ambassadorial positions are never fired. They just retire.)

The entire Iran-Contra investigation and subsequent prosecutions struck me as sheer politics. When I first heard that North and his associates had sold weapons to Iran to ransom us and then used the profits to support the Contras I thought it was a brilliant maneuver. I favored both goals. To this day, I

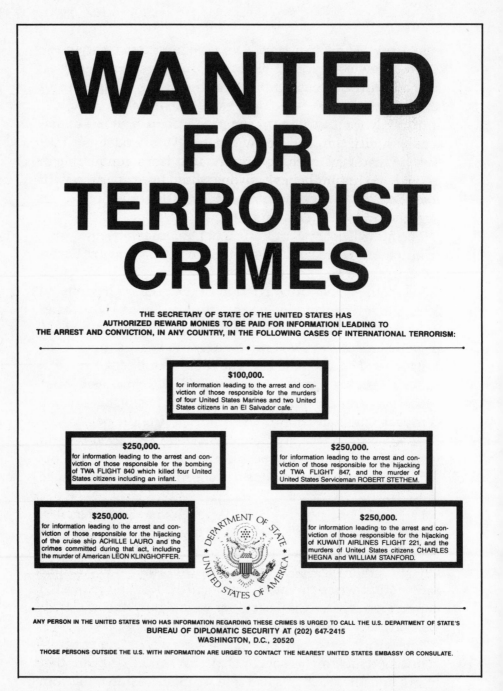

WANTED
FOR
TERRORIST
CRIMES

THE SECRETARY OF STATE OF THE UNITED STATES HAS
AUTHORIZED REWARD MONIES TO BE PAID FOR INFORMATION LEADING TO
THE ARREST AND CONVICTION, IN ANY COUNTRY, IN THE FOLLOWING CASES OF INTERNATIONAL TERRORISM:

$100,000.
for information leading to the arrest and conviction of those responsible for the murders of four United States Marines and two United States citizens in an El Salvador cafe.

$250,000.
for information leading to the arrest and conviction of those responsible for the bombing of TWA FLIGHT 840 which killed four United States citizens including an infant.

$250,000.
for information leading to the arrest and conviction of those responsible for the hijacking of TWA FLIGHT 847, and the murder of United States Serviceman ROBERT STETHEM.

$250,000.
for information leading to the arrest and conviction of those responsible for the hijacking of the cruise ship ACHILLE LAURO and the crimes committed during that act, including the murder of American LEON KLINGHOFFER.

$250,000.
for information leading to the arrest and conviction of those responsible for the hijacking of KUWAITI AIRLINES FLIGHT 221, and the murders of United States citizens CHARLES HEGNA and WILLIAM STANFORD.

ANY PERSON IN THE UNITED STATES WHO HAS INFORMATION REGARDING THESE CRIMES IS URGED TO CALL THE U.S. DEPARTMENT OF STATE'S
BUREAU OF DIPLOMATIC SECURITY AT (202) 647-2415
WASHINGTON, D.C., 20520

THOSE PERSONS OUTSIDE THE U.S. WITH INFORMATION ARE URGED TO CONTACT THE NEAREST UNITED STATES EMBASSY OR CONSULATE.

The State Department distributed thousands of these posters offering rewards for arrests and convictions of terrorists but failed to include the criminals who kidnapped the hostages.

still support Ollie North and his associates, but in hindsight, I now have some doubts about the political wisdom of linking controversial aid to the Contras with the more benign hostage ransoms.

Already the bully boy of the Middle East, Iraq had started the war with Iran and was winning. It was prudent, as most recent history proves, to prevent Iraq from conquering its neighbor. I cannot believe anyone would have quarreled with the trade of basically defensive arms to Iran to gain the freedom of innocent American citizens. The shibboleth "We don't negotiate with terrorists or kidnappers" defies common practice. On the domestic scene, all law enforcement agencies talk to those who hold hostages or demand ransoms. The top priority is the freedom of the victims. Although ransom payments are technically unlawful, money is paid and demands met—if reasonable. Once those seized have been released, the authorities pursue and punish the guilty.

Bargaining to strike a deal is also a well-established prac-

Oliver North testified at the Congressional Hearings on Iran-Contra. I believe I owe my freedom to the efforts of North and his associates. (Courtesy AP/Wide World Photos)

Iranian-born Albert Hakim, a business associate of General Richard Secord, played a significant role in the arms-for-hostages negotiations.

tice in hostage situations abroad. The infant U.S. Congress voted almost $1 million, a formidable sum in those days, to pay off the Dey of Algiers for some one hundred Americans held in North African dungeons. In the Administration of President John Adams at the beginning of the nineteenth century, the United States gave ships and cash to the Barbary Coast pirates as ransom for hostages.

Directly or indirectly, our government in recent years has dealt with countries and overseas groups to liberate Americans. The Carter Administration eventually struck a bargain with the government of Iran to release $8 billion in frozen assets in return for the freedom of U.S. diplomats held more than a year in Tehran. We have negotiated for hijacked airplanes, for Nicholas Daniloff, and on other occasions.

Those who refuse to open a dialogue with the kidnappers claim that negotiations only encourage further acts of terror. The facts say otherwise. During the period in which the United States avoided contact with the terrorists, they continued to snatch people and to commit hijacks.

"We do not negotiate with terrorists" is not really a policy; it's a bumper sticker. A policy sets goals, and designs a strategy and tactics to achieve those ends.

Unfortunately, associating the desirable goals of blocking Iraq and securing release of the hostages with the conflict in Nicaragua, confused the issues. In the matter of Iran-Contra, the Congress specifically had banned U.S. government aid to the Contras. To protect their operation, those involved felt obliged to deceive the legislators. In an open society like ours, it's impossible to expect this kind of covert stuff to remain secret. When the scandal hit the fan, it not only destroyed some promising careers but it also shut down an operation that had produced results, probably buying freedom for three of us hostages.

Although I think those engaged in Iran-Contra may have made a mistake, I feel their efforts on behalf of the captives, which included putting themselves in physical danger as well as risking their careers, deserved better. I testified on behalf of Ollie North at his trial, but the special prosecutor would not let me take the stand in defense of John Poindexter. I wrote a fund-raising letter to aid Gen. Richard Secord. And when Judge Gerhard Gesell was to sentence North and Hakim, I wrote to plead he not sentence them to prison time.

My support for North and his associates is based on their willingness to put themselves on the line and negotiate for the release of the hostages. They arranged for a ransom, just as law enforcement officials would in a domestic ransom case. And I am convinced that if there were an opportunity, once the hostages were all free, Ollie North would spearhead a drive to arrest and prosecute the hostage-takers as the criminals they are.

Indeed, North was the key figure when it appeared the hijackers of the Italian oceanliner *Achille Lauro*, who murdered the elderly wheelchair-bound passenger Leon Klinghoffer, were about to escape on an Egypt Air jet scheduled to fly them from Cairo to Tunis. U.S. intelligence learned all of the details—the type of aircraft, its tail number, schedule, and the list of passengers and crew. North convinced his boss, John Poindexter, that "we can do an Admiral Yamamoto." (During World War II, American forces learned the flight plans of the Japanese admiral and shot down his plane.) Through North's initiative, with approval all the way from President Reagan down, American fighter planes forced the Egypt Air plane carrying the terrorists to land at a base in

I came to Washington to offer my support to Admiral Poindexter during the Iran-Contra hearings. (*Courtesy AP/Wide World Photos*)

Sicily. Although the head of the kidnap-murderers, Abu Abbas, was permitted to leave because of delicate relationships between Egypt and Italy, the other criminals were tried by Italian courts and sentenced to jail, all as a result of Ollie North's efforts.

Although George Shultz served as President Reagan's Secretary of State and implemented the policy that condemned the hostages to languish in their cells, I continue to believe in Ronald Reagan's sincerity and devotion to our interests. I think he was never informed in an official memorandum of the facts of our situation. In their zeal to immunize Reagan, his circle protected him.

In his memoirs, *An American Life*, he says, ". . . whenever one of our citizens, even the least among us, through no fault of his or her own, was denied the right to life, liberty and the pursuit of happiness, it was up to the rest of us to do everything we could to restore those rights, wherever it took us, anywhere in the world."

I feel Reagan's advisors persuaded him to assume publicly the no negotiations stance because they viewed it as politically sound. Meanwhile the National Security Adviser's office went through its exercise with the Iranians. It was probably naive of the President to believe these were not weapons-for-hostages swaps. But I can easily see how his desire to bring us home could have overcome doubts about the fig leaf tales of Iranian moderates exercising influence over "the barbarian Hizballah" (Reagan's phrase). How could he have resisted after "Bill Casey and the NSC staff suggested we authorize a small additional shipment of spare missile parts to the Iranian military forces as a demonstration of goodwill and gratitude. If we didn't, our principal contact in the government might lose face and even be executed by those in Iran who were opposed to what he was doing. He also said one or more of the remaining hostages might be killed. I authorized this additional shipment."

On the other hand, I was disappointed by his response after word on the arrangements with the Iranians leaked. From that point on he refused to commit his people to further efforts to release the remaining hostages. And so far as I can determine, President Bush has also erred in not negotiating.

But I am also grateful to President Reagan. I owe my freedom and perhaps my life to the actions taken by those serving him. The day does not pass that I do not give thanks to Robert McFarlane, John Poindexter, Oliver North, Richard Secord, and Albert Hakim.

Together with Alec Collett's son David, Jenco, Eric and I have formed a non-profit organization, The International Hostage Association. Its purpose is to educate the public about terrorism, and to assist the families of victims.

In the spring of 1990, three and a half years after I breathed

Hostage Frank Reed was jubilant when he arrived in Germany after gaining his freedom. (Courtesy AP/Wide World Photos)

my freedom, two more Americans left the ranks of the hostages. Robert Polhill, seized in January 1987, and Frank Reed, taken in September 1986, were released. Polhill suffered from cancer of the throat and doctors were forced to remove his larynx. If his release could have been secured earlier, such drastic surgery might not have been necessary.

Frank Reed and I shared our experiences. To my delight he revealed himself as the artist who used an olive pit to scratch the picture of father and son on the ceiling of my last cell. Finally, I knew the answer to the nagging question of what happened to those in that drawing. Frank and his son, ten, were reunited when Frank was released in April 1990.

In a letter to Frank, I suggested how he might handle the onslaught he could expect. "One irritating question you will be asked is, 'Why did you stay in Lebanon after the State Department ordered you to leave?' Your response should be forceful and direct such as, 'I was taken hostage on September 9, 1986. That was five months before the State Department ordered private American citizens out of Lebanon. If the U.S. government had asked me to leave before then, I would have done so. Lebanon at that time was probably less dangerous than the streets of Washington, D.C., the murder capital of this country. We do not hear the State Department ordering citizens to leave New York, Detroit, or Los Angeles, where crime is epidemic.'"

I advised him he had no obligation to speak to the press. If *People* magazine called, I recommended he sell his story for at least $25,000, the going price. I named my contact at a speaker's bureau and counseled him to be aggressive if he intended to return to work. Otherwise, he would be defeated by the kind of put-downs I had encountered.

I warned him not to expect support from the State Department, saying it "has no sense of urgency regarding the hostages. This is because many innocent people had their careers destroyed by the partisan politics of Iran-Gate. So they are extremely cautious." On the other hand, I said my experience with the CIA, the FBI, and the Department of Defense had led me to trust these institutions.

Reed had spent many months entombed with Terry Anderson and Tom Sutherland. He reported that Tom had taken over my role as opponent to Terry and the pair of them had frequently engaged in the same sort of devil's advocacy that marked my period in captivity. Unlike me, Reed once actually escaped from his cell. But he was recaptured and physically chastised by the guards. The injuries may have been one reason he was released along with Polhill.

In 1988 the three Americans were joined by a pair of Britons, Brian Keenan and John McCarthy. Keenan, a teacher originally from Belfast, Northern Ireland, holds both British and Irish citizenship. At the end of August 1990 his captors freed him. He reported seeing Anderson and Sutherland almost a year before and both seemed well. Although his treatment had improved over the final nine months of his incarceration, Keenan spoke of beatings and the regimen of

Americans Robert Polhill (left), Jesse Turner (center) and Alann Steen, professors at the AUB, were all kidnapped in January 1987 along with Indian Mithileshwar Singh, who was freed nine months later. Polhill, seriously ill with cancer of the throat, left captivity with Frank Reed April 22, 1990. (Courtesy AP/Wide World Photos)

The nastiness of the terrorists was displayed in a December, 1987 shot of Robert Polhill. (Courtesy AP/Wide World Photos)

blindfolds, darkness, poor food, and isolation. He recalled Terry pacing the floor in tattered socks, endlessly chattering, debating, it seemed, with himself if no one accepted his challenges.

At the date of my release, five Americans along with nine other Westerners remained captives. More than four years later, the cast of characters had changed somewhat but there were still more than a dozen men, including six Americans, locked up in Islamic Jihad cells.

I had written to Frank Reed, "You will have times of real frustration and a little depression. You will probably not have nightmares of disturbed sleep, but there will not be a day that you will not think of the men held in Lebanon. They will flash through your thoughts during the day. It still happens to me and to Father Jenco."

There are three images that bring tears to my eyes: the celebration of the Eucharist, the raising of an American flag as our national anthem is played, and the vision of Anderson, Sutherland, and Waite still locked up and chained.

Chapter 16

The Final Awakening

After my return home, a major preoccupation of mine was examining how I had survived. It was important to me not only in understanding my own personality but also because the answers might contribute to the body of knowledge about coping with the hostage phenomenon.

Although some think that as a political weapon hostage-taking is a late twentieth-century piece of barbarism, it is actually an ancient evil. The Romans often seized the sons of leaders from vassal states to insure parents stayed loyal to Rome. Early French and English imperialists took hostages to pressure submission in Africa and India. During World War II, the Germans and Japanese sought to eliminate resistance movements by taking hostages, frequently executing large numbers as reprisals.

The Palestine Liberation Organization turned the Munich Olympics of 1972 into a bloodbath with their Israeli hostage operation. A number of revolutionary groups in the Far East have turned to kidnapping as a form of political action. The mass imprisonment of civilians has continued to be a weapon of choice for diverse governments. The Israelis have employed detentions in southern Lebanon as a means of quelling unrest. And not the least of Saddam Hussein's criminal acts was his use of foreign civilian "guests" to deter an assault on Iraq. In addition, an increasing number of news stories tell of innocent people seized as shields for common criminals. The phenomenon has become so widespread that most big police units possess a hostage negotiating unit.

Those who have been acquainted with individuals trapped

Dr. Calvin Jeff Frederick (left), and I shared information on the experiences of hostages. He is an internationally known researcher into Post Traumatic Stress Disorder, a common problem among victims of kidnappers.

as hostages have learned that the ordeal does not always end with freedom. Frequently, scars remain for sustained periods. Furthermore, mental health experts are aware of potentially severe problems among the "co-victims," the loved ones and families of hostages and other traumatized persons. Psychologists have labeled the problem, Post Traumatic Stress Disorder (PTSD). Among the symptoms are substance abuse, inappropriate flashes of anger and irritability, hypertension, insomnia, headaches, sexual inhibition, nightmares, phobias, marital discord, diarrhea, weight loss, even back pains.

Dr. Calvin Jeff Frederick, a psychologist at UCLA and the Veterans Administration Medical Center in West Los Angeles, had started studying the coping mechanisms of hostages as part of an overall investigation into PTSD. He interviewed me along with others from the Beirut experience. Frederick also compiled data on people who were victims of crimes and catastrophies that were more commonplace or non-political: kidnappings, robberies, attacks by berserk snipers, harrowing war experiences, and natural or man-made disasters.

The research is vitally important. Given the nature of our society, victims of crime will continue to number in the tens of thousands. Eventually, the hostages in Beirut should come home. And then there are the hundreds who were trapped by Saddam Hussein in Iraq. PTSD may afflict many of them. The findings of Frederick and others offer a basis for treatment programs.

Survivors of a traumatic event may wrestle with enormous guilt. Often the victims blame themselves, feeling they somehow put themselves in jeopardy. They ask themselves, could have I resisted. Such a reaction is quite common among rape victims, particularly when criminal defense strategy attacks the woman's behavior and reputation. A robber's prey may accuse himself of carelessness, carrying too much money or traveling in a questionable neighborhood. And a hostage might reproach himself for being in the wrong place, for not fighting hard enough.

None of the hostages I knew during my time of incarceration, nor any of those released, have ever voiced any sentiments indicting they felt culpable for the misfortune that befell them. We were then and still are convinced we were in the right place at the right time doing the right thing. I did my best to fight off the kidnappers. Had I packed a gun, the result might have been my death and that of Dr. Azoury. If I happened to have toted along a hand grenade, pulling the pin and brandishing the grenade is probably the only way I could have put my assailants in full flight.

There is also a syndrome known as "survivor's guilt." For example, those who lived through the Nazi death camps watched parents, siblings, children, friends die. "Why me, why am I here and they are not?" is a persistent feeling.

None of the hostages, including me, really feels someone else should have come home in his place. During one of the angrier debates he had with Terry and Tom, Frank Reed recalled arguing, as I had, "We all want to go home. It is just a question of who follows whom."

Ben Weir was the first of our number released. At the time

he was the oldest and longest held. A
selection, one had only to look at hir
was. And under the circumstances, h
After Weir's release Marty Jenco beca
too deserved his freedom as much a

They picked me over Terry and To
was seventeen years Terry's senior
doubtedly figured he was in better
longer ordeal. Our hosts regarded me
in humanitarian activities by virtu
hospital. Tom was my age but he ha
captivity. Both he and Terry had ir
Anderson's naturally cantankerous w
his attempted bribe to a guard probab
erland's discursive style coupled with
that he belonged to an intelligence ag
his chances for an early release.

These were all matters beyond my
tained before the selection of Ben We
who was released would be made b
masters. I had no reason to feel guil
had paid my dues with seventeen har

People who avoid Post Traumatic S
ing to the research of Cal Frederick an
a result of factors in their personalit
kind of trauma they endure, and the a
From interviews with me, Marty Jenc
(an American diplomat held by the I
General James Dozier (held hostage fo
terrorists), and other similar victims,
the literature on the subject, Cal deve
mechanisms. These come into play bot
stress and after the ordeal ends.

In no particular order of importance
lief in the innate strength of oneself."
characteristic of all of my companions.
the mild Rev. Ben Weir, could be clas

and still are assertive. I don't recall anyone ever surren-
g a strongly held belief after one of our discussions. Our
nalities did not change from the first day of captivity
we separated. I continue to possess enough self-
dence to speak my mind freely, to think I am a compe-
productive person.

eflections and thoughts of loved ones and friends" is a
d coping mechanism. I spent hours thinking of my
ren and Kerrie. Indeed, while chained to the floor dur-
ny first days of incarceration, I spun out an elaborate
sy in which I attended my son Paul's wedding. I pic-
I myself with the family, completing the chores re-
d of the father of the groom. I saw myself traveling to St.
venture's Church on Springdale Street where the wed-
would take place. I drove to the Huntington Harbor

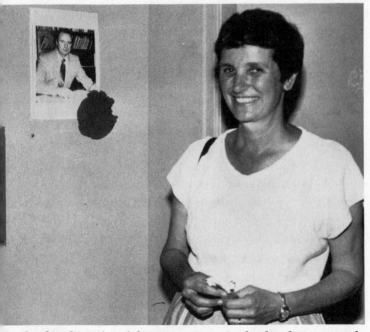

Sutherland, wife of hostage Tom Sutherland, managed a
: smile, although at the time of the picture her husband had
n his third year in captivity. At this writing he is in his sixth
as a hostage. (Courtesy AP/Wide World Photos)

French journalist Roger Auque, a hostage from January 1987 until November of that year, believes he saw Terry Waite. (Courtesy AP/Wide World Photos)

Club for the reception. And I continued to imagine my participation in family celebrations. I was there for Eric's birthday, a month or so after the wedding, and a few days later I motored to my father's home to share his ninety-first.

From the frequency with which Terry Anderson spoke about his ten-year-old and then the infant daughter he had never seen, I knew he too dwelled on his family. He made it obvious that his sister Peggy, who had been almost a surrogate mother to him, was someone he thought of often. Tom Sutherland constantly alluded to his "wonderful" wife Jean and three daughters. Marty Jenco concerned himself with his brother and sister, nieces and nephews. Ben Weir was devoted to his wife, son, and daughters.

My love for my family, which has grown with the seven grandkids plus two daughters-in-law and one son-in-law, is greater than ever and if anything it grew from my ordeal.

"Faith in some superordinate power" is another item named by Frederick. Our devotion to the Church of the Locked Door demonstrates the strength of our commitment to forces beyond mortals. Before I was kidnapped, much of my churchgoing was more of an intellectual habit than an act of faith. Now, my participation in services and my private prayers are freighted with deep, deep emotion.

"Hope that captivity will end favorably" is a fourth requisite. We all had our low moments, but I think we all foresaw freedom someday. The release of others encouraged us. We took heart from the stern insistence upon blindfolds, a restriction imposed by our captors because they too expected us to be freed.

"Use of calculating powers to interact and plan for possible escape" was not a universal element. I certainly plotted to break out. And Frank Reed actually made the attempt. Frank managed to get through his door and make his way into the street. But neighbors noticed him and returned him to his captors. The guards broke several bones in his body and knocked out a few teeth when they beat him in punishment for this attempt.

A Frenchman, Roger Auque, seized after I was released,

Among the most recently released hostages is Brian Keenan, kidnapped in West Beirut on April 11, 1986. He is shown here hugging his sisters, Elaine Spence, left, and Brenda Guilham, right, at the Syrian Foreign Ministry in Damascus, where he was handed over to the Irish Foreign Minister. Keenan was released in Beirut by his kidnappers, a little-known group calling itself the Organization of the Islamic Dawn. (Courtesy AP/Wide World Photos)

I served as the photographer when Marty Jenco baptized my grandson John David Duggan on March 15, 1987, while the parents, my daughter Diane and her husband Dwight Francis (Jake) Duggan, beamed.

My former hostage roommate also officiated at the baptism of my grandson Joseph. Priest and infant are flanked by parents John and Lori, my son Eric (at far left), and daughter-in-law Cathy (extreme right).

pulled off an escape right out of a thriller novel. After the guards had retired for the night, he slipped a sheet of paper under the door. Then he jiggled the key loose from the lock. The key fell onto the paper and he slid it back inside. But when he opened his door, he discovered the only possible route led to a balcony. There was no means to get down to the ground and run away. Auque simply returned to his room and no one realized he had come so close to a getaway.

At one point, Auque shared his quarters with a South Korean, almost certainly the diplomat Do Chae Sung. I believe he was the man I heard from my cell calling, "Pee pee" and "Yah, yah." Auque, who is now free, says the South Korean was fluent in English but kept that from the guards. While the two of them were incarcerated together, they scraped a small hole in the mortar between the cement blocks of their wall. Peering into the adjoining room, they saw a very tall, bearded man who appeared to weigh about 250 pounds. Although they could not make contact with him, they heard him talk and joke with the guards in English. I'm sure it was Terry Waite.

In any event, counting Jeremy Levin, that makes at least four of us who actually took steps to escape. But even Terry Anderson's rejection of escape indicates still one more who at least plotted to flee and worked through the details. His ill- fated bribe proposal to a guard counts as an escape plan.

Their ministerial beliefs, their adherence to "thou shalt not kill" may have inhibited Ben Weir and Marty Jenco from trying to break away. An escape always entailed the risk of deadly combat.

"Physical exercise," the sixth coping mechanism, was heartily embraced by all of us except Marty Jenco. Even he joined our tight-ranked promenades around the cell confines. Physical exertion prevented the loss of muscle tone. Flabby, weak sinews add susceptibility to mental fatigue and depression. I had been a jogger before I was captured and continue to work out at a local gym.

"Expression of anger via appropriate self-assertion" governed conversations among us and with our captors. There is a definite inverse relationship between adrenalin flow and depression. The more the glands of anger pump out their hormones, the less the mind and body droops. We became pissed off for good reason. Alone, we went at one another giving no quarter. When I noticed Tom Sutherland seemed discouraged I picked on him until he got mad. Later, he would thank me for boosting him out of the doldrums. I understand that after I left and Frank Reed joined the group, the quarreling became so bitter that Frank refused to speak with another hostage for months. That was carrying things a bit extreme, but I'm sure it kept the juices flowing.

A smile accompanied my more bitter remarks or I employed sarcasm when speaking to the watchdogs. The tactics enabled me to vent my rage without creating painful ill will. Both Ben and Marty turned the other cheek faster than the rest of us but they retained hostile feelings toward our captors. Neither I nor my associates ever became servile.

My anger still boils over at injustice, with particular focus on the lack of effort to bring home the others. The State Department treats the hostage problem as if it were a pesky gnat buzzing around, interfering with its grand operations. They wave a hand at the bug, wishing it would just go away. There are moments when I would dearly love to grab those in charge by the throat and demand an accounting.

"Ability to focus attention and become task oriented" rounds out the Frederick list. Our fixation on maintaining a sense of time and calendar, the routines by which we kept our quarters as clean as possible, the regularity of religious services, points to fulfillment of this component.

There are, as Frederick notes, two aspects to stress management. Coping techniques also confront specific factors. In general, Frederick concludes that duration of trauma, physical environment during the experience, and premorbid vulnerability— the threat of death—correlate only moderately with the amount of stress experienced subsequent to release. From what Frederick has learned and from my own experience the length of time in captivity has not been a controlling factor among the Beirut hostages. Those who have gained their freedom—Levin, Weir, Jenco, and myself, among others—seem to function without significant deficits. On the other hand, there are individuals whose trauma lasted only a few minutes—witnesses to a murder, victims of an assault or rape—and yet they have suffered severe emotional handicaps.

Our dismal living conditions and the threat of death could have left residues that reduced our capacity to function. But apparently these elements did not exact a toll.

Stronger correlation with Post Traumatic Stress Disorder occurs with the severity of the trauma, restrictions on movement, being alone, and the absence of support systems. I don't know how one could compare the severity of impact upon a rape victim with what the hostages endure. In varying degrees our bodies were violated. Both Frank Reed and I received terrible beatings. Jenco lost some of his hearing from blows to his ears. But these physical assaults do not seem to have had a significant long-term emotional effect upon us, neither while we were hostages nor since being liberated, except to increase our resolve to help the others gain their freedom.

We were extremely limited in our mobility, in some cases spending months chained to the floor, wall, or a radiator. And even when unbound, we occupied a cramped space, needed permission and an escort to go to the bathroom. Again, that often highly stressful element of close confinement failed to emotionally injure us. (Gen. James Dozier spent most of his six weeks confined to a box. Yet, he too mustered the coping mechanisms to overcome the trauma.)

The Beirut hostages gained strength by the comparative absence of one high-stress factor: loneliness. Tiny as our space was, none of us regretted the presence of the others once they moved in. Humans are social animals and few of us thrive in total solitude. We worked at staying in touch, even when locked in separate cells. We used our code of knocking on the walls. When talking to guards we raised our voices so the others would know we were alive and well.

Being together also enabled us to develop another critical element, support systems. For all of our bickering, even anger, we worked at keeping one another's spirits up. We listened to gripes and outpourings of the soul and offered inspiration and compassion. And if we felt our captors mistreated one of us, the others protested vigorously.

An important element of the support system was our individual stress management devices. I cannot count how many times I raised and lowered the golden ball or made an out-of-body trip through the streets of Huntington Beach. I know the others also resorted to mnemonic tricks and mental gymnastics to lower their anxieties.

As a group, we would discuss various key elements of stress management. We would play games such as twenty questions; we would offer each other riddles. We would take turns leading the group on an imaginary dinner outing in Paris or London or Tokyo or, in my case, my hometown of Huntington Beach, California. I tried to stress the crucial importance of exercise: "If you really start to get discouraged, you have to exercise." We all contributed to the group effort of survival through mental—and physical—exercise.

Frederick detected one personal characteristic that enabled some individuals to endure stress better than others. The factor, surprisingly, is age. At thirty-eight, Terry Anderson was the youngest of our group. Tom Sutherland, Marty Jenco, and I were all in our middle fifties and Ben Weir was over sixty. Middle-aged people, even those approaching the status of senior citizens, seem to have the advantage of an established value system, a set personality, that can better withstand the vicissitudes of a traumatic experience—at least mentally.

Out of his research into what has happened to victims since their release, Frederick has arrived at some tentative conclusions. He has his doubts about the use of pharmaceuticals as a way of coping with PTSD in former hostages or their co-victims ("co-victims" is the jargon term for the loved ones of those who have suffered the actual trauma), but he does not rule it out completely. (I have not tried any drugs to relieve me of stress.) He sees far more positive results from the use of a variety of psycho-therapies that range from relaxation techniques through deconditioning via biofeedback procedures, specific recounting of the trauma and/or recreation of traumatic events in a lab or in simulated life scenes.

Supportive reassurance is extremely important; the victim needs to feel it's okay to be mad, to be sad, to experience the emotions generated by a terrible trauma. It is because I accept the value of support that I praise the work of the National Organization for Victims Assistance and Friends of the West. It's also one more reason I fault the Department of State. It has done damn little to inform and comfort the families of those held or to aid in the readjustment a hostage must undergo after release.

Frederick cites "gratuitous trauma," the role of the media, as another potential problem. As my family and I discovered, the presumed right of the public to know can become a rationale for irresponsible statements that expose a hostage to danger and in the case of Terry Waite nominate a person for kidnapping. Furthermore, the pursuit of a sound bite or a provocative quote in print often adds nothing to further understanding but piles more grief upon survivors and those sweating out a captive's return.

For my part I believe I have weathered the threat of PTSD. My health is good, my blood pressure remains normal. I have plans for the future and I pursue them.

Frederick looked into one commonplace of hostage situations, "the Stockholm syndrome." It drew its name from an incident in a Swedish bank where a gang of robbers held several employees hostage. When the siege finally ended, some of the captives turned on the cops and defended the criminals.

The phenomenon results from a dynamic that begins with

the hostages' recognition they are powerless over their own destiny. Out of fear, individuals in this situation may identify with their aggressors. Those under the gun develop hostility against the law enforcement authorities and their families for the failure to accede to the criminal's demands. Indeed, those who have taken them prisoner now serve as the protector against would-be rescuers who are seen as jeopardizing their safety.

Unequivocally, I can say that none of the people taken in Beirut, whom I know, ever suffered the Stockholm syndrome. I loathe those who took me prisoner. For all of the gentle words from the Hajj and the kindly gestures of the guards, we knew they were the enemy, ready to kill us without hesitation if it suited their purposes. I would be delighted to throw away the keys to their cells if they were ever convicted of the crimes against us. There is a single, possible exception. Of all of them, only Sayid seemed to have a genuine interest in our welfare. Were he suddenly to appear in the United States and ask my help, I might be favorably inclined.

Nor do I subscribe to certain myths associated with the kidnappers and those behind them. They are not, for example, men driven by desires for martyrdom that will guarantee a quick trip to Paradise. They all showed normal human fears of death.

For that matter I refuse to dignify them as "political extremists" or "religious zealots." I regard them as a gang of thugs who have committed a series of brutal crimes. The perception that they are more than murderous extortionists contributes to the failure to negotiate or effectively deal with them. Gilding them with a value they do not deserve has led U.S. authorities to treat them as a kind of entity our officials insist they are not, a political or religious group with some kind of legitimacy. The American authorities act as if these people were organizations that should accept all of the rules and niceties of international affairs. Their actions obviously demonstrate that this is not the case.

To set the record straight and for the release of any current and future hostages, there are a number of things we should remember. First and foremost, we should identify who is behind these international abominations. For a long time, I believed the root of the evil was Hizballah and its Islamic Jihad wing. The representatives of Islamic Jihad, Hajj Habib and Imad Mughniya, talked about their brethren, the Dawa prisoners in Kuwait. But I, along with others, missed a vital clue. The kidnappers opened the cells, first for Weir, then Jenco, and finally me after the U.S. government began a dialogue that put arms in the hands of Tehran.

There were no Dawa people exchanged. There were no diplomatic missions by the United States to insure that living conditions for the bombers in the Emir's jail improved. The sole beneficiary of our release was the government of the Ayatollah Khomeini.

Furthermore, after Iraq overran Kuwait, the Dawa prisoners disappeared. The U.S. State Department believes that "some or all escaped from jail during Iraq's invasion." That happened in the summer of 1990, yet we saw no freedom for the Americans held by Islamic Jihad.

This has led me to the conclusion that while my captors spoke in terms of the Dawa prisoners, their real aims were to further the goals of Iran, with the Dawas held in Kuwait a relatively minor matter. It's time to declare to the world, that when it came to the American and other Western hostages in Lebanon, Iran was the Great Satan. The entire business had been masterminded, generated, and financed by Iran. Indeed, Sheik Fadlallah, responding to a private initiative from me, sent back a message that only the Iranian chargé d'affaires could release those held. He described the Lebanese Hizballah agents as nothing more than the Iranian "hunting dogs." On the other hand, so far as I could determine, those directly involved in the hostage-taking, with the exception of the Hajj and Mughniya, were unaware of the strength of the Iranian connection. They operated on behalf of their Dawa brethren. The guards held little more status than employees and were not informed of the how and why of policy.

The Dawa case thus served as an effective red herring, blurring the trail to Tehran. Another Iranian pretext for hostage-taking was the disappearance of four Iranians at a Christian militia checkpoint in Lebanon in 1982. The U.S. did try to supply information about the quartet but could not satisfy the Iranian officials. The best guess is that a Lebanese gang murdered the missing men.

It is logical now to to ask why the Iranians chose to take Americans and what they hoped to gain. Tweaking the nose of the West has become something of a national pastime in the land of the ayatollahs. When you are the number one world power, you are always going to generate hostility. Leaders of a certain political bent frequently will seek to strengthen their image by demonstrating defiance of the United States. Also, some nations may unify their followers by vitriol and low blows at those who have a different ideology. We should be aware of these factors in the future.

In the case of Iran there was an additional aspect, money. When the Revolutionary Guards seized the U.S. Embassy in 1979, Washington retaliated by freezing all of the Iranian assets in American-controlled institutions. Under an agreement reached in Algiers, in return for the freedom of the hostages taken then, some funds were handed back to Iran. But a sizeable chunk went into escrow accounts to satisfy the claims of U.S. creditors. According to DOS, less than half a billion of the disputed assets remain in the escrow accounts awaiting disposition by the Claims Tribunal created through the Algiers Accord.

However, the Iranian Government also has outstanding billions of dollars in claims arising chiefly from the military purchase program under the Shah, who was ousted in 1979. The Claims Tribunal has agreed that the military items, already paid for by Iran, need not be exported by the U.S. to the purchaser. The amount of a refund is under arbitration by the Tribunal. In addition, Iran also insists that it never received billions more in military equipment which was supposedly shipped and was improperly billed. There are big bucks involved and the failure after more than eleven years to reach an agreement most definitely affected the status of the hostages.

Under the circumstances, the American authorities had a number of options. Rather than a policy of no negotiations, it could have opened up a dialogue with Hizballah in Lebanon. Although the organization is financially supported by Iran, its membership is Lebanese. Genuine efforts to improve the lot of the Dawa, in the past, would have stripped away this figleaf coverage of Iranian objectives. It could have helped drive a wedge between the Lebanese Hizballah and Iran. If we entered into a discussion with Hizballah in Lebanon, perhaps offering some humanitarian aid for the beleaguered people of their land, we might have weakened, or even severed, the leash of Iran's "hunting dogs." We should also have sought to break down the support enjoyed by the terrorists through announcements of substantial rewards for anyone supplying information leading either to the arrest of the kidnappers or enabling those opposed to hostage-taking to free the victims. Had we done so in the past, Terry Anderson, Tom Sutherland and the others might have come home years ago.

We should also have initiated serious bargaining with the Rafsanjani government in Tehran. In the wake of the war with Iraq, Iran embarked on an ambitious five-year development plan. Any assets tied up by the U.S. Government could have contributed towards success. Although the amounts in dispute are debatable (Iran has put the figure as high as $23 billion, while others estimate anywhere from $4 billion to $8 billion), there is no question that a considerable sum is due Tehran. Restoration of what legitimately belongs to a country could hardly be classified as ransom.

The assumption made by Ronald Reagan and some of his advisors that it was in the United States' best interest to establish communication and rapport with the modern forces trying to exert control in Iran was, I believe, a good policy. However, achieving this goal, which would aid in combatting international terrorism and the liberation of the hostages, has been complicated by the power struggle that continues to shake Iran.

The fact is that the political process there does not fit the traditional modes ordinarily understood by Americans. The structure of the Iranian government's management of both internal and foreign affairs lacks firm definition. Think of a corporate organization chart, which consists of a pyramid. At the top is a chief executive and at the bottom are the unskilled workers. Between the two extremes are a widening series of executives, managers and foremen, with horizontal and vertical lines that define authority and responsibility. In the Iranian system, however, the lines have been erased, or perhaps never existed. As a consequence, there is neither discipline nor accountability. People act according to their own agendas. A subsidiary, such as Islamic Jihad, may free lance operations or refuse to follow the orders issued from Tehran.

The chaos is compounded by a tenet of the Islamic faith, which holds that all men are equal before Allah. Therefore, the people at any level of the political structure may feel they can act as if they were at the top, setting policies, determining strategies and tactics. Ironically, that egalitarian belief replicates American attitudes, but the difference between our two countries is that we have created strong, well-defined government bodies to fulfill the needs of our society. With agencies and organizations in place, we agree to work through them. The Iranians have not yet reached this point.

Prior to the Ayatollah Ruhollah Khomeini, the Shahs ruled with autocratic hands. The Shah had *carte blanche* from the United States to buy any weapons systems, for use against either external or internal enemies. The secret police, the Savak, terrorized dissenters. Iran never developed the tradition of democratic government of operating with the mass consent of the governed. The revolution is now little more than a decade old. Its founding fathers have little time to create a real structure, and the war with Iraq has further delayed maturation.

Within the context of the country's religious revolution, the current, nominal leader, Ali Akbar Hashemi Rafsanjani and the spiritual successor to Khomenei, Ali Khamenei, represent a somewhat moderate approach. Rafsanjani has reduced his opposition to three factions which bitterly oppose him. One group believes in carrying the revolution beyond the borders to international terrorism. These individuals have been in league with the terrorist campaigns carried out by Syria, Iraq, Libya and the PLO.

A second group is fiercely nationalistic and fanatically opposed to any foreign influences within Iran. They are against all outside investments in the country. A third bunch, led by Khomeini's son, is violently opposed to any contact with foreigners, particularly from the West.

Although this trio of forces espouses slightly different doctrines, they are bound together in an unrelenting hatred for the United States as "the Great Satan." It is a popular theme in Iran, and in opposing them, Rafsanjani has been treading on eggshells. However, he has been successful in preventing them from dominating the important Council of Wisemen. He has forced the three groups into the role of an opposition. Consequently, the choices of Iranians are clearer. Parliamentary elections are scheduled for June or July of 1991. At that point, Rafsanjani may achieve firm control of the government, and be able to finally establish accountability and responsibility. It will indeed be unfortunate, not only for the hostages but also for other American interests, if the attempts begun in the Reagan Administration to establish informal relationships with this more moderate element prove to have been derailed.

Even if the Iranian government takes on a more stable and accommodating stance, the problems in our dealings with them will not magically disappear. There are still vast cultural differences that, as hostages to myths, stereotypes and ignorance, we seem not to comprehend.

We need to begin with an understanding of Middle Eastern history. The bulk of the population there believes the West, including the United States, has exploited the area for cheap oil and to protect our interests. We firmly supported the Shah as our friend in the Middle East, to the perceived detriment of many Iranians. We tried to give him asylum after the revolution. We shot down a civilian Iranian airliner during the period our ships escorted vessels in the Persian Gulf. The United States Navy made a terrible mistake in identifying the jet as a military plane on the attack, but the error cost 290 civilians their lives.

Although the United States supplied military hardware to Iran in return for three hostages, we generally aided Saddam Hussein, the bitterest enemy of Iran, until he marched into Kuwait. The combination of these elements means that distrust for us will not be easy to overcome, and we should be aware of it.

On the other hand, it must be said that crowds of Iranians charging through the streets, yelling "Death to America," while leaders label us as "the Great Satan" hardly generate sympathy for the Iranian cause.

Also, for better or worse, we are understood to have favored certain policies for Israel which, in the eyes of Iranians, are detrimental to Palestinians, believers in the Moslem faith. The "I and my brother, I and my cousin" syndrome has a very powerful hold on the Iranians, even though they are not Arabs. We need to be cognizant of this factor when dealing with Iran and the Arab countries. At the same time, Israel is the one democracy in the Middle East, the one country that has stood as an unwavering friend of the United States.

Culturally, we should also recognize the Iranian tradition as traders. From birth they seem conditioned in the ways of bargaining. When a child refuses to drink or eat, his parents don't lecture him on nutritional values. Instead, trade enters into the discussion. The children are promised a reward if they will eat. This trade concept permeates the entire fabric of social, economic, political and religious life in Iran.

Negotiations will be complicated by Iranian demands for multi-billion-dollar compensation for overcharges and errors during the fifteen-year period the Shah purchased military and industrial hardware from the U.S. The Iranians, I am told, have never offered any evidence of skullduggery or improper billing from U.S. suppliers. They want us to simply accept their assertions that they have been cheated. At this point, our negotiators just throw up their hands and open the aspirin bottles.

The major point in all of this back and forth for the past twelve years, including the swap of arms that brought my freedom, is that we *have* negotiated with a terrorist organization, the state of Iran. There is no logical reason to distinguish between its activities and those of the Lebanese Hizballah.

It should be noted that the French government secured the release of all of its citizens held as hostages in Lebanon through repayment of a $9 billion loan from the Shah on which the French had defaulted. It took a lot of hard-nosed bargaining by the French, but they had the good sense to recognize the Iranians as traders, and as a result, their once-captive citizens now enjoy freedom.

Some sources suggest to me there are powerful people in this country who oppose any accommodation with Iran that accepts its claims. They resist return of the money even if it means continued imprisonment of hostages. There is a small army of attorneys and financial experts who are being paid handsomely throughout the drawn-out negotiations. They will continue to pocket their fees until the business comes to an end. They see no reason to hurry things along.

Other mercenary individuals are profiting from payments to cover the storage of items bought and paid for by Iran but as yet undelivered. The U.S. companies have the funds in their control and they are not inclined to make it easy for the current government of Iran to retrieve either the goods or the money.

Some may think I'm spouting wild conspiracy talk. But I have discussed this with people in Washington. They have quietly told me that this is an avenue worth pursuing.

Suppose talks in good faith have failed? We should have let the Iranians know that their continued role in holding hostages is a criminal act and our actions would be guided by that judgment. Then I think we should have proceeded on the basis employed in any confrontation with outlaws; escalate the pressure. Go to the American people and the world to explain the situation. Then enforce total economic, political, and social sanctions against Iran. Boycott all products from that country, everything from carpets to oil. Do what-

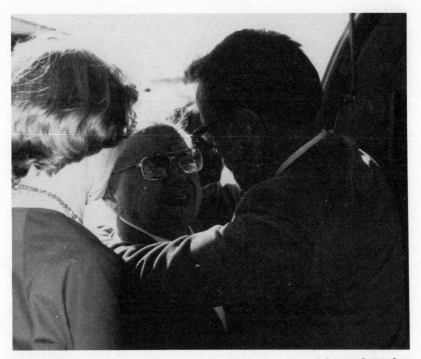

Reunited with my father after my release, I was able to share his remaining six months of life.

In the less than five years since I was freed I have been blessed with seven grandkids.

ever is possible to thwart that five-year rebuilding campaign.

Simultaneously, we should have vigorously explored military or covert operations to rescue the captives. The first step in this option would put the safety of those imprisoned on the agendas of outfits like the CIA and the FBI rather than the State Department, which is not equipped by nature or training to deal with criminals. The former, in both domestic and international situations have shown themselves, in my opinion, to be capable of taking the necessary steps. Let us not be held hostage to bureaucratic tradition.

The Syrian army in the autumn of 1990 re-established a new central government for Lebanon. With the aid of the Damascus forces, the infamous Green Line in Beirut was erased. The militias moved away from the city. Indeed, the hostages apparently were shifted to a site in the Bekaa Valley or in south Lebanon.

There are several countries to which we might contract out the assignment of a rescue. Particularly with the militias losing power, precise intelligence on the location of the

Western captives should have been available, for the right price. Either the military from another nation or perhaps even the Delta Force could have effected a successful operation.

My prescription describes the case of the hostages in Lebanon, taken under the aegis of Iran. However, I think it can be tailored to fit other circumstances should they arise. Unlike the still current DOS shibboleth of "we will not pay ransom for hostages," I offer a policy. It is a series of measured steps. It begins with an effort to identify the real offenders, moves on to negotiations. Rewards for aid should be tendered. If these fail to win freedom, then we move on to the next tactics, mobilizing economic and public opinion pressure. As a last resort we should employ force.

I have now been a free man for close to five years. I have been home for the births of all of my seven grandchildren: John, Jake, and Dylan Duggan; Joseph, Philip, and Stephen Jacobsen; Erika Ann Jacobsen. I have held these blessings in my arms, fed them, changed their diapers, babysat them, and have been privileged to shower them with all the grandfatherly love within me. As I typed these words Terry Anderson has never seen or held his daughter, born in 1985. Tom Sutherland had never held his granddaughter.

I was able to spend the last six months of my father's life with him. I will always be grateful to my father and mother, who endowed me with the basic moral, ethical, and spiritual values that enabled me to endure the hideous fate of a hostage locked up by Iran and Islamic Jihad.

I am truly a lucky man. I do not suffer bad dreams or flashbacks to my time in chains, under the muzzles of guns. But my nightmare in Beirut will continue until I see Terry, Tom, Joe, and the others set foot in the land of the free.

Index

Index